THE HORSE
ENCYCLOPEDIA

JOSÉE HERMSEN

THE HORSE ENCYCLOPEDIA

FIREFLY BOOKS

A FIREFLY BOOK

First published in The Netherlands by Rebo Productions Ltd.
Published in The United States in 1998 by Firefly Books (U.S.) Inc.

Cataloging in Publication Data

Hermsen, Josee
     The horse encyclopedia

Translated from Dutch.
Includes index.
ISBN 1-55209-305-0

1. Horses – Encyclopedias. 2. Horsemanship – Encyclopedias.
I. Challacombe, Stephen J. II. Title.

SF278.H4713 1998   636.1'003   C98-931354-9

Firefly Books (U.S.) Inc.
P.O. Box 1338
Ellicot Station
Buffalo, NY USA
14205

Printed and bound in Slovenia
98 99 00 01 6 5 4 3 2 1

Text: Josée Hermsen
Translation: Stephen Challacombe
Editing for the North American edition: Olive Koyama
Cover design: Ton Wienbelt, The Hague, The Netherlands
Coordination, editing, and production: TextCase, Groningen, The Netherlands
Typesetting: Hof&Land Typografie, Maarssen, The Netherlands

Contents

Foreword 7

Part 1:   Breeds of Horse 9

Part 2:   Caring for Horses and Equestrian Sports 59

   1 The Horse and Its Characteristics 59

   2 Caring for a Horse 91

   3 Riding 119

   4 Dressage 147

   5 Showjumping 169

   6 Driving 191

   7 Western Riding 213

   8 Other Equestrian Sports 241

   9 Illness and Disorders 263

  10 A Horse of Your Own 287

Appendix 304

Acknowledgements 306

Index 307

Foreword

The horse world is so wide-ranging that writing an encyclopaedia of horses is no simple task. To start with, there are around two hundred breeds of horse and pony in the world. These alone could fill an entire book.

The general horse-lover in Europe is only likely to encounter a few of these breeds and therefore this book has selected the more important breeds for the first section of this book in which those breeds are described, and where possible, also illustrated.

The second part of the book turns its attention to looking after horses and the various types of sporting activities that can be enjoyed with horses. The chapters are arranged thematically; to find specific information, you can refer to the index.

It is my intention to provide as complete a picture as possible of those things that horse-lovers want to know.
Many people have helped me to bring this book about and I would like to thank them all very sincerely for their enthusiastic support.

Josée Hermsen

Left: black Arab

Part 1 Breeds of horse

The Thoroughbred is renowned for its quick gallop

Horses at a market

horses for their strength, Arabs for their grace and beauty, and Hanoverians for their qualities as riding and sporting horses.

Terms used in describing breeds

The most important terms that are used in describing breeds are explained below. Terms that are mainly used to describe a horse's build or conformation are mainly dealt with in Part 2, in the Chapter *The horse and its characteristics*.

Native breed

A native breed is one that can survive in a particular place without the introduction of new bloodlines from other breeds at home or abroad.

Shetland ponies, a native breed

Horses are not all the same: there are small, stocky horses and tall, slender ones. The individual horses can be grouped together in large families of breeds. The majority of these breeds are the result of centuries of intentional breeding to an end but there are also semi-wild breeds that have occurred naturally.

There are roughly speaking seven groups: Arabs, Thoroughbreds, Warmbloods, Trotters, Coldbloods, and ponies.

The geographical distribution of the breeds was originally largely determined by living conditions. In countries where the winters are severe, the horses generally had thick winter coats and could survive on meagre food supplies. In contrast, those horses from hotter climates were adapted to higher temperatures.

Man's intervention has somewhat changed this situation. In some areas, the breeds died out but in other parts of the world new breeds were introduced. Man has also made a significant contribution to the cross-breeding between species. Each breed is differentiated from others by certain characteristics. Thoroughbreds, for instance, are known for their turn of speed, Dutch draft

Left: a chestnut Arab

warmblood's nobility depends on the proportion of hotblood in its breeding. The ancestors of the eastern horses are the Tarpan and Przewalski's horse.

Pony

All horses with a height to the withers of 15hh or less (1.52m) are considered to be ponies. Ponies are also differentiated from horses by the build of their bodies. Ponies have larger bodies in proportion to their height than horses, and they move differently due to their shorter legs.
In comparison to their height, ponies have a deeper, more solid body than horses and they generally move differently, chiefly because they tend to have shorter legs than horses.

Arab

Heavy or draft horse

A heavy horse is a working horse that has the stature, muscles, and stamina to make it suitable for pulling heavy loads.

Arabs

There are pure Arabs, part-bred Arabs, and Anglo-Arabs. The full-blood Arab is known as a hotblood and is the only true hotblood, because this breed has been kept pure of other bloodlines for centuries.
Thoroughbreds though are also regarded as hotbloods because they are directly descended from Arab blood. Anglo-Arabs are the product of crossing Thoroughbreds with Arabs.

Coldbloods

The coldbloods originate from the heavily built horses that lived in the forests of Central Europe. Most coldbloods are heavy working horses that are suitable for use as draft horses.

Warmbloods

The term warmblood indicates that a horse has some eastern blood in its pedigree. The addition of Arab blood is known as ennobling or improving. The extent of a

Warmblood

D pony

Light horse

Light horses have a build and movement that make them suitable for riding. The gait must be loose, correct, in line, and with good thrust from the hindquarters. In addition to the walk and trot, canter and gallop should be performed properly.

Light horse

European pony height categories are A, up to 11.2hh; B, to 12.2hh; C, to 13.2hh; D, to 14.2hh; and E (actually small horses) to 15.2hh. In North America a pony is officially 14.2hh or under.

Pony families characteristic to North America are the Chincoteague/Assateague of coastal Virginia, the Sable Island pony of Nova Scotia, and the Newfoundland pony, a category E or small horse.

Foal and dog both measuring 60cm (2ft)

Foal and dog both measuring 60cm (2ft)

Harness horse

Stud

A stud is the place where colts and mares are brought together and where through careful selection the breed is improved.
Some breeds are named after their studs of origin. A stud stallion is also known as a stud.

Founding sire

Various stallions will have played their part in the breeding of ponies and horses. These horses have been responsible for the inheritance of certain characteristics that are important for the breed and they therefore become known as the founding sires of the breed.
See the appendix.

Stud Book

A studbook is a register in which the origins of the breed are listed and in which all the progeny from these progenitors are then entered. Certain breeds assess the conformation of candidates for entry by having them led round in front of a jury.

Showing for conformation

Horses are not only shown for their studbook registration, but also when they are to

Bridle with leading rein and snaffle but without noseband

Harness horse

The characteristics of the harness horse are the upright neck, the less pronounced withers, and knee action when trotting. The trot is the most important gait, and this must be loose, powerful, and high.

Showjumping horse

Although showjumping horses are a type of light horse, they need to have certain specific properties. The back, which is very important, needs to be short and strong. Horses with longer backs will not jump so well. Good lungs and sound leg joints are essential.

be sold. The horse will be led by a groom who will ensure that the potential purchaser can watch the horse's gait from every angle. Horses also have to be walked round for a vet if they are lame.

The horse is walked round using a halter or bridle with a snaffle. The most suitable bridle is one without a nose-band. For showing, the horse's mouth must not be interfered with and it must have sufficient room to move its head and neck. The horse should hold its head up during both the walk and trot. If this is impeded, the horse will walk crookedly with an irregular gait. The ends of the halter lead or reins are held by the groom in his or her left hand.

If the horse moves too quickly, the groom can bring the left hand in front of the horse's head, which is usually sufficient to curb them. When the horse stands still, it should stand straight and square with its head held in a natural position. For checking its conformation, the horse is required to stand so that all four legs can be seen from the left hand side.

Stance for checking the conformation

Profile

The profile of a horse's head is often a particular characteristic of the breed.
There are three different profiles: a concave or dished profile, a straight profile, and convex or rounded profile.

Measuring rod

A measuring rod is needed to measure the height of a horse. The height of a horse is measured to the highest point on its

back where the neck extends, known as the withers. The horse needs to stand on a level surface for measuring.

Height is traditionally expressed in hands: 4 inches. 15 hh (hands high) equals 60 in. (5 ft. or 1.52m).

Breeds

In this part of the book, a summary is given of the best known breeds of horse. This is in no sense exhaustive; instead the focus is on breeds that have made a name for themselves in competition or for recreation, and those breeds which are famous for their exceptional characteristics. For each breed, the same set of characteristics is described (where relevant).

- The origin: where did the breed originally come from?
- The height: what is the average height to the withers?
- The color: what color should the horse's coat be?
- The character and nature: what type of character does the breed generally have?
- The appearance: is the horse heavy, broad, slender, or muscular etc.?
- Applications: is the horse a trotter, dressage horse, or showjumping horse etc.?

- The action: what are the characteristic gaits of the particular breed?
- Special remarks: such as how the breed came into existence and where they are bred.

Akhal-Teke

ORIGIN
Russia, Turkmenistan, Kazakhstan, Uzbekistan, Kyrgyzstan.

HEIGHT
15.1–15.2hh (1.45–1.57m).

COLOR
The color of this superb creature is literally quite sparkling. They usually have a gold or silver sheen with greys and bays being less prevalent. White markings are possible.

CHARACTER
The Akhal-Teke is not an easy horse: they tend to be strong-willed and high-spirited.

APPEARANCE
The head is small with a long, straight profile with large, expressive eyes, wide, sensitive nostrils, and long ears.
The horse is slender, tall, with high withers. The back weak with a low-set tail. The legs are

Albino Akhal-Teke

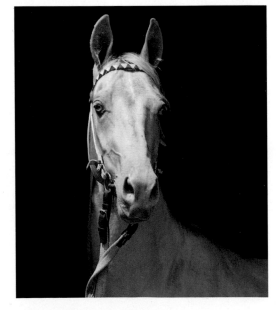

long with muscular thighs. The hair is sparse and both mane and forelock are often missing.

APPLICATIONS
The Akhal-Teke is a typical nomadic horse renowned for its tremendous stamina. They are also now used in some countries as racehorses.

ACTION
The first-class action of this riding horse is smooth, lithe and extended in all gaits.

SPECIAL REMARKS
The Akhal-Teke can cover tremendous distances without eating or drinking. The horse was traditionally protected under seven blankets and given a diet that is high in albumin.
The blankets were only removed during racing, breeding, and for a few minutes before sunset.

American Saddlebred (Kentucky Saddler)

ORIGIN
United States of America.

HEIGHT
15–17hh (1.52–1.72m).

COLOR
Bay, brown, black, or chestnut with markings.

CHARACTER
The American Saddlebred is a superior

American Saddlebred

American Saddlebred x Arab

riding horse with an exceptionally friendly nature.

APPEARANCE
The American Saddlebred shows to perfection: it has a noble head with straight profile, expressive eyes, and large, sensitive nostrils. The head is carried on a fine arched neck.
The overall impression is one of strength, elegance, and agility. The tails are bound to develop the unusually high carriage of the tail.

APPLICATIONS
The Saddlebred is first and foremost a horse for showing.

ACTION
The American Saddlebred has 3–5 actions that are collected and precise. These horses are said to "dance."

SPECIAL REMARKS
The Saddlebred has much in common with the Tennessee Walking Horse that was originally bred to convey plantation owners around their property in a fitting, elegant, but above all comfortable manner.

American Standardbred

ORIGIN
United States of America.

HEIGHT
14–16hh (1.42–1.62m).

American Standardbred

COLOR
The American Standardbred colors are solid chestnut, dun, black, or dark brown.

CHARACTER
The American Standardbred has an excellent sportive temperament and considerable stamina.

APPEARANCE
The overall impression is of strength, and with speed being the most important requirement, some variety in the conformation is acceptable.
Generally this is a small, muscular horse with short forelegs, longer hindlegs, well-formed hooves, and a plain head with long

Andalusian horse

ears. Power is important, so the breed has a broad chest, strong withers, and well-developed hindquarters.

APPLICATIONS
The American Standardbred is the world's foremost breed of harness racing horse, seen in trotting races, both saddled and drawing a sulky.

ACTION
A racing trot or a pace are the principal gaits, typified by long sweeping movements. The steps are not extended and must not break into a canter or gallop.

SPECIAL REMARKS
The American Standardbred has a tremendously powerful trot or pace and is considered one of the fastest horses in the world.

Andalusian horse

ORIGIN
Spain: Andalusia, provinces of Cadiz, Seville, and Medina Sidonia. Stud: Jerez de la Frontera.

HEIGHT
15–15.2hh (1.52–1.54m).

COLOR
The Andalusian is predominantly grey.

CHARACTER
The Andalusian is gentle and docile, proud, intelligent, and can be high-spirited. These horses enjoy working and learn readily.

APPEARANCE
The Andalusian is an elegant and beautiful horse to behold. The long head frequently has a rounded nose, with large, expressive eyes. Other characteristics are the luxuriant mane, small ears, and muscular shoulders. The shoulders are low and rounded, as is the back. The tail is low-set. The limbs are medium length, clean cut but strong. The mane and tail consist of silken hair. See also Special Remarks.

APPLICATIONS
The Andalusian is a light riding horse and an excellent dressage horse. Ennobled with Thoroughbred or Anglo-Arab blood, they make excellent jumping horses.

Their tremendous popularity as circus horses is remarkable.

ACTION
These horse have a raised action, with short but even steps and typically high knee-action.

SPECIAL REMARKS
A misconception about the Andalusian horse is that its origins are in Arab blood. Spain could be one of the few areas in which the horse survived during the last Ice Age. There are primitive paintings on rocks in Spain made by Neolithic man which depict horses. The Sorraian pony, which could be the primitive ancestor of the Andalusian, still exists today in Portugal where it is used by the people living in hilly regions as a working horse, which has saved it from extinction. The outward appearance of the Sorraian pony is similar to the Tarpan.
The original ponies of the Iberian peninsula were crossed centuries ago with the horses brought from the north by the Vandals. The original name for the province from which these horses derived their name was Vandalusia which became corrupted to Andalusia. These horses were further crossed with the Barbs during the Moorish rule of southern Spain. The breed has been carefully bred since the fifteenth century by Carthusian monks and these lighter horses are known as Carthusian Andalusians. There are two different types of Andalusian horse. One of them is more heavily built, with more robust limbs than most riding horses, the other is more lightly built.

Anglo-Arab

ORIGIN
Great Britain, France, Poland, Sardinia, and Spain. There are consequently British, French, Polish (Malopolski), Sardinian, and Spanish Anglo-Arab strains. An Anglo-Arab is always a cross between a Thoroughbred and an Arab. The Anglo part of the name refers to the English origins.

HEIGHT
15.3–16.3hh (1.55–1.65m).

COLOR
The color of the Anglo-Arab is usually chestnut, bay, or brown. The color is always plain.

Arab purebred

CHARACTER
The Anglo-Arab is always spirited, courageous, lively, intelligent, and trustworthy.

APPEARANCE
The Anglo-Arab has a fine head with a strong body, and broad chest, with a short, strong back, high loins, and well-developed hindquarters; the eyes are expressive, the neck long and arched. The tail is high-set, and the limbs are long and slender.

APPLICATIONS
The Anglo-Arab is a good dressage and outstanding jumping horse.

ACTION
The Anglo-Arab has an extended pace in all gaits, canters moderately well, and has a natural aptitude for jumping. The horse's movement is fine and smooth.

SPECIAL REMARKS
The Anglo-Arab is bred from Thoroughbreds and Anglo-Arabs in a number of countries. An Anglo-Arab bred in Britain must have at least $12^{1}/_{2}$ per cent Arab blood to be accepted for the studbook, but in France this has to be a minimum of 25 per cent, although the permutations of sire and dam are wider than in Britain. The temperament of these horses calls for an experienced rider.

17

Selle Français (French Saddle Horse)

ORIGIN
France.

HEIGHT
The minimum height is 15.3hh (1.55m) and the larger horses can reach over 16.1hh (1.63m).

COLOR
The Selle Français is usually chestnut, though other colors are permissible.

CHARACTER
The Selle Français is a friendly, well-behaved but spirited horse.

APPEARANCE
The medium-sized head can have either a concave or straight profile and the ears are somewhat long. The strong, long neck raises from very pronounced withers. The length of the back and loins is quite long. The overall impression is of a large, distinguished looking horse.

APPLICATIONS
The Selle Français is an excellent riding and jumping horse.

ACTION
The movements of this breed at the walk, trot, canter, and gallop are lithe, springy, and extended.
The Selle Français has a remarkably high knee action for a riding horse. The horse is a natural jumper.

SPECIAL REMARKS
The breed has a long history extending back to the Moorish conquest of southern France.

In the Middle Ages, this breed was very popular with those of high society but then its popularity waned until the breed was re-invigorated in the nineteenth century with an infusion of Thoroughbred blood.

French Trotter (Anglo-Norman)

ORIGIN
France.

HEIGHT
Between 16.2 and 16.3hh (1.60–1.65m).

COLOR
Mainly bay or dark brown, also chestnut, and to a lesser extent, grey.

CHARACTER
An energetic horse that is a good stayer, well suited for driving. The French Trotter is

Mounted trotting races

certainly a willing horse but its character is not entirely stable.

APPEARANCE
The appearance of this horse can vary somewhat. Generally, the French Trotter has an alert head carried on a long neck. The back is sound, with raised withers. This trotting horse has immensely powerful sloping hindquarters and long, strong legs. The overall impression is of a large light horse.

APPLICATIONS
The French Trotter is a harness racing horse that is also used in France for mounted trotting races.

ACTION
These horses have an impressive trot. The trot is extended, the walk and canter are satisfying. In addition, this trotter has an ability for jumping.

SPECIAL REMARKS
The French Trotter is a special branch of the Anglo-Norman breed, with selection of breeding stock based on trotting ability. The breed has had its own studbook since 1922. The French Trotter is a finer looking horse than the American Standardbred and is an influential breed in the development of European harness racing horses.

Appaloosa

ORIGIN
The Appaloosa originates from the Palouse country surrounding the Palouse river in northern parts of the United States. Today, the Appaloosa is bred in the west of both USA and Canada, particularly in Alberta where they are bred by the Cree Indians.

HEIGHT
14.2–15.2hh (1.44–1.54m).

COLOR
The most striking characteristic of the Appaloosa is the markings of their coat, described below.

- Leopard: white with dark spots over the entire body.
- Snowflake: spotting on entire body but dominant over hips.

Leopard-coat Appaloosa

- Blanket: dark with a white "blanket" over the hindquarters that is either plain or spotted.
- Marble: mottled all over the body.
- Frost: white specks on a dark background.

CHARACTER
Appaloosas have tremendous stamina and are docile and very tough. They are willing and good-natured.

APPEARANCE
The head is broad, with lively, expressive eyes. The ears, as with all American horses, are small and pointed, the neck is well-formed, and the chest is broad.
The Appaloosa has rounded, powerful hindquarters with a high-set tail. The mane and tail is unusually silken.

Appaloosa with white-blanket coat

Snowflake-coat Appaloosa

Blanket-coat Appaloosa

APPLICATIONS
The Appaloosa is a popular western horse and they are used for all forms of western riding (see Western riding, Part 2).
The friendly nature of these horses make them exceptionally reliable riding horses.

ACTION
The Appaloosa is a typical western horse and therefore has an outstanding canter and gallop, with a great turn of speed. These horses are also excellent jumpers.

SPECIAL REMARKS
The name is derived from the area surrounding the Palouse river (in the north of the USA). It is thought that the Spanish introduced spotted Neapolitan horses to North America in the seventeenth century. The colorful horses were bred by the Nez-Percé Indians of the Palouse valley for hunting and war.

The horses were known as Palouse horses, which in turn became "a Palouse horse", and eventually Appaloosa. The present day Appaloosas result from crossing Palouse horses with Quarter horses.

Arab

ORIGIN
The Arab originates from North Africa and the Middle East, particularly Egypt.
Fullblood Arabs are horses that portray clear breed characteristics and are the issue of horses imported from the above areas.

HEIGHT
14.2–15hh (1.44–1.52m).

COLOR
Arabs are predominantly chestnut, bay, grey, and more rarely, black.
They often have white markings on their legs and head.

CHARACTER
Arabs are exceptionally intelligent animals with tremendous stamina.
They are also renowned for their spirited character.

APPEARANCE
The head is an outstanding characteristic of the breed, with a wide forehead, a small, slender muzzle, and dished profile.
The small, pointed ears almost touch each

Pure-bred Arab

other and the eyes are exceptionally large and expressive.

This sense of expression is added to by the large, sensitive nostrils. The arched neck and relatively broad chest are typical breed points. The legs, however, can be a weak point with the breed. Arabs carry their tails in an unusually high arch.

APPLICATIONS
The Arab is first and foremost regarded as an attractive and fine riding horse but they are also raced in some countries. The breed is also used to improve or ennoble other breeds and provided the foundation of the Thoroughbred.

ACTION
The Arab is famous for its graceful, floating action that is particularly apparent at the gallop. The trot incorporates a great deal of knee action but the walk is not the strongest point for this breed. The action is harmonious and supple but not very extended.

SPECIAL REMARKS
Sources exist that are more than 5,000 years old that record the existence of this breed. Many modern hotblood breeds are related to the Arab – often through the Thoroughbred. Arabs are bred throughout the world these days.
The Arabian horse is renowned for centuries for its tremendous reserves of stamina

and ability to withstand the harsh conditions of its desert homelands. Arab legend has it that Allah created the Arab with a breath of southerly wind. Mohammed bid the nomadic tribes to keep the breed pure from other bloods.

Greek legend maintains that Poseidon conjured the animal out of the waves of the sea with his trident. What is certainly true is that man has regarded the Arab as something special since ancient times. Although the Arab is a muscular animal, they do not weigh more than about 500 kg (1,100lb).

Ardennais

ORIGIN
Belgium, in particular the Ardennes, and France.

HEIGHT
15–16hh (1.52–1.62m).

COLOR
Ardennais are mainly roan, iron grey, or chestnut.

CHARACTER
Ardennais are renowned for their docile, friendly nature and readiness to work.

APPEARANCE
The Ardennais is a medium-heavy cold-blood horse with all the usual characteris-

An Ardennais horse working

This Ardennais horse takes a well-earned rest

tics of such animals. It is solid, strong, and very muscular, the head is heavy and borne on a strong, arched neck and enormous chest. The hindquarters are also very well developed. The legs are fairly short, strong, and muscular. A second, lighter form of this breed was developed in the nineteenth century that is a lighter heavy horse or somewhat slow, but outstandingly strong working horse.

APPLICATIONS
Ardennais are widely used by foresters to haul trees out of places that cannot be reached by tractors. They are amazingly sound draft horses.

ACTION
Despite its cumbersome nature, the Ardennais has a remarkably energetic walk and trot. The trot can be quite extended.

SPECIAL REMARKS
This very old breed has inherited its size, weight, and character from the ancient Forest horse.
It is likely that ancestors of the Ardennais were praised by Julius Caesar in *De Bello Gallica*. It is certain that this breed was influential in the development of the Medieval war horse. The breed has seen additions of Arab blood over the centuries. Napoleon used Ardennais to haul his guns. The importance of the breed dwindled with the mechanization of agriculture. The Ardennais horse weighs about one tonne.

Brabant (Belgian Heavy Draft/Flanders Horse/ Dutch Draft Horse)

ORIGIN
Belgium and The Netherlands (Belgian type of Dutch Draft Horse).

HEIGHT
17.2hh (1.70m) but 16.2hh (1.64m) for the Dutch Draft Horse.

Brabant or Belgian Heavy Draft

COLOR
The predominant colour is red-roan but chestnut, bay, and sorrel also occur.

CHARACTER
The Brabant is a good-natured horse that is animated, tough, courageous, and prepared to work hard.

APPEARANCE
The Brabant has a short, thick neck and a double-crested mane. The head is small in proportion to the powerful, stocky body. The short, strong legs have plenty of feather.

APPLICATIONS
The Brabant was a very popular farm horse and is still much used as a working draught horse.

ACTION
The walk and trot action is quite energetic but not always entirely regular.

SPECIAL REMARKS
The Romans referred to the Brabant or Belgian Draft Horse and these animals were used from the eleventh to sixteenth centuries as war horses in both Brabant and Flanders.

These horses continue to be bred by farmers in Belgium and The Netherlands. The Belgians founded the studbook for *Le Cheval de Trait Belge*, as the breed was then known, in 1866, and the Dutch founded their studbook for the "Belgian type" of Dutch Draft Horse in 1914.

Barb

ORIGIN
North Africa.

HEIGHT
14.2–15.2hh (1.44–1.54m).

COLOR
Predominantly bay, dark brown, chestnut, black, and grey.

CHARACTER
The Barb is a tough, reliable horse that is highly spirited, with considerable stamina,

making them a plain-looking, yet still elegant, riding horse.

APPEARANCE
The Barb has a narrow head with a straight or convex profile and large muzzle. The neck is long and graceful, springing from high withers and a short back. The hindquarters are small with a low-set tail. The horse has long, thin, sinewy legs, with small but hard feet.

APPLICATIONS
The Barb was originally a cavalry horse but these days they are elegant hacks.

ACTION
The action is not particularly extended. The trot exhibits some knee action. The Barb jumps well.

SPECIAL REMARKS
The Barb was introduced to Spain in great numbers from 800AD by the Moors and has contributed to the development of the Andalusian horse. Many Barbs were imported to England from the seventeenth century, where they were used in the breeding of race horses.

Camargue

ORIGIN
The Camargue, southern France.

HEIGHT
13.1–14.1hh (1.33–1.43m).

COLOR
The Camargue is predominantly grey.

CHARACTER
These are tough, down-to-earth but spirited riding horses of good character.

APPEARANCE
A pure-bred Camargue is spotted by its goatee beard that grows from under the cheeks to the chin. The large, very expressive eyes and luxuriant manes are very striking.
The head is fairly coarse, usually with a large muzzle. The neck is long and these horses have no apparent withers. The legs are long in proportion to the body, with strong joints. The general impression is of a strong, muscular, and robust pony.

APPLICATIONS
The horses are used in the Camargue to round up the black bulls. The guardians (or cowboys) use a trident prod to drive the cattle.

Cleveland Bay

ACTION
The Camargue horse is not fast but does have considerable stamina at the walk, trot, or canter.

The Camargue horse comes from the Camargue in the south of France where they are raised in semi-wild herds. These horses sure-footedly move around the marshlands of the Rhône delta.

They are so well adapted to their surroundings that they can even close their nostrils in order to graze on young reed shoots under water.

The foals are born dark but change to a snow-white grey as they mature.

Cleveland Bay

ORIGIN
Cleveland, North Yorkshire, England.

HEIGHT
16–16.2hh (1.62–1.64m) though smaller horses are acceptable.

COLOR
Bay to chestnut with black legs, mane, and tail. White markings are not acceptable although a few slip by. Originally, the Cleveland Bay had faint zebra markings on their legs.

CHARACTER
Cleveland Bays have enormous stamina and a delightful, docile nature. They are also intelligent and sensitive.

Connemara Pony

APPEARANCE
The Cleveland Bay's large and not very distinguished-looking head has friendly eyes. Their necks, back, and loins are long, while their legs are short but well-formed with powerful hindquarters. The tail is high set.

APPLICATIONS
The Cleveland Bay is a warmblood with a wide range of uses as both a carriage horse and mount for riding. They are crossed with Thoroughbreds to produce Hunters.

ACTION
The action of the Cleveland Bay is a reason why these horses are popular hunting horses. The walk is extended, the trot energetic, and these horses also canter, gallop, and jump well.

SPECIAL REMARKS
The Cleveland Bay is the oldest unchanged breed in Great Britain. This powerful warmblood derives its name from the Cleveland area of Yorkshire.

Before the roads were built, the breed was used as pack-horses. Cross-breeding with Thoroughbreds in the eighteenth century completed the development of the breed. With the coming of motor vehicles, the Cleveland Bay is now bred as an outstanding hunting horse.

Connemara Pony

ORIGIN
Originally from Connemara in Ireland but now bred throughout Ireland and the United Kingdom.

HEIGHT
13.2–14.2hh (1.30–1.44m)

COLOR
The original color of these ponies was sallow or dun with an eel-stripe, black legs, nose, and ears but this color is now fairly rare. Greys and browns, black-browns, and other black variations are now more common.

CHARACTER
The Connemara Pony has great stamina, an exceptionally good nature, and equable temperament.

APPEARANCE
The Connemara Pony has a well-formed, noble head with fine long arched neck. The build is compact, with short, sound, and sturdy limbs.

APPLICATIONS
The Connemara makes a first-class riding pony for children.

ACTION
Connemaras have an extended action with a powerful canter and they jump well.

SPECIAL REMARKS
The Connemara is an ancient breed that has lived wild in the mountains of Ireland for centuries. They are hardy animals that can survive on sparse fodder. There are still semi-wild examples that breed freely without human intervention.

Dartmoor Pony

ORIGIN
Dartmoor, Devonshire, England.

HEIGHT
Not taller than 12.2hh (1.25m).

Dartmoor Pony

COLOR
Mainly bay, black, or brown but no color is barred except skewbalds, piebalds, or other excessive markings.

CHARACTER
The Dartmoor Pony is an exceptionally friendly and sensitive pony.

APPEARANCE
The Dartmoor Pony has the appearance of a mini-Thoroughbred with a noble head and small alert ears. The look is of a strong, muscular pony. The limbs are slender with well-formed hooves and their tails are full and high-set.

APPLICATIONS
Their height makes them ideal first ponies for children.

ACTION
The action is extended and smooth.

SPECIAL REMARKS
Dartmoor Ponies originate from the high moorland of Dartmoor in South-West England where they still live in wild herds. The Dartmoor Pony studbook was founded at the end of the nineteenth century, since which time the breed is virtually unchanged. Dartmoor Ponies are very fertile and can live to a very old age.
During World War II, Dartmoor was even more extensively used for military training than today so that the ponies suffered greatly.

Thoroughbred

ORIGIN
Originally the breed was founded in England but Thoroughbreds are now bred throughout the world.

HEIGHT
Up to 17hh (1.72m).

COLOR
The Thoroughbred has all solid colors and white markings are permissible.

CHARACTER
Thoroughbreds are renowned for their brave, almost fearless, and lively nature.

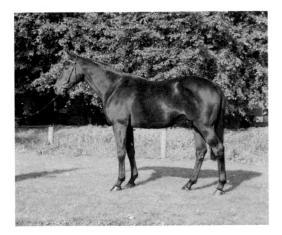

Thoroughbred

APPEARANCE

The Thoroughbred is generally a gracefully-built horse with a powerful and muscular form. The height and build can vary according to bloodlines. Riding horses are generally of light build, racehorses are compact and muscular. The head is noble, with a straight profile, and intelligent eyes. The neck is proudly arched above pronounced withers and a short, sound back. The hindquarters are muscular with either sloping or level shoulders. The clean, hard legs are impressive. The flesh is spare with veins showing and a thin, silken coat.

APPLICATIONS

The Thoroughbred is best known for its prowess as a racehorse. They are also suitable for use for dressage, showjumping, and hunting.

ACTION

The Thoroughbred has a naturally extended action through its size with a smooth trot, an impressive gallop and jumping ability. Thoroughbreds are extremely fast horses.

SPECIAL REMARKS

The progenitors of the Thoroughbred were the three Arab stallions that were brought to England in the seventeenth and eighteenth centuries. Their resounding names are Byerley Turk, Darley Arabian, and Godolphin Barb. These horses were cross-bred with horses that were then being used for horse-racing. Their offspring were so fine that horse-racing developed rapidly. The studs of Newmarket and Ascot are a direct result.

A horse may be termed a Thoroughbred if both its parents are entered in the General Stud Book in England or the studbooks of other countries. Thoroughbreds are widely used throughout the world to improve other breeds.

Exmoor Pony

ORIGIN

The Exmoor Pony originates from the rough moorland of Exmoor in South-West England (Devon and Somerset).

Exmoor Ponies

ACTION
The action is extended and these ponies have great stamina. They are also excellent jumpers.

SPECIAL REMARKS
The Exmoor Pony is an ancient breed that was probably used by the Celts as a pack-horse. They can withstand severe winters outdoors without shelter or additional food.

Fjord Pony

ORIGIN
Norway.

HEIGHT
13–14hh (1.32–1.42m).

COLOR
The Fjord Pony is mainly different shades of dun with a partially darker mane with a black eel-stripe. Stripes are also sometimes visible on the legs.

CHARACTER
The Fjord Pony is a self-willed but friendly horse that is pleased to work.

APPEARANCE
The Fjord Pony can easily be picked out from other breeds by the combination of its pale yellowish dun color and the erect crest of its mane with a black eel-stripe, that runs from the poll, along the back to the tail.

Fjord Pony

HEIGHT
Stallions not exceeding 12.3hh (1.24m), mares not exceeding 12.2hh (1.23m).

COLOR
Bay, brown, or dun with black points, no white markings but a mealy-colored muzzle.

CHARACTER
The Exmoor Pony is intelligent, friendly, and fast.
The Exmoor is a trustworthy pony for children provided the pony has been accustomed to humans from a young age.

APPEARANCE
The Exmoor Pony characteristically has an elegant head, with large, open nostrils, expressive eyes, and short ears.
The neck is strong and short, carried on a strong medium-length body.
They have clean, short limbs with neat, hard feet. The summer coat tends to have a coppery sheen while the winter coat is matt and coarse.

APPLICATIONS
The Exmoor Pony makes an ideal first riding pony for a child provided it has been schooled from a young age.

The likeness with Przewalski's Horse is unmistakable. The head is fairly large with the eyes widely separated. The neck is short and thick.

The Fjord is tremendously strong, with a powerful, muscular body, long back and rounded hindquarters. The short legs have a pronounced fetlock.

APPLICATIONS
The Fjord Pony was originally used by Norwegian smallholders as a working pony. These days, in addition to this role, they have become popular recreation ponies and are widely used for covered wagon rides. A Fjord Pony pulling a two-wheeled Norwegian *karjol* gig is a traditional sight.

ACTION
The Fjord Pony has a powerful striding walk and somewhat short trot.

SPECIAL REMARKS
The Fjord Pony is more or less unaltered from the Viking horses that were used for horse fighting. The breed has been bred in Norway for centuries without outside bloodlines, principally for use as a working horse. The breed is also popular and widely used in Denmark.

Frederiksborg

ORIGIN
Denmark.

HEIGHT
15.3–16hh (1.55–1.62).

COLOR
The horses of this breed are usually chestnut.

CHARACTER
The Frederiksborg is a spirited and willing worker.

APPEARANCE
The Frederiksborg is a fluent, medium-weight, noble warmblood. The horse has a small head with plain nose and an attractively-carried neck. The shoulders and chest are exceptionally strong; the back is broad and both the loins and hindquarters are muscular. The horse has good legs with sound joints.

APPLICATIONS
The Frederiksborg was originally used as a schooling horse for the high school of equitation but with the addition of Arab and Thoroughbred bloodlines in the nineteenth century, an all-round riding horse has been created.

ACTION
The present-day Frederiksborg has a sound walk, extended trot, and fine canter.

SPECIAL REMARKS
This is the oldest breed in Denmark, named after the stud founded with Andalusian and Neapolitan stallions in 1562 by King Frederick II. Denmark became one of the foremost suppliers of first-class riding and cavalry horses during the sixteenth century. The subsequent addition of substantial Arab and Thoroughbred blood means that the original type of Frederiksborg is quite rare.

Friesian

ORIGIN
The Province of Friesland in The Netherlands.

HEIGHT
15–16hh (1.52–1.62m)

COLOR
Friesian horses are always jet black; any kind of marking is not permitted. A few escape the net.

Friesian

CHARACTER
The Friesian is best described as an easy-going, spirited but willing worker. They are loyal and sensitive.

APPEARANCE
The Friesian is an attractive carriage horse with plenty of feather. Both the mane and tail arc wavy. These horses have fine heads born on long, upright and arched necks above no discernible withers. The legs are rather short but sturdy with ample feather and prominent fetlocks; the hooves are blue. These horses deport themselves with pride.

APPLICATIONS
The Friesian horse is regularly seen at shows between the shafts of a traditional Friesian high-wheeled gig. In The Netherlands, the occupants are likely to be dressed in traditional costume. The Friesian also makes a first class riding horse with a definite aptitude for dressage and strong reputation as a schooling horse for the high school of equitation.

ACTION
The Friesian catches the eye during the trot because of their high knee action.

SPECIAL REMARKS
The Friesian is one of the oldest of all European breeds. It is probable that the Friesian horse has been in use for more than 3,000 years. These horses were highly regarded by the Romans who took them with them when

they invaded Britain, and Friesians were widely used in the Middle Ages as war horses. Andalusian blood was introduced in the seventeenth century to produce a fast trotting horse. The introduction of mechanization in agriculture almost saw the breed disappear but there has been a resurgence in interest in the breed, for which a studbook was instituted in 1879.

Hackney and Hackney Pony

ORIGIN
England.

HEIGHT
Hackney Pony not taller than 14hh (1.42m); Hackney 15–15.3hh (1.52–1.55m).

COLOR
The Hackney is usually dark brown, black, bay, or chestnut, with the occasional grey.

CHARACTER
The Hackney is a spirited horse that is eager to work.

APPEARANCE
The graceful upright, strongly muscular neck, with small, noble head with a straight profile, and high-set tail that is carried high are typical for the Hackney. The legs are strong with exceptionally flexible joints. The hooves are small and hard.

APPLICATIONS
The Hackney is a harness horse that is never raced. They are solely prized for their unusual action and clean lines of a typical show horse.

Hackney

Hackney Pony

ACTION
The extended, high action, particularly of the forelegs in the trot, of this elegant coach horse is impressive.

SPECIAL REMARKS
The name Hackney is thought to be derived from the Old French word *haquenée*, meaning "an ambling horse or mare, especially for ladies to ride on," that was perhaps used to differentiate them from the knight's steeds.
The Hackney Pony is a related, smaller horse, that is registered in the same studbook as the Hackney.

Haflinger

ORIGIN
Northern Tyrol, Austria; Bavaria, Germany; Hafling in South Tyrol, Italy.

HEIGHT
About 14hh (1.35–1.45m)

COLOR
The Haflinger is chestnut with a flaxen mane and tail.

CHARACTER
The Haflinger is an intelligent pony that is eager to learn, with a friendly nature.

APPEARANCE
The noble head of the Haflinger betrays its hotblood origins (see Special Remarks). The Haflinger is a plain, tough, and exceptionally strong pony with short legs and muscular legs and quarters.
The strong, broad hindquarters are quite striking. The feet are hard and extremely sound.

APPLICATIONS
These ponies make excellent riding and carriage ponies. They are used in the Alps to pull sleighs.

ACTION
The action of the Haflinger is perfect for their role as mountain ponies. All three gaits are good but not very extensive because of their adaptation to climbing.

SPECIAL REMARKS
The Haflinger was bred in the nineteenth century by crossing a Shagya Arab stallion

Haflinger

with a local Tyrol mare. It is likely that the mare's ancestry included eastern influences.
Hafling now lies in Italy (in South Tyrol) where a heavier type of Haflinger is now bred. In the Austrian North Tyrol, the efforts are directed towards a modern, multi-purpose Haflinger that is as pure-bred as possible.

Two Haflinger ponies

Hanoverian

ORIGIN
Hanover, Lower Saxony, Germany.

HEIGHT
15.3–16.2hh (1.55–1.65m).

COLOR
Predominantly chestnut with white markings but also brown, black, and occasionally grey.

CHARACTER
The Hanoverian has a sound character and generally a quiet temperament.

APPEARANCE
The Hanoverian is large and imposing with a clean cut and expressive face rather than noble head. The neck is long and muscular, as is the back. The horse is generally large, with breadth as well as length, robust bone structure and powerful legs, with somewhat small feet. The tail is high-set and is carried high.

APPLICATIONS
The Hanoverian is one of the most successful dressage and jumping horses, making it an ideal riding and competitive horse that can be used in various sporting disciplines.

ACTION
These horses have a long walking stride, energetic trot, and springing canter and gallop. They are excellent jumpers.

Hanoverian

SPECIAL REMARKS
In common with the other German warmbloods, the Hanoverian is a horse of outstanding quality. The breed, that was developed in the eighteenth century from Mecklenburgs, Holsteins, and Thoroughbreds, is somewhat heavily built but this does not detract from its excellent characteristics.
Breeding is almost entirely a state enterprise, with the Hanover stud's 16,000 mares making it the biggest in the world.

Holstein

ORIGIN
Holstein, Germany.

HEIGHT
16–17hh (1.65–1.75m).

COLOR
The Holstein varies from bay with black points to brown-black, but grey and chestnut also occur.

CHARACTER
The Holstein is a well-behaved horse with an impeccable temperament and therefore entirely trustworthy.

APPEARANCE
In common with the Hanoverian, the Holstein is a large horse but the addition of Thoroughbred blood gives it a noble appearance. The head has a straight profile with expressive eyes and large nostrils. The

Holstein

neck and withers are very powerful, the long back has strong, sloping shoulders, and muscular hindquarters. The short legs are well positioned with strong joints. The feet are large and round.

APPLICATIONS
Originally, the Holstein was a carriage horse but through the continual improvement of the breed, they are now primarily riding horses greatly suited to horse sports with considerable ability as jumpers.

ACTION
These horses have a long walking pace, extended and powerful trot, a springy canter, and great jumping ability.

SPECIAL REMARKS
The Holstein was an elegant carriage horse with both German and Spanish blood in its veins to which some eastern blood had been added.
In the nineteenth century, the demand for riding horses increased and breeders improved the breed by using Thoroughbred stallions. Care was taken to retain sound legs and hooves. These improvements have made the Holstein look more like a true riding horse.

Hunter

ORIGIN
England and Ireland.

HEIGHT
15–18hh (1.52–1.83m). The height varies for Hunters. Horses for women are usually towards the lower end of the height scale.

COLOR
All colors are possible.

CHARACTER
Hunters are energetic, fast, and have great reserves of stamina.

APPEARANCE
Since the Hunter is more a part-bred type rather than a true breed, bred specially for hunting, their appearance can vary significantly. Generally, they are large, tall horses, with sound legs and a strong back. Hunters are specifically bred for the type of country across which they must hunt.

Hunter

There are therefore three categories of Hunter: heavy, middle-weight, and light, denoting the type of build.

APPLICATIONS
The Hunter is bred for hunting but they can also make good event horses.

ACTION
The Hunter is an outstanding jumper and also possesses an extended walk, very extended canter, and fast gallop that can be maintained over quite some distance.

SPECIAL REMARKS
The Hunter is bred by crossing Thoroughbreds with various coldblood mares such as the Cleveland Bay in England, and the Irish Draft Horse in Ireland. The Hunter is therefore a "Part-bred" or half-breed.
As its name implies, the Hunter is particularly suitable for hunting with a pack of hounds. The good Hunter remains fit all season and can perform well at all times.

Icelandic Pony

ORIGIN
Iceland.

HEIGHT
12.3–13.2hh (1.25–1.35m).

COLOR
Icelandic Ponies are mainly black or dark brown, but chestnut, grey, and sometimes

even piebalds or skewbalds occur. Chestnuts usually have light manes and tails.

CHARACTER
The Icelandic Pony is friendly, good-natured, and trustworthy. It has considerable stamina.

APPEARANCE
The Icelandic Pony has a fairly heavy, large head for its size, with small ears, a stocky body, and strong limbs. Their tails are low-set and they have a coarse, dense coat.

APPLICATIONS
The Icelandic Pony is by origin a mountain pony that can withstand harsh conditions. They have been used for centuries as pack horses and for riding.

ACTION
The remarkable characteristics of the Icelandic Pony are its two unusual additional gaits.
It has a pace *(skeid)* in which the right front leg and right rear leg move forward together followed by the same for the left legs and a unique running walk *(tølt)*. This means that the Icelandic Pony has five different gaits. Each gait is confidently performed in whatever terrain. These ponies are also excellent jumpers.

SPECIAL REMARKS
Icelandic Ponies are not permitted to be broken for riding before they are five years old because of their late development. This enables them to strengthen themselves through eating for longer than other ponies which makes them more expensive.
On the plus side, they are very hardy and healthy, remain fertile longer than normal, and can continue working until an old age. The Icelandic Pony needs no stable, being able to remain out of doors the entire year, which is better for their muscles, skin, and lungs.
Their thick waterproof coat keeps them warm and dry, even when it is bitter cold. By contrast, they need shelter from the strong sun in summer. The breed is reared naturally in semi-wild herds in Iceland, but they are also widely bred and used elsewhere.

Irish Draft Horse

ORIGIN
Ireland.

HEIGHT
Stallions 16hh (1.63m) and over, mares 15.2hh (1.55m) and over.

COLOR
The most usual colors are bay, black-brown, chestnut, and grey.

CHARACTER
The Irish Draft Horse is a keen worker that performs well, with a reliable nature, all of which make it a suitable basis for Irish Hunters.

APPEARANCE
The Irish Draft Horse is a large, muscular horse with a long back and four strong, hard legs with pronounced fetlocks – which points to the significant amount of cold-blood in its origins.

APPLICATIONS
Cross-breeding with hotbloods has produced a popular all-round sporting horse. Many Hunters have Irish Draft Horse blood.

ACTION
All these horses' gaits are extended and energetic and they have astounding jumping ability.

SPECIAL REMARKS
The Irish Draft Horse is an Irish warmblood with which the coldblood traits are still clearly visible. The original Irish Draft

Irish Draft Horse with foal

Kladruber

has probably had infusions of blood from Connemara Ponies, Spanish horses, and English warmbloods. The coldblood influences date from the nineteenth century.

Kladruber
(Czechoslovakian Warmblood)

ORIGIN
Kladruby stud in the Czech Republic.

HEIGHT
16.2–18hh (1.65–1.80m)

COLOR
Kladrubers are black or grey, depending on the stud from which they come (see Special Remarks).

CHARACTER
These horses have a friendly, docile character but can show spirit when it is required of them.

APPEARANCE
The Kladruber is of Spanish and Neapolitan origins and they have a large, rather coarse head with prominent blunt nose. The neck is proudly carried upright, the withers are barely discernible and the back can be

weak. The quarters are broad and short and are crowned with a high-set tail. The legs are strong with sound joints. The feet are hard and large.

APPLICATIONS
During the time of the Austro-Hungarian Empire, all the greys from the Kladruby Stud were sent to the Imperial stables in Vienna to be used for festivals. The black horses were used for funerals and for hauling the coaches of the clergy.
The Kladruber is however also an excellent riding horse and they are being increasingly used in equestrian sports.

ACTION
The action is short with a high knee action. This majestic, exalted action is at its best with the trot. The canter is ponderous.

SPECIAL REMARKS
The Emperor Maximilian II chose Kladruby as the site for a stud to breed coach horses for the state. His son Rudolf II turned the stud into the official court stud.
The horses were bred for their color: greys from Kladruby, and blacks from the stud at Slatinany.
These horses mature late and are slow in their development but they have long lives.

Konik

ORIGIN
Poland.

HEIGHT
12.3–13.2hh (1.25–1.35m).

COLOR
The Konik is drab dun with an eel stripe along its back. Some of this breed turn white in winter.

CHARACTER
Most Konik horses have a kind temperament though they can be spiteful.
They look like wild ponies and can act like them.

APPEARANCE
The Konik has the characteristic appearance of a primitive horse and resembles the Tarpan. It is a tough, plain-looking, versatile horse that is very hardy. The profile of the head is concave and the ears are small. The neck is somewhat stocky, while the back is both long and sound. The legs and feet are both strong. The full tail is quite low-set. In winter, the coats become thick and woollen. Some Koniks have feather around the fetlocks and hooves.

APPLICATIONS
Koniks are down-to-earth horses that can happily survive living wild so that they are being widely used for nature conservation projects. They are virtually only used in harness by man to pull carts.

ACTION
The action is fluent in all three gaits. The Konik canters and jumps well.

SPECIAL REMARKS
Koniks are rough horses with all the characteristics of a primitive pony, such as the eel stripe along the back. Their mousy grey is similar to the extinct Tarpan. The name Konik literally means "little horse" in Poland where these horses have been

known for centuries. Although the Konik has been ennobled with oriental blood, it retains the primitive constitution of its forebears.

Dutch Warmblood, Groningen and Gelderlander

Gelderlander mare

ORIGIN
The Netherlands.

HEIGHT
About 16–17hh (1.65–1.70m).

COLOR
These Dutch warmblood horses are bred bay, dark brown, and chestnut. Some white markings are permissible, particularly for driving horses. Black and grey are both rare.

CHARACTER
These horses are willing, good-natured, friendly, and energetic.

APPEARANCE
The Dutch Warmblood has a fine head with alert appearance, while the two breeds that are the core of its breeding, the Groningen and Gelderlander, have plainer heads. All three horses have long bodies.
The Groningen is heavier built than the Gelderlander. The Dutch Warmblood inherits the good points from the two other breeds but other bloodlines have been introduced to produce a quality horse.

APPLICATIONS
The Dutch Warmblood is much in vogue for dressage and jumping competitions. The Groningen and Gelderlanders are popular carriage driving horses.

ACTION
The Dutch Warmblood has good level paces in all gaits and they are energetic and outstanding jumpers. The Groningen and Gelderlander both have fine, high trotting actions for carriage work.

SPECIAL REMARKS
The current Dutch Warmblood is a modern breed specially created by crossing Groningen and Gelderlander horses with each other but other bloodlines were also required to produce the perfect sporting horse, so Thoroughbred, French Trotter, and Holstein blood was also introduced.

Dutch Warmblood

Groningen stallion

Lipizzaner

ORIGIN
The Lipizzaner originates from the former Yugoslavia (present day Slovenia) and Austria.

HEIGHT
About 15hh (1.57–1.60m).

COLOR
Most Lipizzaners are grey but the Slovenian horses include black and brown.

CHARACTER
The Lipizzaner is an intelligent horse that is eager to learn and exceptionally well-behaved.

APPEARANCE
The expressive head often has a ram nose. The neck is low-set, not particularly long, and makes a strong impression. The body with its rounded quarters and heavy shoulders portrays power. The luxuriant tail is squarely set and the legs are short and sturdy with small but perfectly-formed feet.

APPLICATIONS
The Lipizzaner is famous for its appearances at the Spanish Riding School in Vienna. The character and springy trotting action make them ideal for the art of high school equitation.

Lipizzaner

ACTION
The pace is fairly short and there is a high knee-action in the trot that is exploited in the "Spanish trot." The canter and gallop are somewhat ponderous.

SPECIAL REMARKS
The Lipizzaner is famous for its part in the Spanish Riding School in Vienna. The Arch-

Duke Charles of Austria started breeding them in 1580 with 33 horses that he imported from Spain. German blood was subsequently added to these horses. The breed is named after the stud at Lipizza (Lipiça) in present day Slovenia, where the horses were bred for the Austrian court until 1918.

The training in the high school airs takes about seven years. Some Lipizzaners have shown that they can perform well to an age of twenty and beyond. The springing trot action of these horses in particular makes them ideal for high school equitation.

Mecklenburg

ORIGIN
Germany.

HEIGHT
15–16hh (1.52–1.63m).

COLOR
The Mecklenburg is acceptable in any solid color.

CHARACTER
These horses have a willing and friendly nature and they are above all brave, making them very trustworthy mounts.

Miniature Appaloosas: Pony of the Americas

APPEARANCE
The Mecklenburg is closely related to the Hanoverian and it also closely resembles it. The Hanoverian is both larger and longer though, and the Mecklenburg is stockier. The general impression is of a sturdy, down-to-earth, and sound horse.

APPLICATIONS
The Mecklenburg is mainly used as a general hack.

ACTION
The movement is steady and smooth in all gaits.

SPECIAL REMARKS
The Mecklenburg was bred principally as a cavalry horse but since World War II, the effort has been directed towards producing good general riding horses.

Miniature Horses

ORIGIN
Europe, Argentina, USA.

HEIGHT
Less than 9hh (.87m).

COLOR
Miniature horses match the color of a full-size horse. Miniature Appaloosas, for example, have the same colors and markings of their greater brothers.

CHARACTER
Miniatures enjoy human companionship. They are mischievous and playful, and learn quickly.

APPEARANCE
Miniature horses are bred to look, not like ponies, but like their larger brothers.

APPLICATIONS
Miniature horses are much in vogue as pets. They make good stable companions for horses. Although they are not suitable for riding, they can easily pull an adult in a small-scale carriage.

ACTION
Miniature horses' movements at all gaits are short and brisk.

SPECIAL REMARKS
Long the pets of royalty and nobility, some were bred for work underground in the mines of Europe. In the 1860s the Fallabella family in Argentina bred miniatures by crossing Thoroughbreds with Shetland Ponies. The American Miniature Horse Registry was founded in 1972, the American Miniature Horse Association in 1978.

Dutch Draft Horse

Miniature Shetland Ponies

ORIGIN
The Netherlands.

HEIGHT
About 16hh (1.60m).

COLOR
Dutch Draft Horses are bay, grey, and chestnut.

CHARACTER
The Dutch Draft Horse has a calm manner and outstandingly good nature.

APPEARANCE
The small head is in strong contrast to the heavy, muscular body.
The limbs are short with heavy feet and feathering. These horses weigh 750–1,000kg (1,653–2,204lb).

APPLICATIONS
The Dutch Draft Horse is a typical working horse that was previously used on the land.

Dutch Draft Horses

ACTION
The Dutch Draft Horse has a remarkably light-footed and energetic pace for such a heavily built horse. The trot is easy and extended.

SPECIAL REMARKS
The Dutch Draft Horse is the only heavy draft horse breed originating in The Netherlands. It was bred from native Dutch coldbloods at the beginning of the twentieth century and is an impressive horse that is immensely powerful.

Its progenitors were used for centuries before that to haul loads and work the land throughout Europe. Today the breed is fairly rare and the breeding is limited to a few private owners.

New Forest Pony

ORIGIN
The New Forest in Southern England.

HEIGHT
13.3–14.2hh (1.35–1.45m).

New Forest Pony

COLOR
All colors are permissible except piebald and skewbald.

CHARACTER
The New Forest Pony has a docile, reliable temperament and has a good, friendly nature.

APPEARANCE
The head has something of the Arab in it, with expressive eyes and large nostrils. The long, strong back has pronounced withers. The legs are sound but not always of regular conformation.

APPLICATIONS
The New Forest Pony is a favorite mount for children.

ACTION
The pace and trot are nothing exceptional but these ponies canter well and are good jumpers.

SPECIAL REMARKS
The New Forest Ponies get their name from the heath and woodland of the New Forest in Hampshire, England which draws many

The New Forest Pony makes a first-class mount

visitors. The ponies run free in the New Forest and meet many humans from an early age. They are consequently less shy than other breeds of pony that roam free.

The New Forest Ponies were crossed in the past with both Thoroughbreds and Arabs to improve them and this can be clearly seen with many of them from their large but slender heads.

Noriker

ORIGIN
The Alps in Austria and Germany.

HEIGHT
16–17hh (1.65–1.75m).

COLOR
The most usual colors are dark brown, black, and chestnut with few markings. The tiger-haired Norikers that used to be quite common are now rare.

CHARACTER
The Noriker has an easy going and willing nature. They are sound work horses.

Noriker

APPEARANCE
The Noriker has a long, friendly looking face with a ram's nose. The sturdy neck is festooned with a wavy mane. The broad back has little discernible form to the withers but the long broad quarters are, typically, ridged. The tail is low-set and also consists of wavy hair. Norikers' sturdy, short but widely placed legs have delightful socks.

APPLICATIONS
In addition to its use as a working horse, the Noriker is also suitable as a general hack.

ACTION
The Noriker is more of a pacer with an extended action. The trot is not so smooth.

SPECIAL REMARKS
The name of this breed stems from Noricum, the vassal province of the Roman Empire that roughly corresponds with the Austrian and Bavarian Alps, close to the home of the Haflinger.

The two breeds are clearly related. The breed was recognized by the Archbishop of Salzburg in 1565, when the Salzburg studbook was established. The breed was regularly crossed in previous centuries with Kladruber, Clydesdale (a Scottish heavy horse), and with other coldblood breeds.

Oldenburger

ORIGIN
Germany

HEIGHT
16.2–17.2hh (1.65–1.75m).

COLOR
The most usual colors were bay, dark brown, and black but chestnut now occurs as well.

CHARACTER
The Oldenburger is an equable, energetic horse, with an excellent temperament.

APPEARANCE
The Oldenburger used, typically, to have a ram's nose. These horses have a proud stance with a strong neck and powerful body. The quarters are broad and muscular but the back can be slightly weak.

The body is generally rounded. With the injection of Thoroughbred blood, Oldenburgers now have a more noble appearance.

Applications

The Oldenburger was bred as an elegant and powerful coach horse. Cross-breeding with Thoroughbreds, Hanoverians, and Holstein horses has produced a more general riding horse.

Action

The action is light, extended, and spring-like. The Oldenburger is also an excellent jumper.

Special remarks

The Oldenburger is a warmblood of German origin that was developed in the seventeenth century as a powerful carriage and farm horse. Since then, it has evolved to become a modern sporting horse although the original characteristics can still be recognized in the solid build.

The Oldenburg is certainly the heaviest of the warmbloods but this does not harm their performance in equestrian sports.

Orlov Trotter

Origin
Russia.

Height
15.3–16hh (1.55–1.62m).

Color
The most usual colors are grey (often dappled), black, and brown.

Character
The Orlov Trotter has a spirited temperament and excellent nature.

Appearance
Although the conformation varies widely, the Arab influence is usually clearly apparent. The eye is consequently often very expressive and the neck tends to the characteristic arched form.

Orlov Trotter

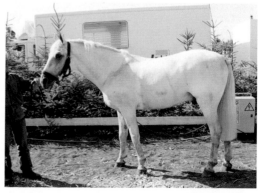

Paint (Overo)

Paint (Overo)

at the end of the eighteenth century when Count Orlow Tschesmensky brought together breeding stock that included eastern stallions and Danish and Dutch mares. The stud is now State run.

Paint

ORIGIN
USA.

HEIGHT
14–17hh (1.42–1.72).

COLOR
Paints are predominantly Quarter Horses which have white on their bodies above the knee. There are two types of markings, Tobiano and Overo. The Tobiano marking is the more usual, with large and evenly arranged white markings running over the back. With Overo horses, the white markings are rarely on the back. Instead, they run upwards from the belly and tend to be irregular blazes. A typical Overo may have a white head with dark-colored legs and this type will often have blue eyes.

CHARACTER
The character of Paint Horses tends to be similar to Quarter Horses from which most of them stem. This means that they are generally intelligent with a first class temperament.

The backs can be somewhat weak and have pronounced withers. The quarters slope and the tail is low-set. The legs are long, muscular, and have large, sound feet.

APPLICATIONS
The Orlov Trotter is a harness horse that is also used in Russia for harness racing with both sulky and sleigh. The Orlov Trotter is also used to improve the bloodlines of working farm horses.

ACTION
The Orlov Trotter has a short pace and a quick, forward-moving trot with a powerful knee action.

SPECIAL REMARKS
Before the Russian Revolution in 1917, the breeding of horses was reserved for the aristocracy. The Khrenov stud was no exception and this stud first bred the Orlov

Paint (Tobiano)

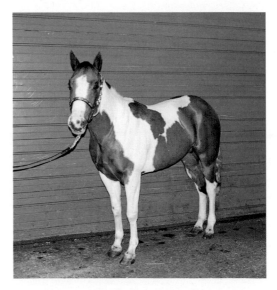

APPEARANCE

The color is the only specific type characteristic for a Paint Horse. Most of them in all other respects resemble Quarter Horses which are the predominant blood: a broad forehead with friendly, expressive eyes, an Arab's nose, little discernible withers but strongly developed muscular hindquarters. (See also *Quarter Horse.*)

APPLICATIONS

The Paint is a typical Western horse and is used for all forms of Western riding.

ACTION

Most Paint Horses share the smooth gait and rapid acceleration of Quarter Horses.

SPECIAL REMARKS

The American Paint Horse Association was set up to register marked horses that could not be registered as Quarter Horses. Two plain Quarter Horses can throw a marked foal.

Unlike the Pinto Horse Association, that registers any horse with appropriate color markings, Paint Horses must meet breed criteria, being bred from Quarter Horse, Thoroughbred, or Paint Horse stock.

Percheron

ORIGIN

The Perche region in Normandy, France.

HEIGHT

15.2–17.2hh (1.55–1.75m).

COLOR

The permitted colors for Percherons are grey and black.

CHARACTER

The Percheron has a good-natured temperament, is characteristically full of gusto and a true stayer that is determined to finish a job.

APPEARANCE

The Percheron is a heavy coldblood but the addition at some time of Arab blood makes them more finely and elegantly built than other coldblood breeds. This is clearly to be seen from the broad, rather noble head with expressive eyes, and small hooves. The neck

Percherons

is short and thick, the withers are barely discernible, and the quarters are broad and muscular. Unlike other coldbloods, the Percheron has little feather on the legs.

APPLICATIONS

The Percheron is the world's most popular draft horse and is often to be seen hauling a dray or wagon.

ACTION

The Percheron has an extended, easy but forceful action at both walk and trot.

SPECIAL REMARKS

It is suggested that Charlemagne's knights rode the ancestors of today's Percherons into battle. An outstanding more recent example was the Percheron Dr. Le Gear who was 21hh (2.13m) and weighed 1,372kg (3,024lb). The Percheron is now bred throughout the world. They have been bred with great care in the United States since the nineteenth century and in Britain they are crossed with Thoroughbreds to produce excellent Hunters. The Canadian, a riding and driving breed based in the province of Quebec, is thought to have descended from eighteenth century Percherons shipped to France's North American colonies.

Pinto

ORIGIN

USA.

HEIGHT

15–16hh (1.52–1.63m).

Pinto

COLOR
The colors of a Pinto are similar to those of a Paint Horse. The difference between a Pinto and a Paint Horse is that the Pinto Horse Association accepts a wide range of breeds provided they are part-colored. The preferred color is the piebald – black and white – but the skewbald – white and any other color – is more common. In the United States they use the terms Tobiano and Overo that are used for Paint Horses. There are also Morocco markings with a dark head and neck but white body and legs.

CHARACTER
The Pinto is usually a friendly and willing riding horse.

APPEARANCE
The head normally has a straight profile with large expressive eyes. In common with most American horses, the withers are not pronounced. The back is sound with rounded and sloping quarters.

APPLICATIONS
The Pinto is generally a reliable riding horse.

ACTION
All gaits are energetic but not always smooth. Otherwise, these horse canter well.

SPECIAL REMARKS
The Pinto Horse Association was founded in 1941 to register Pinto Horses. The Pinto originates from stock introduced by the Spanish and these horses were bred by the Indians. The Pinto should not be confused with the Paint Horse.

Przewalski's Horse/Asiatic Wild Horse
(Equus przewalskii)

ORIGIN
Mongolia.

HEIGHT
About 13hh (1.32m).

COLOR
Przewalski's Horse is recognized by its sandy-yellow dun coloring.

CHARACTER
These horses are hardy and rather plain with all the characteristics of a wild horse.

Przewalski's Horse

APPEARANCE
The Przewalski's Horse stands out because of its coarse upright mane. The head is rather large and the muzzle is grey. The mane, back, and tail have a clearly discernible eel stripe and the dark legs also have zebra stripes.

APPLICATIONS
The Przewalski's Horse is not domesticated but is used to graze nature reserves.

SPECIAL REMARKS
The Przewalski's Horse is deemed to be the forefather of the Arab and other eastern breeds. It is the only truly primitive horse still in existence.

Colonel Przewalski discovered that a herd of truly wild horses still existed while he was exploring Mongolia for the Russian Tsar. He discovered them in the Tachin Schah, which literally means the Mountains of the Yellow Horses.
He published an account of his discovery in 1880 and since then these Asiatic wild horses have been named after him.

Przewalski's Horse

Their survival was uncertain for a long time and they only survive today in reserves, zoos, and collections.

Because a number of countries have made efforts to protect the species, their numbers have increased in recent years and horses have been returned to the wild in reserves.

Quarter Horse

ORIGIN
USA.

HEIGHT
15–15.3hh (1.52–1.60m).

COLOR
The Quarter Horse is permissible in any plain color.

CHARACTER
Quarter Horses generally have an excellent

Black Quarter Horse

Bucksin-colored Quarter Horse

Quarter Horse

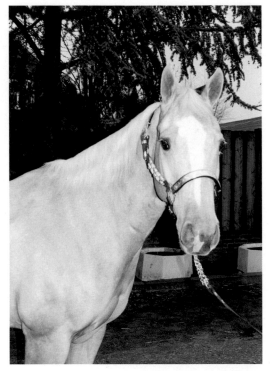

temperament and are very intelligent. They are quite calm and reliable.

APPEARANCE
The head of the Quarter Horse is small with a broad forehead, wide jaw, and large expressive eyes. The withers are hardly discernible but the rear legs in particular are strongly muscular.

The limbs are good with short cannons, broad, flat, low-set hocks, and muscular thighs and gaskins.

APPLICATIONS
Quarter Horses are ideal for Western riding.

ACTION
Quarter Horses are fast, well-balanced, and very maneuverable. These horses' muscular hindquarters and legs enable them to sprint quickly, turn, and stop.

SPECIAL REMARKS
The Quarter Horse is the oldest and most popular of American breeds.
The breed is derived from the Arab-based horses brought to the Americas by the

Quarter Horse

Spanish, and further ennobled by Thoroughbred bloodlines with horses brought from England.

Horse racing became very popular in the seventeenth and eighteenth centuries in America but because they had no racecourses the horses were usually raced on a road over a fixed distance that was rarely longer than a quarter of a mile (about 400m).

To win, a horse needed a quick turn of speed to out-accelerate the opposition and because this breed was quicker than any others, they became known as the Quarter Horse.

Shagya Arab

Morgan

ORIGIN
USA.

HEIGHT
14.2–15.2hh (1.45–1.55m).

COLOR
Dark bay, brown, chestnut.

CHARACTER
Spirited, intelligent and easily managed; courageous and willing.

APPEARANCE
Compact and sturdy with a short back, broad breast and well-muscled hindquarters. Head has a dished, 'Arab' profile.

APPLICATIONS
A versatile pleasure horse for both riding and driving. Favored for endurance rides and as a cowpony.

ACTION
Moves freely and smoothly with little elevation.

SPECIAL REMARKS
About 1795 Vermont schoolteacher Justin Morgan acquired the young stallion Figure. The little horse proved himself as a riding hack, weight and stump puller, swift sprinter and speedy in harness. The only stud to sire a distinctive breed, his get are the chosen cavalry mounts of the U.S. Army.

Shagya Arab

ORIGIN
Originally Hungary but now also Czech Republic, Slovakia, Poland, and Russia.

HEIGHT
About 15hh (1.52m).

COLOR
The color is always grey.

CHARACTER
The Shagya Arab is a multi-talented horse, that is eager to learn, and intelligent.

APPEARANCE
The Shagya Arab closely resembles the pure-

bred Arab but on average they are slightly larger and stronger.
The limbs are sounder than those of the true Arab.

APPLICATIONS
The Shagya Arab was originally bred as a cavalry horse but their qualities shine out today in their main role as carriage-driving horses.

ACTION
The movement of this noble horse in each gait is impressive and they are also good jumpers.

SPECIAL REMARKS
The Shagya Arabs are not pure-bred Arabs but result from cross-breeding between native Hungarian mares and Arab stallions of which the most successful import in 1836 was the grey stallion Shagya.

Shetland Pony

ORIGIN
The Shetland and Orkney Islands in North Scotland.

Shetland Pony

Shetland Pony

HEIGHT
Not exceeding 40in (102cm) at three years or under. Not exceeding 42in (107cm) at four years or older. Those under 34in (86cm) are called Miniature Shetland Ponies.

COLOR
Almost every color is possible, including piebalds and skewbalds. Black and brown are the most usual colors.

CHARACTER
Shetland Ponies are exceptionally friendly and docile, making them excellent first ponies for children. They are also intelligent and therefore easy to train.

APPEARANCE
The Shetland Pony is exceptionally strong – weight for weight, it is the strongest of all horses – capable of pulling twice its own weight, which is more than other cold-bloods can manage. This power is clearly to be seen in its build. The Shetland has a small head with a concave profile, small ears, expressive eyes, and large nostrils. The back and legs are both short and strong. The luxuriant mane and tail together with their

woolly and feathery coat contrive to make the Shetland look like a cuddly toy.

APPLICATIONS
Shetland Ponies are used throughout the world as first riding ponies for children but they also perform well in harness in front of a cart or trap.

ACTION
With their very short, sturdy legs, it is not fair to expect an extended action from this semi-wild breed. The action is short, straight, and smooth.

SPECIAL REMARKS
The Shetland Pony is a fairly ancient breed. Remains of ponies have been found on the Shetland Islands dating from 500 BC. These are descendants of the tundra ponies that possibly came from Scandinavia to Scotland some 10,000 years ago.

Thanks to its diminutive size, the Shetland Pony can survive without shelter on the windy slopes of the Shetlands and Orkneys. Previously, these ponies were used as working horses on farms and in the nineteenth century, they were employed as pit

Shetland Pony

The grey Shires of Whitbread's Brewery

ponies in the coal mines of Northern England. There were still 11,000 pit ponies in 1957.

Shire

ORIGIN
England.

HEIGHT
Over 17hh (1.73m).

Grey Shires

SPECIAL REMARKS
The Shire is the best known of the English heavy draft horses.
This descendant from the Old English Black – the most important breed in Medieval England – was probably crossed with Friesian Horses and later in the sixteenth and seventeenth century with the Flanders Horse. These giants weigh about 1,200kg (2,645lb).

COLOR
Shire Horses are black, brown, and grey. The two darker colors often have white markings.

CHARACTER
The Shire has – in common with most coldbloods – a good-natured and docile temperament.

APPEARANCE
Shires are huge coldblood horses. The head is enormous with a broad forehead and a ram's nose.
Shires have the appearance of coldbloods, except much larger: the neck is fairly long for a coldblood, the back is short and strong, and the quarters broad and muscular. The bushy tail is high-set. Much of the Shire's tremendous height comes from its long legs with their sound hooves. An eye-catching feature is the silken feather on the lower limbs.

APPLICATIONS
The Shire has all the properties that make a good draft horse and they used not only to be widely used on the land but also hauled brewers' drays.
These days, they are extremely popular at shows and other events, in their harness, decorated with brasses, pulling traditional wagons and drays.

ACTION
The Shire has an extended pace and a forceful trot.

Tennessee Walking Horse

ORIGIN
The southern states of USA.

HEIGHT
Average height 15.2hh (1.55m).

COLOR
The Tennessee Walking Horse is usually black, brown, chestnut, or grey.

CHARACTER
These are very intelligent horses with a fine character.

APPEARANCE
The head is small and is topped by small, alert, and pointed ears. The profile is straight, the neck strong and arched. Their backs are strong with high-set luxuriant tails that are carried high in the American manner. The overall impression is of a limber, strong, and elegant horse.

APPLICATIONS
The Tennessee Walking Horse is used as both a riding and driving horse.

ACTION
The distinctive gaits of a Tennessee Walking Horse are the flat-foot walk – the horse's hindleg treads in the hoof-print of the opposite foreleg and the horse shakes its head with every step – the running walk – when the hindleg continues 12–20in (30–50cm) beyond the fall of the foreleg and the horse can reach 8–11 miles per hour (13–18km per hour) – and a rocking, strongly developed canter. The horse can maintain the running walk for hours on end.

SPECIAL REMARKS
The Tennessee Walking Horse originates from the southern states of the USA.

In the eighteenth century Flemish and Shire stallions were imported to improve the small native Scots draft animal. Clydesdales became especially popular in the USA and Canada, and have been widely exported. The American Clydesdale Society was founded in 1878.

The horse was bred to provide a means of quickly inspecting the far-flung plantations without damaging the crops. This called for a nimble, light-footed horse.

Clydesdale

ORIGIN
Scotland.

HEIGHT
About 16hh (1.65m).

COLOR
Brown, bay or roan with white blaze and socks or stockings.

CHARACTER
Docile and good natured; gentle and tractable.

APPEARANCE
Somewhat less massive than the Belgian, Percheron or Shire. It is particularly noted for its finely sloped shoulder, and abundant feathers at the fetlocks.

APPLICATIONS
Originally bred for agricultural work, in cities the Clydesdale became favored for heavy delivery. Recently 6, 8, or 10-horse hitches have appeared in parades and exhibitions to advertise large commercial concerns.

ACTION
The walk and trot are springy, free and extended.

Trakehner

ORIGIN
Germany.

HEIGHT
16–17hh (1.60–1.70m).

COLOR
The most usual colors are brown, roan, chestnut, and red roan.

CHARACTER
The Trakehner has a lively and good nature; they are tough and hardy.

APPEARANCE
The Trakehner is the most noble of the German breeds. The graceful small head with its large eyes is very striking. The neck is long, ending in a raised withers. The back is both strong and supple. The legs are very sound and fine looking.

APPLICATIONS
The Trakehner is an elegant riding horse that was previously used in Germany as a cavalry mount and hunter.

ACTION
The Trakehner has an extended walk and trot, without knee action, and a powerful canter.

SPECIAL REMARKS
The Trakehner was developed using Arab and Thoroughbred blood. The result is a warmblood with a high level of hot blood influences.

The Trakehner stud was founded by King Frederick Wilhelm I of Prussia in the eighteenth century.
The stud suffered greatly during World War I. During World War II, 1,200 of the 25,000

Trakheners were dispersed throughout Europe to prevent them falling into the hands of the Russians. The animals had to travel 1,450km (almost 1,000 miles).

Welsh Pony and Cob

ORIGIN
Wales. The American Welsh Pony is bred in the United States.

HEIGHT
Welsh Mountain Pony (Section A): 12hh (1.22m); Welsh Pony of Riding Type (Section B) and Welsh Pony of Cob Type (Section C): 13.2hh (1.37m); Welsh Cob (Section D): above 15hh (1.52m).

COLOR
Welsh Mountain predominantly grey, though bay, chestnut and palomino occur. Any solid color is permitted for any of the four breeds; piebald and skewbald are not accepted.

CHARACTER
Ponies of the Welsh Section are generally intelligent, eager to learn, and have considerable stamina.

APPEARANCE
All four types of Welsh Pony have a noble appearance with fine heads and large nostrils. The high-set tail also points to the influence of Arab blood.
The back is short and rounded with well-formed quarters. The legs are sound and hard.
The forelegs are set forward with straight forearms.

APPLICATIONS
The smaller types are popular riding ponies, while the cobs are frequently hunted. All types are shown.

ACTION
There is zest in all the gaits and sound, well-developed legs make them potentially good jumpers.

SPECIAL REMARKS
The Welsh Pony and Cob Society Stud Book recognizes four different Welsh Breeds that are categorized in Sections A–D. The Welsh Mountain Pony is Section A and this is the foundation stock for the other breeds.
The Section B ponies are very similar to the Welsh Mountain Pony but are a larger riding pony for children. The bloodlines of these ponies includes that of a Thoroughbred stallion Merlin that was let loose with the ponies in the eighteenth century. Locally, these ponies are known as "Merlins."
The ponies in Section C (Welsh Pony of Cob Type) have Arab blood in the veins. The Arab bloodlines were introduced to improve the riding characteristics of these ponies. They are also popular driving ponies. Finally, Section D are the true Welsh Cobs which were created by cross-breeding with larger horses. At the beginning of the twentieth century, the Welsh Cob was used both as a riding pony and as a pack horse. Through cross-breeding with Thoroughbreds, they have developed into good hunting and jumping horses.

Welsh Pony

Part 2: Caring for horses and equestrian sports

1 The horse and its characteristics

The horse in its many types as we know it today is the result of eons of evolution. The oldest known type of horse lived about sixty million years ago and was 10–18in (25–45cm) high to the withers.

The forelegs of this horse had four toes with only three on the hindlegs. This horse evolved across time as a result of climatic changes. The ancestor of today's horse was an omnivore that lived within the shelter of tropical forest.

Changes in climate saw wide open plains replace these forests and the horse adapted

The horse has undergone eons of evolution and development

Left: an exceptionally handsome-looking horse

Horses on the land

to become a herbivore that could run fast to escape predators. Because only the middle toe was used in this role, the outer toes grew smaller and smaller.

As the outer toes disappeared, the bones in the lower legs also adapted into the cannons and fetlocks of today, culminating in a relatively sturdy hoof. The horse also became taller with a longer neck and the teeth adapted to the requirements of the new diet.

Horse riding as recreation

The changes in climate may have played a major role in the evolution of the horse but man has had the greatest influence on its further development. Right from the first moment that man domesticated the horse for his own ends, horses have been selected and bred to enhance and develop useful characteristics. This led to the development of different types of horse: draft horses, riding horses, and pack horses.

With the rapid increase in mechanization of farming after World War II, the demand for working horses was greatly reduced. The mechanization also meant an increase in leisure time and the horse found a new role for sport and recreation. This has meant a change of emphasis in breeding from heavier working horses to lighter riding types.

This chapter deals with the appearance and senses of the horse; their characteristics, how they convey their feelings; their breeding; and their bad habits and behaviour.

Appearance

The appearance of a horse is described in terms of the physical proportions of its body, known as *conformation,* and the color of its coat and any markings. The purpose for which a horse is bred and the requirements of its specific breed lead to different emphases in conformation.
A driving horse that has to pull a trap or carriage is built differently from a show-jumping horse. With a child's pony, conformation is less important than temperament and behavior.

Conformation

POINTS OF A HORSE
From front to back, the following points or parts of the body are commonly recognized: the head with muzzle, nostrils, chin, fore-

1. forelock, 2. muzzle, 3. chin, 4. throat, 5. shoulder, 6. point of shoulder, 7. breast, 8. forearm, 9. knee, 10. cannon bone, 11. pastern, 12. hoof, 13. heel, 14. ergot, 15. fetlock, 16. chestnut, 17. elbow, 18. flank, 19. stifle, 20. gaskin, 21. hind cannon, 22. hock, 23. point of hock, 24. buttocks, 25. root of tail, 26. croup or rump, 27. point of hip, 28. loins, 29. back, 30. withers, 31. mane, 32. poll

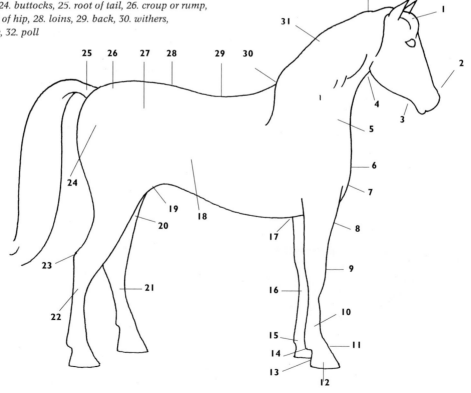

head, poll, and cheek; the neck with jugular or vascular groove, crest, and mane; the forelegs with elbow, forearm, cannon bones, fetlocks, and hooves; breast; shoulders, withers; the girth with chest, belly, and back; and finally the hindquarters with loins, flank, point of hip, croup, root of tail or dock, buttocks, thighs, gaskins, stifle, and hind-legs with hocks, pasterns, fetlocks, flexors (rear tendons), hind cannons, ergots, and hooves.

GOOD CONFORMATION

If the parts of a horse are properly in proportion to each other and soundly formed, the horse is said to have good conformation.

Each breed has different standards for the size and shape of the different parts of the body.

FOREHAND

By forehand, we mean the head, neck, shoulders, withers, and forelegs. It is that part of the horse in front of the rider. The position in which the neck is carried can be important for both jumping and dressage horses.

The line of shoulders and withers should be sloped and flowing.

The breast should not be too small for this can mean a weak horse and lead to grazes and scratches.

THE BODY

The back, chest, and flank together form the part of the horse on which a rider sits. A horse should be deep and broad through its girth to provide room for the many organs inside its chest. The back should be short and sound without too much of a hollow.

Good conformation

The quarters

THE QUARTERS

The quarters include the croup, loins, point of hip, the buttocks, and hindlegs of a horse. The legs should be strong and straight with straight, smooth stifles.

If these are too greatly bowed there is a risk of the horse stumbling. The hindquarters are so important because they are the motor that propels the horse. The extent to which a horse can perform is largely determined by the build, muscles, and fitness of the hindquarters.

FORELOCK AND MANE

The forelock is the uppermost part of the mane that falls forward. The mane runs from the poll – the very top of the head – to the withers, across the neck.

WITHERS

The withers should be the highest part of a horse's back. They are located at the bottom of the neck, where the shoulders of the forelegs come together.

CANNON BONE

The cannon bones run between the knees or hocks and the pasterns. If the cannons are too long, they will be less sturdy.

The fetlocks and tendons (flexors) should be clearly apparent.

Black forelock and mane

Croup-high

PASTERNS
The pasterns are the small parts of a horse's legs that form the sloping connection between the lower legs and the hooves.

Without the off-set of the pasterns, a horse's action would be very jarring. However, if the pasterns are too angled they put a strain on the legs.

FETLOCKS
The fetlocks are situated at the bottom of the legs, just above the pasterns.
The hair is usually somewhat longer over the fetlocks. Fetlocks need to be strong and not susceptible to inflammation from strains.

ERGOT
The ergot is a horny growth at the bottom of the fetlocks.

CROUP-HIGH
A horse is croup-high when the croup – highest point of the rump – is higher than the withers. This is not uncommon in young horses but the trait usually disappears as they mature.

Height

MEASURING THE HEIGHT
To measure a horse, it is essential that the horse stands square, that is with its weight evenly carried on all four legs.
The horse must also stand on level ground.

STANDING SQUARE
A horse is standing square if when viewed from the side, only one foreleg and one

SOUND LEGS
Horses with sound legs have very apparent skeletal structure.
A horse with sound limbs has little problem with windgalls (swelling caused by strains to the tendons or joints).

KNEES AND HOCKS
The knees of the front legs and hocks of the hind legs are found between the cannons and forearm or gaskin. Good joints are essential if a horse is to have a good action and jumping ability. The angle between the forearm or gaskin and the cannons should be about 150 degrees.

Thoroughbred with sound legs

hindleg can be seen, with the opposite pair hidden from view.

Coat colors

The color of a horse is partially determined by the color of the base coat of its hair.

Horses are divided into two main coat categories: *whole* or *solid-colored* and *part-colored* or *colored* which have patches of different colors.

The latter group comes in many different varieties. The illustration on the next page indicates the most common colorings.

BASE COAT
The base coat consists of short hairs that lie flat and which protect the horse.

These hairs also determine the color of the horse.

BLACK
Plain black horses are quite rare. If a horse is truly black or not can be seen from the groin and muzzle.

A black-brown horse will have brown hair in these places but a true black horse has almost no brown hairs. The coat of a true black horse can look somewhat brown in the bright summer sun.

BLACK-BROWN
With black-brown horses, the main coat is black but the groin and muzzle are brown.

BROWN OR BAY
Although the color can vary from light to dark brown, the coat is always solid-colored and the mane and tail are always black.

The first hairs of the base coat fall out

CHESTNUT

Chestnuts range from light golden-brown to dark reddish-brown. The mane is usually the same color as the body. Markings are possible.

GREY

Whether a horse is almost pure white or grey-white, it is always referred to as a grey.

Greys are always born dark and there are those that lighten to almost white with age and others that retain their adult coat coloring for the rest of their lives.

Some almost pure white horses have white or off-white hairs on pink skin but with dark eyes.

Chestnut

Those with blue eyes and unpigmented skin are called cream or cremello.

Black

Red roan

Cream

Grey

CREAM
A cream horse has unpigmented skin and will also often have a similarly deficient iris of the eye, resulting in a blue or pink eye.

DUN
Dun is a yellowish color that covers a darker base coat.

Those horses with darker reddish-yellow hairs over a dark base coat and with dark manes and tails are known as Claybank dun.

PALOMINO
Palomino horses ideally are the color of a new-minted gold coin, but may range from cream to very light chestnut with flaxen mane and tail.

DAPPLE GREY
A dapple grey is a changeable grey that gradually loses its darker hair and the distinctive dappled markings.

ALBINO
An albino horse is one with a congenital absence of skin pigment, resulting in white skin and pink eyes.

They are unable to stand strong light and see best in the twilight.

Palomino

Flecked coat

Dapple grey

Liver chestnut

Spotted

SKEWBALD/ODD-COLORED/PIEBALD
Skewbald horses have white patches and another color other than black.

Odd-colored horses are similar but have more than two colors in their coats. Piebald horses are like skewbalds but are restricted to white and black.

FLECKED/FLEABITTEN/GREY-TICKED COAT
A flecked coat has small irregular groups of white hairs, fleabitten is the name given to the brown specks that develop with age on grey horses, and grey-ticked is the name for coats with a small number of grey hairs throughout the coat.

SPOTTED
Horses with small, regular patches or flecks on a white background are spotted.
The best-known spotted horses are Appaloosas.

LIVER CHESTNUT
A liver chestnut is so-called because it has a coat the color of raw liver.

Eel stripe

1. star
2. small diamond star
3. round star
4. diamond star
5. half-moon star
6. extended star
7. narrow extended star
8. interrupted stripe
9. broad stripe
10. blaze
11. stripe
12. blaze
13. interrupted stripe with snip
14. irregular blaze with partially white muzzle
15. irregular blaze with darker "snip" and lip marks

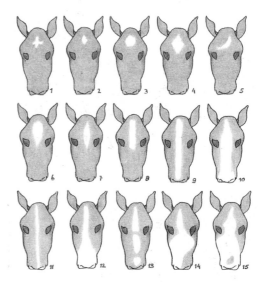

EEL STRIPE

An eel stripe is a dark line of hairs that run through the mane and along the back to the tail.

BALD PATCHES

Sometimes the saddle, girth or carriage harness wears a bare patch in a horse's coat. These are not natural coat markings.

Markings

Small and larger white markings on the head and legs of a horse have different names.

FACIAL MARKINGS

No two horses are precisely the same. This is particularly true of the markings on the face and legs.

There are certain recognisable patterns such as the star – a white patch on the forehead, and the snip – a white patch between the nostrils.

Mealy muzzle

Star

Blaze

Two white socks

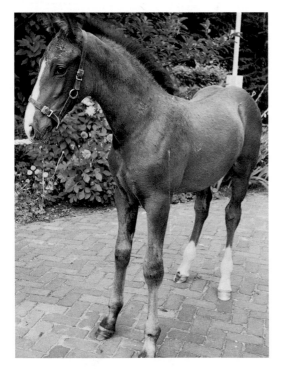

Striped hoof

These also appear in combination with other markings.

A blaze runs from the forehead to the muzzle and can vary in width. A horse that has a white patch that covers the eyes and nostrils is known as a white face.

MUZZLE MARKINGS

Some ponies have white muzzles, others have flesh-colored muzzles or flecked muzzles. Exmoor Ponies in particular have muzzles the color of oatmeal, known as mealy muzzles.

LEG MARKINGS

There are three principal types of leg markings: pastern, which runs from the hoof to stop at the pastern, the sock, which runs part-way up the lower leg, and the stocking, which runs from the hoof to the knee or hock.

ZEBRA MARKS

Zebra marks are stripes or bars that can be found on horses' legs.

HOOVES

The color of a horse's hooves is dependent on the color of their legs. White lower legs usually mean light-colored hooves, dark legs give rise to dark hooves and white hooves can sometimes have dark stripes on them. Some people claim that dark hooves are stronger than white ones.

1. white coronet
2. small pastern
3. pastern
4. sock
5. sock
6. stocking
7. stocking
8. partial pastern marking

9. irregular sock
10. irregular sock
11. irregular sock
12. irregular sock
13. irregular sock

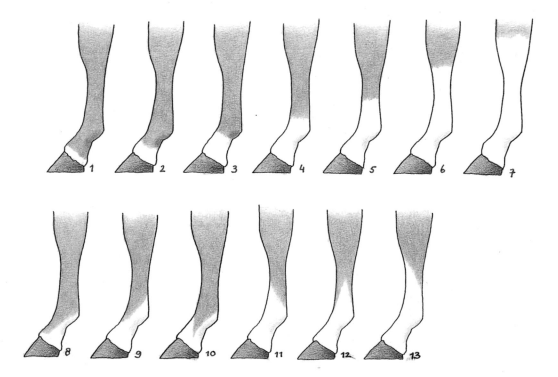

Gender

STALLION

A stallion is an ungelded male horse of at least four years of age. Under this age, an intact male horse is known as a colt.

Stallions are powerfully built and have a strong neck, with a more stocky shape than mares.

Stallions also behave differently to mares, and he is much more aware of his surroundings, and frequently bursting full of energy.

A lively stallion of good conformation is a magnificent sight. However, stallions are said to be easily distracted, particularly when there are mares in season but they are also said to learn more quickly. It is not really possible to generalize about such matters. A stallion which is used for breeding is known as a stud.

UNSOUND STALLION (RIDGELING)

A stallion with which the testicles have not wholly dropped but are retained in the body will be infertile. Such a stallion is unsound. An unsound stallion will react to mares precisely the same way as a sound stallion.

Riding stallion

Mare with foal

Gelding

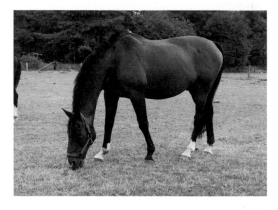

MARE

A mare is a female horse that is four years old or more. A younger female horse is known as a filly. Mares are usually more slender in their build and easier going than stallions but there are notorious examples to the contrary.

Mares that are in heat can be difficult and troubled. A mare that is used for breeding is known as a brood mare.

GELDING

A gelding is a male horse that has been gelded or castrated.

This renders the horse infertile but geldings are generally somewhat easier going than stallions which is the principal reason for neutering male horses.

Age

The age of a horse can be ascertained by examining its teeth. Up to the age of five, a horse still has milk teeth, with molars that are replaced by the permanent teeth.

This provides an accurate indication of the horse's age.

From six years old, a horse is said to be "full-mouthed" with its permanent teeth, when age can only be determined by examining the extent of the wear of the incisors in the lower jaw.

AGEING

When a horse starts to get old, this can clearly be seen. The tell-tale signs are the way that the lower lip hangs down, hollows above the eyes, the grey hairs that appear in

A four-month-old foal with four incisors and four molars

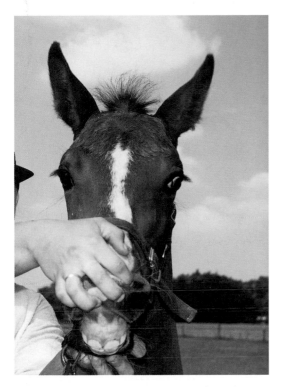

An elderly horse

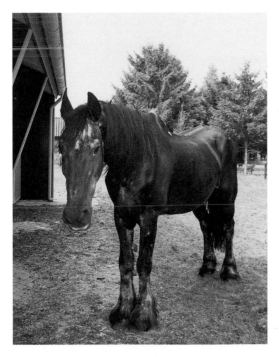

A "tush" or hooked tooth can be seen on the right

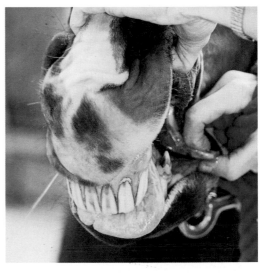

these hollows, and also on the head, mane, and tail.

TEETH

At the front of both the upper and lower jaws of a horse are its incisors or cutting teeth and behind these are the molars, or grinding teeth.

A fully-grown horse has six incisors and twelve molars in each jaw. The incisors are located at the front, with the molars at the back of the mouth as they are with humans. Sometimes a horse grows an additional molar at the front of its molars which can lead to problems with the bit. If this troubles the horse, the tooth needs to be removed.

Stallions and geldings also have an extra "tush" tooth on each side at the rear of their incisors, on both jaws. Rudimentary versions of these teeth can also appear in a mare's jaw. If there are sharp edges to the teeth because of insufficient wear, it is necessary to file the teeth down to prevent the sharp teeth from hurting the horse when it has a bit in its mouth.

Other terms used to describe the appearance of horses

FEATHER

Feather is the long hair on the lower legs and pasterns of a coldblood, or a horse that is predominantly coldblooded. This is an

Forelock and mane

A brand can be clearly seen on the horse's quarters

Feather on the lower legs

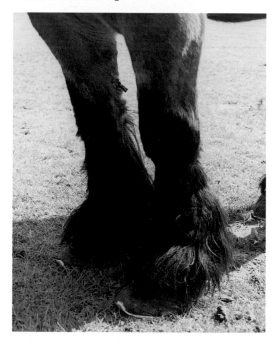

Freeze-burned marking

ing" a mark using dry ice, or freeze-burning, which turns the hair of the coat white. Tattooing is also used to inscribe a number on the lip of a horse and numbers can be marked on a horse's hooves.

WALL EYE
A wall eye is a blue eye. The color of the iris of the eye is determined by the color of the hairs surrounding the eye. If these are white, the chance is high that the eye will be blue. Sometimes a horse will have one brown eye and one blue one. The North American Indians thought that the brown eye was to see by day and the blue "moon-eye" was for the night-time.

RAM'S HEAD OR ROMAN NOSE
A horse is said to have a *ram's head* if the

attractive sight on a heavy horse such as a Shire but it is regarded as a fault in a riding horse, implying a prepotency of coldblood.

BRANDING
A brand is a mark burned into a horse's coat, mainly used by the ranches in North America to mark their horses. The brand indicates to which ranch a horse belongs so that if a horse is stolen, it is easy to prove who the rightful owner is. Another way in which horses can be "branded" is by "burn-

One brown eye and one white one

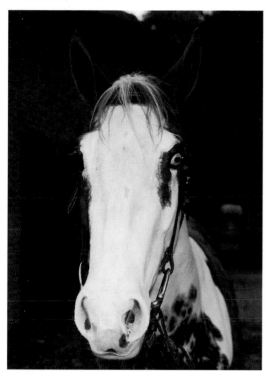

profile has an outward rounded curve as is often the case with Lipizzaner horses.

JIBBAH
The rounded forehead of an Arab is said to form a shield shape called the *jibbah*.

WHISKERS
The longer hairs or "whiskers" around a horse's eyes and muzzle are important to it as feelers, so they should never be clipped too short.

The jibbah, *or Arab profile*

A ram's head or Roman nose

A horse uses its whiskers as feelers

The star and snip are identifying marks for a horse's passport

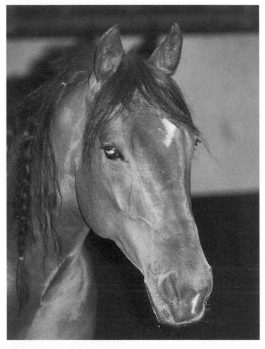

CHESTNUTS/CASTORS
Not the common color of Thoroughbreds and racehorses or the wheels on an armchair but the small, horny outgrowths often found on the inside of a horse's legs. They are also useful for identifying the horse.

IDENTIFYING MARKS
A full description of every identifying mark, such as a star or blaze, or size and position of chestnuts is not only needed for a horse's passport and for breed registration, it forms a valuable aid in the event that a horse is stolen.
Features such as pressure marks that can change are not included in the registration description.

Senses

Horses' senses enable them to be very aware of what happens in their surroundings. In common with humans, the senses can be divided into:
- sight (eyes)
- hearing (ears)
- smell (nose)
- taste (tongue and palate)
- touch (skin)

Sight

A horse's sight is different from that of humans. The eyes are set to the side of the head which has two consequences: it sees quite different images with each eye and it can see almost all around itself without turning its head. Only the central part of this image is truly sharp though and a horse has a blind spot immediately in front and immediately behind itself. This means that when a horse jumps it cannot actually see the fence at the moment of take off.

Although a horse cannot see anything immediately behind itself, it can see things slightly to one side that are behind it. To see them properly though, the horse must move its head.

The horse's field of vision has a range of a few hundred metres or yards. To detect what is happening beyond that range, the horse uses its excellent hearing and first-class sense of smell.

Alert horses have sensed something

To see something further away, a horse needs to lower its head

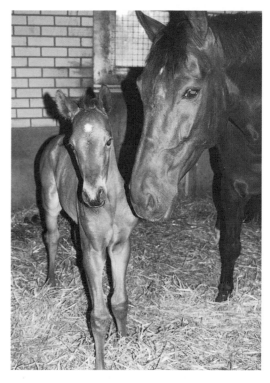

A horse is unable to assess depth, which is why it might shy away from a piece of paper or a shadow. The main reason for a horse taking fright is that it has not seen something properly, so do not punish it for doing so but instead try to calm it by reassuring it that there is nothing to be frightened of.

It is thought that horses can see colors such as red, green, yellow, and blue, with yellow being the color they see most readily.

Hearing

A horse has very much better hearing than humans. The shell-like ears can be turned to catch all kinds of sound from the environment. When a horse lifts its head, tenses its neck muscles, and pricks its ears, it has heard something. Hearing is very valuable for a horse in finding its way in the dark. Sounds from far off and closer sounds such as that of its own hooves ensure that a horse can find its way in the dark better than we can.

Smell

The sense of smell is very strongly developed in horses. They can easily differentiate between different smells and they can detect whether another horse is in the same field. If they smell something unusual, a horse will often stick its nose in the air, and raise its top lip.
With stallions, this is often a sign that they have detected the presence of a mare.
Horses can smell whether their drinking water and fodder is in order and if they do

What a tasty apple!

not like the smell, they will not touch it. The sense of smell is also very important to horses in socializing with other horses. A newcomer is sniffed all over and does the same in return.

Once a horse has recorded the smell of another horse, it will never forget it, whether it liked the horse or not.

Taste

A horse can use its sense of taste to recognise poisonous plants from those that are safe to eat. This is how they eat just the non-poisonous parts of buttercups. Horses also have their own preferred tastes – just like humans – and those they detest too. In general, they prefer sweet things but are unlikely to spurn a sharp-tasting apple. They like to lick salt blocks.

Feel

A horse reacts to the lightest of touches, showing how well-developed their ability to feel is. If a fly lands on their back, a muscle will twitch nervously in reaction. They get to know their immediate surroundings with the long feeling hairs on the lower and bottom lips. Most horses love to be tickled, particularly under their chins and on their noses.

Horses like to be tickled

Characteristics of the horse

HERD ANIMAL
A horse is by origins a social animal that is quite happy living with others in a herd. For a horse to remain on its own in a stable is quite unnatural.

All horses need some diversion, preferably with other horses or with a stable cat or goat as company.

FLIGHT ANIMAL
The horse does not prey on other animals in order to feed itself but it is prey for the larger carnivores. The only way the horse could avoid being eaten was to flee or take flight.

The horse retains this instinct to take flight at a moment's notice and they can accelerate rapidly. They do not wait until they

Taking the stable cat for a ride

Feeding time

have detected the danger themselves but will also react to signs from other horses.

Horses are herbivores

OPEN SPACE
Because in the wild a horse had to seek out its own food and might have to travel great distances to do so, it is happiest when it is not hemmed in, with room to move.

Standing with little movement in a stable is therefore quite wrong for such an animal that needs as much exercise as possible.

HERBIVORE
Behavior studies have shown that if the opportunity exists, a horse will eat vegetable matter at regular intervals. The horse does not have a large stomach and in the wild, they will eat small amounts of grass at a time but do so often.

HABITS
The life of a wild horse is controlled by an "internal clock" so that they rest at specific periods in the day and graze at others. Disturbing these habits unsettles a horse and this applies to its feeding times. Changing the feeding routine or a change in diet can not only unsettle a horse, it can lead to colic.

MEMORY
The horse's natural excellent memory can be used when training it. If a horse is

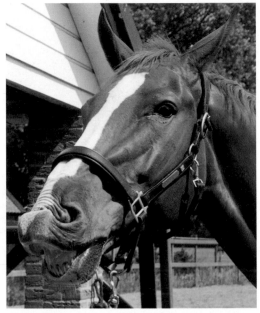

rewarded or punished at precisely the appropriate moment, it will remember the connection between these different experiences.

POSITION IN THE HERD

Horses that live in herds have a definite "pecking order" or status in the herd. Each new animal has to fight for its position in the herd. A stallion always needs to know who the boss is. The position in the herd also decides the order in which horses eat if they are given fodder. The lowliest member must always wait until last.

A rider always has to ensure that they are the master of the horse and not the other way around or a horse will resist. A horse will then struggle with its rider for their respective hierarchy.

Body language

INSTINCT

When a horse acts instinctively, we mean that it is acting according to inborn imprinting rather than that which it has learned.

An example of this is the horse's natural flight instincts, which have not been learn-

ed but are inborn. A horse that is suddenly frightened has a natural instinct to flee.

SCENTING OR FLEHMEN

A horse will often stick its nose in the air and lift its top lip. The horse is scenting the

Horses grazing in a paddock instinctively know which plants are poisonous

air. This behavior, known as *flehmen,* is particularly prevalent with stallions when they detect a mare is close at hand.

WHINNYING

Whinnying is a sound that horses make as an expression of a feeling or emotion. When one horse is calling to another, the tone is usually more high pitched and clear.

When a horse greets the person who brings its food, the tone is usually lower and more friendly. High-pitched whinnying is often used by mares to turn away a stallion or other horses.

DROPPINGS

When a horse moves its bowels, it can be a sign of relaxation and satisfaction, or of

Watch out!

Manure heap

Here comes my food

excitement. Horses often make droppings when they have a new bed of straw or have returned to their familiar territory. If the horse is nervous or anxious, the droppings can be somewhat loose.
The passing of urine can also be stimulated by pleasurable feelings.

LANGUAGE OF THE EARS

Experienced horsemen and women can tell what mood a horse is in by reading the language of a horse's ears. If the ears are set forwards, this means friendly interest but if the ears are set back flat against the neck watch out because this usually means the horse is angry.

RESTING

The lives of horses and ponies living free in a field is regulated by an internal biological clock. The horse will rest at certain times of the day and graze at others. Resting varies from true sleep to a sort of wary doze.
However, the horse will never sleep for long, or deeply.

Swishing the tail

As an animal that was preyed upon in the wild, the horse is instinctively always on its guard. This is why they mainly sleep on their feet. A horse will lie down sometimes but this must never be for very long because its weight makes breathing difficult.

SWISHING THE TAIL

When a horse swishes its tail it can be a sign of displeasure. With riding horses, it can also be a sign of resistance, especially if spurs are worn and used. This is not to be confused with swishing the tail to ward off flies.

Breeding

REPRODUCTIVE ORGANS

The sexual organs of a stallion have the function of conveying semen to the mare's body and fertilising the ovum. The most apparent of these organs are the testes or testicles and the penis.

The reproductive organs of the mare consist of the ovaries, each with a Fallopian tube, the womb, and the vagina, which has its opening under the tail. The opening of the vagina, known as the vulva, has two protective flaps of skin.

IN SEASON

During the time that a mare is in season, there comes a point at which she is ready to be covered. This period lasts from three to nine days. For the following three to four weeks, the mare does not want a stallion anywhere near her but then she becomes eager once more. During this period, the vulva opens and closes and there is some fluid loss.

If this is not immediately apparent, the mare can be tested by using a "teaser" or sub-

Legs bound to prevent a mare from kicking when she is covered

Diagram of the reproductive organs of a mare and stallion

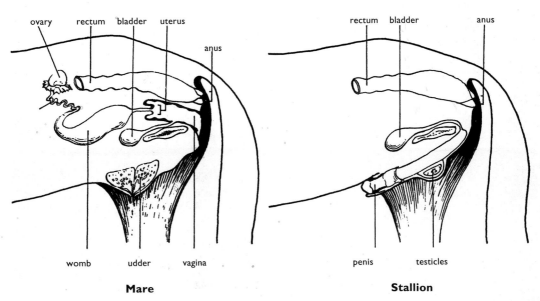

Mare **Stallion**

80

Beneath a stallion's tail there is just the anus

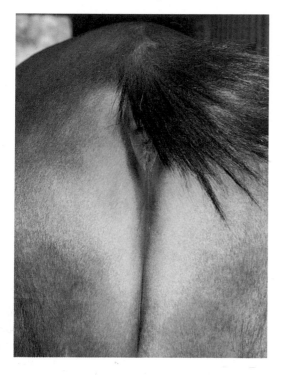

Beneath a stallion's tail there is just the anus

Beneath a mare's tail there is also the vulva with its protective lips

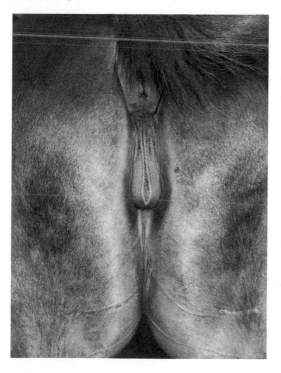

stitute stallion. This is usually an immature or infertile animal that is cautiously introduced to the mare. If the mare is ready, she will acquiesce, but if not, she will become quite angry, shrieking loudly and kicking. Horses come into season usually in the spring and summer.

SAFETY DURING SERVICING
The hindlegs of a mare are often bound and link to a rope around her neck to prevent her from kicking the stallion that is to serve her in case she decides she is not ready.

SERVICING
A mare is covered by a stallion once she is ready. When the stallion comes into contact with her, natural sexual urges ensure that the stallion's penis enlarges and stiffens.

The actual mating takes place when the stallion's penis is located in the mare's vagina. To prevent hairs from getting into the vagina, the mare's tail is bandaged in preparation for mating.

ARTIFICIAL INSEMINATION
Semen can also be introduced to a mare by artificial means, known as AI or artificial

A mare that is ready to mate

The mare's tail is bandaged

The stallion is unloaded from the box and has already scented the mare

During the introduction, the natural sexual drive is awakened

Crush box for inspection by a vet

Servicing or mating

insemination. Artificial insemination can save a great deal on transport costs and also avoids the difficulties with unwilling mares.

FEELING THE WOMB
A vet can inspect the mare to see if she is pregnant. The vet feels the womb by placing his hand in the rectum.

This is easiest performed with the mare in a crush box that prevents the mare from kicking or trampling the vet.

INSPECTING
A mare is inspected three to four weeks after she has been covered. This can be by reintroducing her to a stallion: if she will not have anything to do with him, the chances are that she is with foal.

Other means of checking for pregnancy are a blood test or feeling for the embryo in the womb (see feeling the womb).

The most reliable method is by scanning

Introduction to a stallion

which can be done twenty days after the mare was covered.

PREGNANT
Once a mare has been adequately covered so that her ovum has been fertilized, she becomes pregnant. The period of gestation lasts for about eleven months.
A mare can continue working until about two months before she is due to foal. During the last two months she needs to be spared

Pregnant

and taken care of with additional rations because of the increasing demands made on her by the requirements of the placenta for the foal growing within her, the enlargement of the womb, and the development of the udder.

WAXING UP AND THE BIRTH

The term *to wax up* refers to the way that a wax-like substance appears on a pregnant mare's nipples. Waxing up is a clear sign that the foal will soon be born. After the initial contractions, the mare becomes very restless, tending to walk around in circles, sweating. When the final contractions occur, the mare usually lies down, the placenta detaches, and the contractions become much stronger. First to appear is the water bag that surrounds the foal and provided the foal is lying properly, this is followed by the front hooves, then the head and shoulders. Once this has happened, the rest of the foal appears quite quickly.

Finally, the afterbirth must be expelled within the next few hours.

Although it is a good ideas to be present when a foal is born, intervention is not always necessary. Too much outside involvement can even delay the birth. The mare can often manage entirely on her own. If there are complications or the afterbirth fails to appear, then a vet is needed urgently.

COLOSTRUM OR BEESTINGS

Colostrum or beestings is the first mother's milk that a new-born foal drinks. This is

Waxing up of the nipples

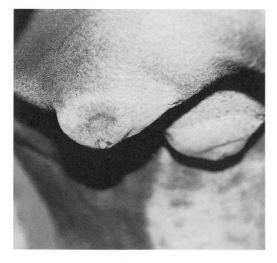

The birth of a foal

A mare eats the afterbirth

A newly born foal with its mother

The mother licks her foal clean after the birth

very important for a foal because it contains antibodies from the mother to protect the new foal from illness and is very rich in protein. Sometimes a mare does not survive the birth and although it is an unpleasant task, the mare must be milked so that the beestings can be fed to her foal by bottle.

The colostrum also ensures that the dark brown to black matter that is in the bowels and intestines of a newly born foal is expelled. If however the foal has not excreted this matter within six to eight hours, consult a vet. If necessary the vet can usually remedy the problem quite simply.

MILK YIELD
Some mares have a high yield of milk but others do not. In this latter case it may be necessary to give the foal additional feeds of milk or to try to increase the mare's milk yield by improving her diet. If it appears that the foal is getting too little milk it is advisable to consult a vet.

COMPACTED FECES
The bowel of a newly born foal has dark brown to virtually black compacted feces

which must be excreted as quickly as possible to avoid the foal suffering from colic.

Nature normally takes it own course because of the laxative nature of the beestings from the mother's first milk. If this does not occur and the foal has not expelled this matter within six to eight hours, you should contact your vet who will be able to clear the blockage.

FOAL
A newly born foal is first licked clean and then dried by its mother. It will quickly try to stand up.
This usually succeeds after a couple of attempts and the foal then searches for its mother's teats.

TWINS
Twins are extremely rare with horses. Only about one in a thousand of the twins that are conceived are born alive. Of these, one of the two foals often dies due to insufficient milk. In order to enable both foals to survive, it is necessary to give additional feeding by bottle day and night for the early days.

Yearling

WEANING

A foal can be weaned from four months onwards but will usually suckle until it is about six months old. When the foal is removed from its mother it is best to put it with other newly weaned foals to help them get over the loss of their mother more quickly. The mare too needs special consideration. After her foal is removed it is best to let her rest for a day or two because her milk does not dry up immediately. The mare should be given little feed and water during this time. If she is really troubled with a full udder, a little milk may be expelled but do not do this too frequently because this will only encourage her to produce more milk.

YEARLING

A yearling is a one-year-old horse. It is very important to take good care of such young horses. This means the appropriate diet, sufficient exercise, and regular attention to their growing hooves. It is also important that a young horse is regularly handled. The bones are still too soft and growing too rapidly for the horse to be worked hard or ridden. This will be the case for the first three years.

Twins

Stable vices and bad habits

Stable vices

Most stable vices are the result of boredom. A horse that spends the entire day in a box with insufficient attention, and too little exercise will channel its surplus energy into mischief.

Stable vices can be passed on to other horses in the stables and can reduce the value of a horse, since any stable vices should be notified to a purchaser. If not, the sale could be put in jeopardy. The following are the most usual stable vices.

CRIB BITING OR CRIBBING (USUALLY ACCOMPANIED WITH SUCKING IN AIR)

This vice results in a horse biting its feeding rack, stable door, sides of its box, and usually also means that the horse sucks in air in the process.

There are special neck collars that if used early enough can cure a horse of sucking in air in this way by restricting the position of their head whilst leaving them free to breathe and swallow their feed. Sucking in air whilst crib biting can lead to severe indigestion and severe wind.

Crib biting can also be deterred by fixing metal strips to the top of the stable door and wood that is coated with creosote is less attractive to a horse. The best way to prevent it though is to keep a horse occupied and to take it out regularly.

WEAVING

Weaving is when a horse sways its head and neck from side to side as it shifts its weight from one foreleg to the other. The forelegs tend to be set apart during weaving and the

A horse ball to minimize boredom

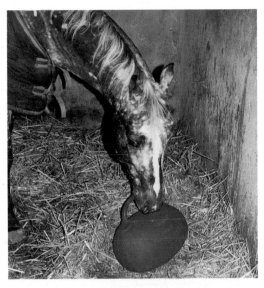

Neck collar to prevent sucking in air

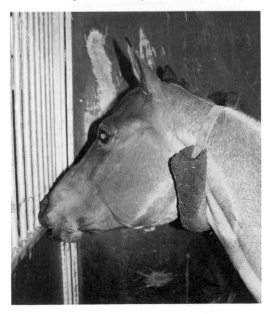

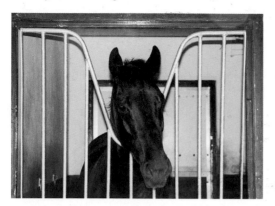

Grill to prevent weaving

process can put undue stress on the legs and hooves with risk of extra wear and even injury. There are special frames for stalls to prevent a horse from weaving that have an aperture for the horse's head and neck that is sufficiently small to prevent the horse from weaving from side to side.

KICKING AND STAMPING

Stamping the floor and kicking the stable door and walls certainly count as vices. These are annoying traits that can damage the stable, and lead to the horse hurting itself.

BLANKET BITING

Finally, there are those horses that bite their blankets. This can be cured by attaching a cloth or "bib" to the halter.

Biting in this way is a form of fondling

Bad habits

Some bad habits are inherited but a horse's surroundings and experiences play a major role.

BITING AND STRIKING OUT

Some horses bite or strike out when they do not like something.
The cause is almost invariably due to their training.

NERVY

A nervy horse reacts with fright to almost anything in its surroundings.
If it sees a sudden movement, it can take fright.

CLINGING

This trait is probably due to a reluctance of a horse to be alone.
Some horses tend to cling closely to other horses but the horse is after all by nature a herd animal.

SCRAPING WITH THE FORELEG

When a horse scrapes the ground with a foreleg, this is a sign of impatience.

OBSTINATE HORSE

An obstinate horse refuses to work and reinforces this by rearing and bucking.

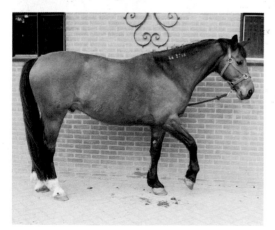

Scraping with the foreleg

Rearing

BUCKING

A horse bucks when it curves its back and jumps off the ground with the front and/or hindlegs. Horses that have kept indoors for some time are likely to buck exuberantly when they are first let out into a paddock. Bucking when saddled is often a sign of resistance and a horse can buck to try to unseat its rider.

TAKE FRIGHT

A horse taking fright is the nightmare of all riders. The horse is suddenly spooked by something, has a pain, or becomes very frightened. It no longer reacts to the aids or any of its rider's signals and takes refuge in flight, galloping as fast as its legs will carry it. It is essential to get the horse back under control before things become dangerous. With a horse that often takes fright, a martingale and a different type of bit may offer some help.

REARING

A horse rears by suddenly raising both of its forelegs into the air. This can be a sign of aggression or nerves. If a rider prevents a nervous horse from moving forwards, it may well rear up.
Horses that are prone to rearing can be controlled better by using a martingale. Rearing is not solely a sign of nervousness, it can also be a sign of exuberance.

Ready to buck

The horse is by nature a herd animal

2   Caring for a horse

Both those who ride as a hobby and those who ride for a living have the daily routine of caring for their horses. This chapter deals with all the important routine tasks that are a part of the daily caring for a horse and is intended as a source of reference on the subject. The subject is treated thematically but items can be looked up alphabetically by referring to the index. Even if you are merely contemplating the possibility of getting your own horse, it is a good idea to read this chapter carefully because it will give you a good idea of what is involved if you buy a horse. Quite apart from its cost, a horse needs a considerable input in terms of time and attention. In the winter particularly, when the horse will probably be in a stable, it is still essential that the horse gets sufficient exercise. An average of some two to three hours per day are needed to look after and exercise a horse at that time of the year. In addition to all this, the horse has to be fed two to three times each day. Caring for a horse in the summer, when it can stay out in a paddock, is certainly easier; there is less mucking out to do and provided there is sufficient grass for the horse's keep, a horse that is only ridden for pleasure should not need supplementary feed. The horse will also not need to be ridden so often because it gets fresh air and exercise on its own.

This chapter deals with matters such as the stable, pasture, putting horses out to pasture, fodder, caring for and grooming the coat, and looking after the hooves. First there is a summary of a few general essentials for a horse whether in a stable or paddock.

A horse demands a lot of time and attention

Left: a halter

Quick release (left), and spring clips for attaching leading reins

Essentials

HALTER (HEAD COLLAR)
When not being ridden, most horses wear a halter or head collar. The halter should fit the horse well without rubbing but closely enough so that it cannot slip out of it. To put a head collar on a horse, first put the halter rope or leading rein over its head to prevent it from walking away. The next step is to calmly pull the collar over the horse's nose and ears and to fasten the check strap. Some head collars also have to be buckled up at the top of the head.

LEADING ROPE (LEAD SHANK)
The leading rope is usually attached to the halter by means of a spring or quick release clip. The quick release clip can be easily released in case of emergency. When leading a horse, always walk on its left next to its shoulder. Do not let the horse walk along behind you. Not only can it step on your heels, it might also be frightened, with all the consequences that could entail.

HITCHING KNOT
The head collar is useful for holding a horse still while you groom it. Always use the special knot for hitching a leading rope because it can be released quickly in an emergency with one tug. The knot consists of a series of loops, rather like a tangled

Knotting the leading rope: form a loop under the rope

Pull a new loop through the first one

Tighten and repeat

Tighten again: the knot is tied

thread, in which each new loop passes through the previous one. Fix the rope high enough to prevent the horse from tripping over it.

MINERAL LICK
Whether a horse is in a stable or paddock, it should have access to a mineral lick to ensure it has sufficient salt in its diet. There are special holders for mineral licks but it can be placed in a feeding trough.

Mineral lick

Feeding trough with anti-spill bar

There are a great variety of mineral licks: some consist of about 95% raw salt but others have additional minerals and vitamins added.
The right lick depends upon the horse's overall diet and whether it is working hard or competing.

FEEDING TROUGH
A feeding trough for supplements needs to be deep enough to prevent much of the feed being wasted by spillage. For horses that are messy eaters, there are special troughs that prevent the feed from being wastefully pushed out of the trough. Feeding troughs need to be cleaned regularly, whether they are made of metal or plastic. This is best done with a damp cloth. If you choose to use a soft, disinfectant soap, make sure the trough is well rinsed afterwards because a horse will not eat from a trough if it has a strange smell. Store the feed in airtight containers to keep it dry and to prevent rodents and insects from getting at it. Pay attention to the use-by date on the feed and only fill the containers with new feed when the previous batch has been fully used up.

RUGS AND BLANKETS
Most horses that are ridden or worked are rugged up in the autumn once the temperature drops below 10°C (about 50°F). The rug or blanket not only keeps the horse warm but prevents it from forming a thick winter coat. The disadvantage of a thick winter coat is that it is almost impossible to get the horse dry when it has been ridden or driven.

From the wide variety of rugs and blankets, you will need least at least two: a stable rug and a sweat blanket. The more expensive stable rugs are usually made of canvas or

New Zealand rug

nylon. Good sweat blankets are entirely made of wool and they are used to cover a horse that has worked up a sweat. Once the horse is dry, the blanket is replaced by the stable rug.

There are also New Zealand rugs, usually of flax or cheap canvas, for horses that are turned out, special riding rugs for specific uses, underblankets for under the stable rug – any old blanket will do – and rugs to protect a horse from the sun and flies in summer. There are also waterproof rugs that are useful to protect a horse that must wait to compete and finally, there are also special head covers with holes for the ears, eyes, and muzzle that will keep a horse warm in severe cold, but which also help to keep it clean. They allow the mane to fall to one side.

Stable

In the winter, a horse spends most of the day in its stable. It is obvious that the stable must meet certain basic requirements.

• There must be adequate ventilation and sufficient daylight. Ideally, all windows should be kept open, except those facing the prevailing wind.
• A constant temperature of 10–15°C (50–60°F). Too warm a stable is not good for a horse. Even when a horse is sweating, it is better to have a window open and to put a blanket on the horse.
• It must be big enough and sturdily built. The manner in which this is achieved depends on the dimensions, installation, and materials from which the stable is built.

A good stable

The right dimensions are very important

DIMENSIONS OF A GOOD STABLE
The internal height of the stable should be at least 3.2m (10ft 6in); higher is beneficial for better ventilation. In any event, the ceiling must be high enough to prevent the horse's head from touching it. The floor area of the box should be at least 3 x 3m (10 x 10ft) with a doorway at least 1m (3ft 4in) wide so that the horse can enter and leave without banging its shoulders. If there is a passageway, bars or a grill can be fixed on a wall at a height of 1.4–1.5m (55–60in) but the uprights must not be more than 50mm (2in) apart to prevent the horse from getting a hoof caught.

BUILDING MATERIALS
Stables can be made of timber or masonry. In either case, the walls need to be sturdy and smooth. The inner walls of a timber box need to be at least 40mm (1½in) thick. If the inner walls are made of brick or block, the masonry must be able to withstand a horse's kick. The roof is also important, particularly in respect of adequate ventilation for the stable. The best solution is a conventional pitched roof of tiles, leaving room beneath it for storing hay and straw

but corrugated sheeting is cheaper and will do the job provided there is a layer of insulation beneath it. Make sure the roof projects well over the stable, especially with an outside box, to prevent rain penetrating the usually open upper door of the box.

The floor is usually made of concrete with a roughened finish and this needs to have channels to carry away water and urine. The floor must slope slightly towards the channel. Well worn concrete floors can become smooth and then a thick layer of straw is essential. Some old stables still

Grill across the window and an automatic drinking bowl

The roof is wide enough to stop rain penetrating the open door

have sand floors with the advantage that liquid drains away immediately. The most modern solution is a rubber floor but these are difficult to keep clean.

FITTING OUT A STABLE
The stable needs to be equipped with a hay rack, a feeding trough, drinking bowl, and a mineral lick. These days, the hay rack is usually fixed at chest height so that the horse can eat the hay in a natural position. The feeding trough should be fixed about 700mm (about 27in) off the ground for most horses and needs to project out about 500mm (20in) so that the horse will not bang its head against the wall or injure its eyes when feeding.

The best solution for drinking bowls are the automatic ones that are connected to the pipes. Take care that they do not freeze up in winter. If you use a bucket for drinking water, place it where the horse is not likely to kick it over.

A window is essential to let in sufficient daylight and this should be sited high up if possible. If this is not possible, the window will need a grill to protect it to prevent the horse from breaking the glass.

STALL
Horses stand with their heads to the wall in a straight stall. The rope holding the horse should be neither too short nor too long. If the rope is very short, the horse will be severely restricted, and if over-long, the horse might trip over it.

The right length is about 800mm (32in). To prevent the horse from standing too far back in a stall, a plastic-coated chain can be fixed across the rear of the stall at buttock height. A horse that is kept in a stall will need plenty of exercise to compensate for the lack of movement.

MUCKING OUT
A horse produces droppings about ten to twelve times each day and produces about seven litres or twelve pints of urine. The manure and wet straw has to be removed each day, and once per week the stable has to be completely cleaned out with new bedding laid. With straw, the best tool to remove the fouled straw is a dung fork but if the bedding is wood shavings, it is easier to use a shovel. It is best to pile the clean straw in the corner while the dirty straw and droppings are removed. This makes it easier to sweep the floor and gives it a chance to dry.

Mucking out

Wood shavings

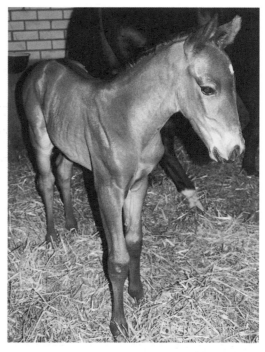

Straw is the best bedding for a newly born foal

BEDDING

A thick layer of bedding material ensures that the horse has a comfortable dry bed. The bedding also provides insulation from the cold stable floor. Make sure some straw is piled up against the walls because horses roll and can hurt themselves or get wedged. A high pile of straw around the edge of the floor can prevent this. The most commonly used bedding materials are straw and wood shavings. Straw is warm and relatively inexpensive but make sure that the ears have been removed because these can cause irritation and choking. Some horses can be rather partial to barley straw and tend to eat it. For these horses, wood shavings are a better option.

Other types of scattering material for bedding include sawdust, but this is dusty and can cause skin irritations in dry weather – especially sawdust from pine; peat dust, which is quite light and absorbs a great deal of moisture but is rather expensive; and shredded paper, which is an ideal choice for horses that are allergic to other bedding materials, or ones which suffer from respiratory problems. Paper is very cheap but wet areas need to removed as quickly as possible or you will be left with a filthy, wet sludge.

Forking over the bedding

97

Stable tools

Washing and grooming corner

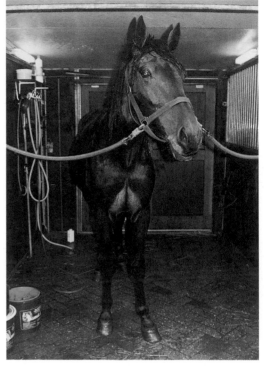

Tack room

FORKING OVER THE BEDDING
Horses in a box or stall will always shift their bedding in a particular direction. The bedding needs forking over to spread it about and to bulk it up again.

STABLE TOOLS
The tools you will need for a stable are a pitchfork, a dung (or manure) fork, a flat steel shovel, a stiff sweeping brush, and a wheel-

"Treadmill" exercise wheel

barrow. Make sure before you leave each time that you have not left any tools in the stalls.

TACK ROOM

An ideal tack room is separate from the stable because the moist stable environment is not the best ambient conditions for leather. Tack is best neatly hung up where it can easily be found again and saddles should be stored on a purpose-made saddle rack.

WASHING AND GROOMING CORNER

A place specially made for washing and grooming a horse is an ideal asset for a stable. The floor can be of rough concrete and should drain well.

EXERCISE WHEEL

An exercise wheel is installed at some stables to ensure that horses get sufficient exercise. These contraptions, that look somewhat like a treadmill, can even have special computer programs to control them which can be adapted to the individual horse.

Pasture for a horse should not be too tender and lush

Pasture and grazing

PASTURE

A paddock or field where horses and ponies graze, should not be too tender and lush – in contrast with milk cattle – because horses' digestive systems cannot cope with too much rich grass. Too lush pasture can lead to laminitis. A horse needs about three quarters of a hectare of pasture (about $1^1/_2$ acres) and a large pony requires about half a hectare (approx. $1^1/_4$ acres).

If concentrates are also fed then the pasture can be smaller. The pasture needs to be checked regularly for any poisonous plants and to remove any rubbish such as plastic and glass.

PUTTING OUT TO PASTURE

Regular grazing is very important for a horse. It resembles their natural living situation and is essential for growing horses. Horses put out to pasture are generally less

susceptible to illnesses such as laminitis and colic, because they are hardier than horses that spend their entire day in a stable.

It is sensible though to visit the field every day to make sure the horse has not injured itself, is not looking ill, or thrown a shoe. Make sure too that there is shelter and shade for the horse from cold winter winds

Wooden fences

Barbed wire is not a good fencing material

and scorching summer sun and flies. If there is no natural shelter such as trees or a tall hedge or fence, build a shelter for the horse.

Finally, horses are sociable herd animals and need company. This can be another horse but a sheep or goat will also suffice.

HORSE DROPPINGS IN THE PASTURE
Horses tend to do all their droppings in one part of the paddock. They will not eat the grass in this area and this gets much longer. This reduces the area of grazing but the solution is to remove the droppings regularly, and to mow the longer grass, or by putting sheep in the field.

Thistles are not poisonous

Sheep will eat almost anything horses do not like, including stinging nettles, and all manner of parasites that are harmful to horses will be killed off in a sheep's stomach.

FENCING
There are both natural and artificial ways to divide up fields. Natural ways include ditching, hedging, or trees.
The artificial means include wooden fences, wire, netting, or an electric fence. Check hedges and trees for poisonous plants and make sure there are no gaps large enough for a horse or pony to escape through.
An electric fence works extremely well: the horse quickly get the message but it can be dangerous during thunderstorms.

The use of barbed wire is not recommended since this can cause serious injuries.

POISONOUS PLANTS
It is important to make sure there are no poisonous plants in the vicinity of a field into which horses are to be turned out.
A horse will usually detect that a plant is poisonous and not eat it but a bored horse might do so anyway. Yew is particularly renowned for its toxicity. Other poisonous

plants include bracken fern, chokecherry, hemlock, horsetail, nightshade, oleander, ornamental yew, ragwort and rhododendron. Pastured horses will avoid dandelion, buttercup, milkweed and thistle.

DRINKING PROVISION

A horse that is put out to pasture still needs drinking water. If there is no natural flowing water, make sure you provide fresh water regularly. One way is to tap into a spring and connect this to an automatic drinking bowl but a trough will suffice provided the water is replenished and changed frequently to ensure it is fresh. This is a cheaper solution but it requires a lot of coming and going with buckets. Natural but stagnant water is not suitable for horses.

When there is a frost it is necessary to keep an eye on the drinking water. With a moderate frost, a ball in the water can prevent ice from forming. During very hot weather water sources should be checked to make sure they have not dried up.

SUPPLEMENTING THE FEED

In winter – that is say from November until May – most horses and ponies that are out to pasture will need additional fodder to supplement their grass. In common with horses that are kept in stables, they need additional food to keep themselves warm and the pasture will also yield less nutrition during the winter.

Feed horses preferably at about sunrise and in late afternoon or early evening. In this way, horses have supplementary feed during the coolest parts of the day. A net of hat is another means of giving additional fodder to horses that are out. This can be hung up

in different parts of the field to prevent one area becoming a quagmire from hoof marks. Check drinking troughs up to three times per day when there is a frost. Ponies that are sufficiently hardy for the winter will try to eat the roots of the grass using their lips to tug at the grass.

Feeding

The amount of food that a horse needs depends on its age, condition, and what is required of it. A young, growing horse needs to be fed differently than a mature one, a general hack needs less food than a showjumper that is constantly competing in tournaments. The temperament of the horse also has a role to play in the amount of food it needs. Some horses get quite wound up and difficult to handle when fed concentrates. Finally, a horse needs to eat more in winter to stay warm. Make sure though that you do not overfeed a horse.

An overweight horse will become shortwinded and out of condition. Generally a

Carrots, horse nuts, bran, and hay

fat horse is more serious than a scrawny one. Generally, the feed should consist of the following elements.

a. Carbohydrate (starch and sugar), fibre, and fat.
b. Protein
c. Minerals and vitamins.

The carbohydrate provides energy, protein is important for building muscles, hooves, hair, blood and milk for mares in foal.
Minerals and vitamins contribute to the formation and maintenance of the skeleton and the good working of the body.

WATER

Like humans, a horse is better able to endure hunger than thirst. The quality of their drinking water is very important: it must be fresh, without any other taste, or a horse will not drink it.
The best temperature for water is about 10°C (50°F). Water that is too cold can cause colic. Automatic drinking bowls are an ideal solution as they always supply fresh water, provided they are kept clean. This also enables a horse to drink when it wants to. Do not let a horse that has just worked

Eager for horse nuts

hard drink too much water at one go. A few litres is sufficient to quench the initial thirst.
Once the horse has been rubbed down it can be allowed to drink once more. Some horses are greedy drinkers but they must be prevented from over-drinking. One way is to leave the bit in the mouth or to strew some hay on the surface of the water.

Types of feed

HORSE AND PONY NUTS OR CUBES

Horse nuts are a mixed feed that is produced to exacting standards to provide high nutritional value. They are easy to use and if fed together with hay and carrots, form an ideal basic diet.

Make sure that you buy the correct formula for your horse. There are feeds that are right for horses that are used for pleasure rides, and pony nuts with a low (10%) level of protein on the one hand but feed for studs, competition horses, and race horses contains twice as much protein. There are also differently formulated meals to which extra vitamins can be added.

OATS

Oats are very nutritious and easily digested. It is important that the oats are of good quality: the grains should be dry and shiny, with no musty smell, and feel loose in the hand. Oats are best fed in combination with hay.
Oats have been given to horses that have to perform well for a very long time.
They keep a horse in good condition and

My friend the rabbit also likes carrots

very spirited. This latter point is the reason why oats are less suitable for feeding to children's ponies. Oats make some horses far too boisterous.

BRAN

Bran is a waste by-product from milled wheat; it is the ears of the grain. Bran makes a suitable feed because it is rich in vitamins and it is easily digested by horses.

The fibre in bran cells aids digestion of other foodstuffs. Bran should not exceed a third of the total diet and it is advisable to moisten the bran before feeding it to your horse. Good bran is coarse and totally dry. Dry bran is good to feed to a horse with loose bowel movements because it binds their droppings.

BRAN MASH

Bran mash is made from wheat bran with cooked linseed meal, mixed with boiling water.
The oil in linseed is good for a horse's coat but linseed is normally only fed to horses that have been working hard but are then resting because it contains little energy-giving nutrition but it is easily digested and will not distend the digestive system while a horse is resting.

A bran mash can be a nice and a healthy treat for a horse when it has been working. Do not make too much at a time and use it up within twelve hours because it deteriorates very quickly.

CARROTS

Carrots are rich in carotene, which is a rich source of vitamin A. They are a suitable supplement to the daily feed.

They need to be washed and have their foliage removed because both sand and carrot tops can cause colic.

MANGELS/SWEDES

Mangels and swedes, like carrots, have little nutritional value but horses like them because they are juicy. If you do not have a mangel chipper, cut them into strips to prevent greedy horses from choking on them. Sugar beet can also be bought as a dry pulp. It is high in calories and makes a good supplement for rather lean horses. The pulp

Hay must be of good quality

Horses are fussy eaters

has to be soaked first since dry pulp can cause colic, choking, and far worse problems. The soaked pulp must be used up within a day or it will ferment.

HAY

There is first cut hay and second cut hay. First cut hay was harvested in the spring or early summer when the grass grew lushly and this hay is of higher nutritional value than second cut hay which was made during August. Hay cannot be given as fodder immediately it is harvested but must first wilt for at least six weeks. Horses cannot differentiate any poisonous plants in dry hay but after six weeks, the poisonous sap has disappeared.

Generally, a horse may eat as much hay as it wishes. It also helps to prevent boredom for the hours in which a horse is restricted to its loose box or stall. Hay must always be of good quality. Unless a horse is very hungry, it will not eat poor hay.

For horses that suffer from allergies or respiratory problems, the hay should first be moistened.

Go easy with sweet titbits

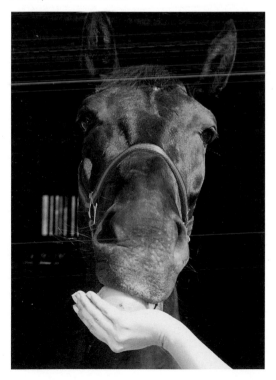

A pause for rest

Put sufficient hay for a feed in a large container and pour several buckets of water over it. Leave the hay to soak for half a day and drain. Wet hay can be fed in a rack or hay net.

GRASS

A horse put out to pasture will largely feed itself. Pasture with sufficient good grass should take care of most of a horse's nutritional needs. They use their flexible lips to select precisely the types of grass they prefer and will certainly not eat any grass they do not like.

Good horse pasture should contain more herbs than cattle pasture. The herbs help to provide the necessary mineral intake.

Horses that get the largest part of their diet from eating grass will tend to have larger bellies than horses that remain in stable. For this reason, race horses and harness racers are restricted in their grazing for fear that a swollen belly will hamper them on the racecourse.

SWEET TITBITS

Sweets are not good for horses but they adore them. Everyone has heard about giving sugar lumps to horses and there are horses that are crazy about peppermints. Try not to give any sweets to horses but if you insist, give them a carrot, an apple (in sections), or some dry bread (but not moldy). There are even horse biscuits with apple and carrot flavours. Sugar lumps and such like should be totally banned. Make

sure that you do not take something tasty
with you every time you visit your horse.
There is a danger that the horse will start to
bite if it does not get something.

Feeding time

In the wild, a horse eats almost all the time
with short rests in between. Horses have a
relatively small stomach, which when empty
is about the size of a football. The food is
quickly moved from the stomach to the long
intestines which should be kept full and the
bowels in motion as frequently as possible.
These natural circumstances are best mir-
rored as closely as possible. In practical
terms this is virtually impossible but feeding
a horse three times per day is a step in the
right direction. If a horse does not have to
work hard, two feeds per day are possible,
provided the horse can eat the entire day. If
a horse has to work hard during the day, it
is best to give the major part of its feed to it
in the evening. Stick to the same feeding
times because if these vary too widely,
the horse will become anxious and suffer
from indigestion. Do not ride a horse for at
least an hour after it has eaten to allow it to
digest its food.

Grooming and skin care

The skin is an important part of the body
with various functions that are important to
the welfare of a horse. The condition of the
skin and the coat reveal whether the horse
is healthy or not. A dull coat indicates poor

Rolling on the ground is a form of skin care

condition and possibly an illness. A shiny
coat indicates a healthy horse.
Grooming is an important part of the skin
care for horses that remain in stables
for much of the time. Horses put out to
pasture rely on natural oils in their skin for
protection against cold and rain. For this
reason, they should not be too rigorously
groomed. Dried-on mud and manure should

Ready to be groomed

be brushed off; rub them down to remove sweat after a ride. Grooming provides an opportunity to check for any irritations or swellings. The legs should also be thoroughly inspected. During wet weather it is advisable to clip any longer hairs around the hooves to allow the skin to dry. A smear of moisturiser will help to prevent the skin from drying out in hot, dry weather.

CONTACT

There is another important aspect to the daily grooming of a horse, particularly if it is your own.

There is no better way to get to know a horse. You will soon become acquainted with the horse from head to toe. In this way, small wounds will be picked up more quickly or any other disorder. Apart from such physical considerations, grooming also forms a bond between you and the horse.

Relaxing

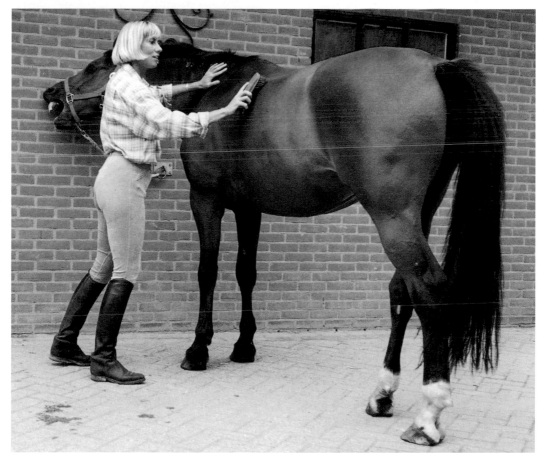

Most horses enjoy being groomed very much and can even move to and fro to indicate just where they want to be itched. Other horses are so relaxed that they almost fall asleep. Whichever it is, you can be sure that your efforts are much appreciated.

GROOMING AND SKIN CARE

The daily grooming session cleans and massages the skin. Excess grease, dead skin, dirt, dust, and dried-in sweat is removed. Without this grooming, the pores of the skin could clog up and it is important that they do not. The skin controls the horse's temperature. Moisture is exuded via the sweat glands which has a cooling action, so it is essential that the pores remain open. In winter, when they have longer coats, horses need grooming with a stiff dandy brush more than in summer. The grooming is best done after a ride, when the coat has dried but the pores are still quite open.

Grooming and skin care equipment

CURRY COMB

A curry comb is made of steel, rubber, or plastic. A metal comb is only used to remove dirt from the dandy or body brush and never on the horse. Soft rubber curry combs can be used to remove loose hairs and caked-on dirt. Start grooming from the top left-hand side of the neck and work an area at a time in small circles towards the tail. Places where the bones are close to the surface, such as the head and legs, are never groomed with the curry or the hard dandy brush.

DANDY (DANDER) BRUSH

The dandy brush is used to remove loose hairs, and dirt from a horse's coat. This is often used instead of the soft curry comb but can be used afterwards. Take care in sensitive areas and avoid using this brush on horses that have been clipped or those that are very sensitive. The dandy brush is good for getting dirt from the mane.

BODY BRUSH

The body brush is used once the coat has been cleaned to make it shine. Work once more from head to tail. Use the soft body brush instead of the dandy brush on the head, skin beneath the mane, the elbows and hocks, and between the forelegs.

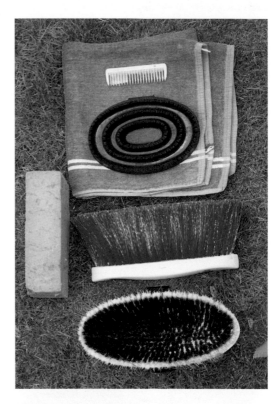

Grooming with a rubber curry comb

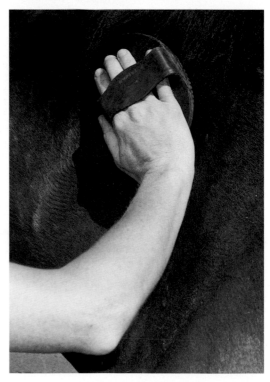

Getting a shine with the body brush

SPONGE

After a ride particularly, a damp sponge should be used to clean the corners of the eyes and the nostrils. Rinse the sponge out regularly while working to prevent infections. Some horses detest this process but much can be achieved with patience and a calm manner. A different sponge, that is kept apart, should be used for cleaning the anus and hind legs. In nature a horse rarely dirties itself from its droppings but in a stable and while riding, it is difficult for the horse to stop and spread its legs apart when it excretes.

HOSING DOWN

Many horses like being hosed down in the summer. Always start by hosing down the legs. Hosing the legs is generally advisable because it massages and cools the tendons but make sure the pasterns are properly dried to avoid catching greasy heel.

SWEAT SCRAPER

A sweat scraper can also be used to dry a horse off after it has been hosed down. Work from top to bottom with the direction of growth of the hair.

Cleaning off with a dandy brush

Remove dirt from the tail by hand

A sponge for the corners of the eyes and nostrils

Start by hosing down the legs

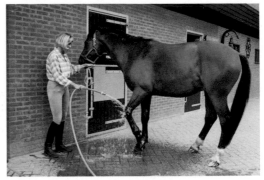

Shedding hair

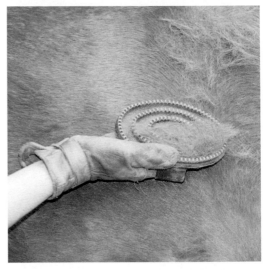

Sweat scraper

RUBBING DOWN

If your horse has been hosed down, or is sweating from working hard, rub it down with a stable rubber (piece of cloth) to dry it. This way the horse does not cool down too quickly and, while you are rubbing it down, it can regain its breath. Once it has been rubbed down, the rest of the grooming can be done in its box or stall.

SHEDDING HAIR

Horses shed and replace their base coat hairs twice a year in the spring and autumn. The spring moult is the most noticeable because the longer winter coat makes way for the thinner summer coat.

Older horses in particular can suffer badly with the shedding of hair and supplements for their diet with linseed or linseed meal is recommended. The oil makes the shedding and replacement easier.

It may be that you wish to prevent your horse from getting a winter coat, which can be difficult to get dry and to keep clean.

Rug the horse up as soon as the weather gets colder and keep the rug on throughout the winter. A horse can also be clipped but this will make the horse hungrier and will usually require increasing its feed. With riding horses, the legs and saddle area are usually not clipped.

Hoofcare

Always clean the hooves out with a hoof pick before and after riding. While doing so check to see if the horse has stood on anything sharp. If this is not noticed for a few days the chances are that a nasty infection will set in. When cleaning the hooves, always stand next to your horse and ask it to lift its foot. Once per week give the hooves a thorough going over. Use a stiff brush and water to scrub the hooves clean. Make sure you do not touch the sensitive coronary band. When this is done, coat the hoof with hoof oil to protect it and prevent it from drying out.

HOOF

The parts of the hoof are known by the following names. Seen from the side, there is the coronary band – the uppermost part next to the hair on the legs; the wall of the hoof, and the sole, which bears on the

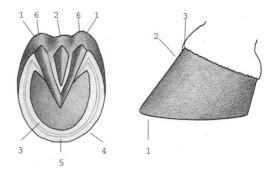

A hoof viewed from below:
1. *bars*
2. *cleft of frog*
3. *sole*
4. *wall*
5. *white line*
6. *bulbs of heels*

A side view of a hoof:
1. *toe*
2. *wall*
3. *coronary band*

ground. Seen from below there are the bulbs of heels above the heel, the cleft of frog and the bars that prevent a horse from slipping, the sole, the wall, and the white line, which is particularly clear on horses that have just had their hooves trimmed by the farrier. The

A well cared-for hoof

A hoof pick, a stiff brush, and a paintbrush

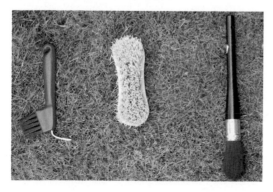

Horseshoes in every size

Cleaning out a hoof

The farrier removes the nails

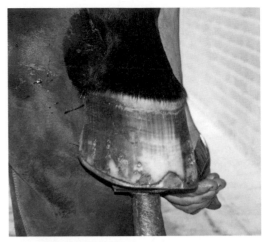

and pulls the shoe off

Worn horseshoe

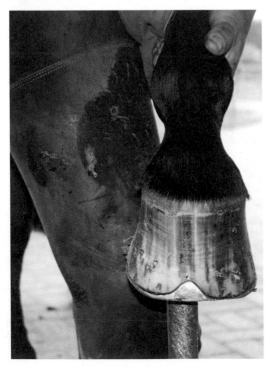

He trims the hoof

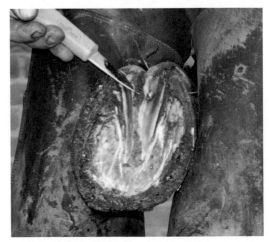

white line is uniform in thickness around the bottom of the wall of the hoof. It is into the white line that the farrier hammers his nails.

HOOF PICK

The hooves are cleaned out with a hoof pick, paying special attention to the grooves

heats up the shoe

...and works it to size and shape.

around the frog, the edge of the sole, and shoe. Work from the point of the wedge shaped frog towards the rear.

SHOES

A horse that is regularly ridden on the road will need new shoes about every six to eight weeks. Horseshoes protect the sole and rim of the hoof, which would wear quickly on paved roads.

Only horses that are never ridden on a hard surface can manage without shoes but even these horses need a regular visit by the farrier.

Because their hooves do not wear down evenly, an unshod horse will need to have its hooves trimmed from time to time.

The nails are driven into the white rim of the hoof

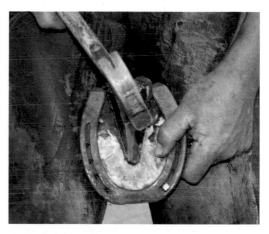

The nails are trimmed off

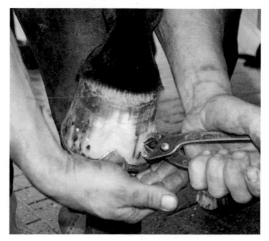

CALKIN

Calkins are metal studs that can be fixed to shoes to provide extra grip on slippery and wet surfaces.

SHOEING

For shoeing a horse, horseshoes, nails, special tools, and a skilled farrier are needed.

The farrier first removes the nails so that the old shoe can be taken off. Before fitting a new shoe, the farrier trims down the hoof and then adapts the new shoe to fit the hoof. The shoe is heated and beaten to shape and then fixed to the hoof with six to eight nails.

The nails must be driven precisely into the white rim of the hoof. If they were driven deeper, they would hurt the horse and probably make it go lame. If the farrier drives them too shallow, the nails will quickly fall out and the horse will shed a shoe.

The nails should exit the hoof about 2.5cm (1in) above the sole. These clenches as they are called, are nipped off with pincers and turned over into the hoof.

Preparing for showing

When a horse is shown or entered in competition, it needs to look its very best.

Preparing a horse for showing is only really possible once they have lost their winter coat. The horse must first be groomed

thoroughly and during this process any excess hairs can be removed or clipped. The

A well turned-out harness horse

Trimming the whiskers

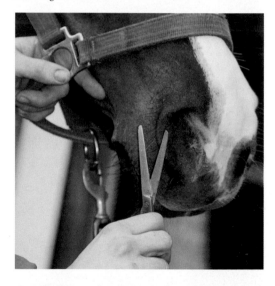

A horse well turned-out for showing

Clipping shears and trimming comb

Thinning or pulling the mane

Clipping the bridle path

style in which a horse is turned out for showing depends on the breed.

Check with the breed society what the requirements are before preparing a horse for showing.

Tools for clipping and preparing for showing

SCISSORS
Use special scissors with rounded tips for

Trimming the tail

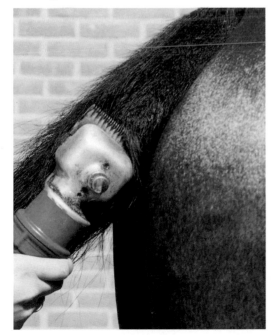

Clipping the legs

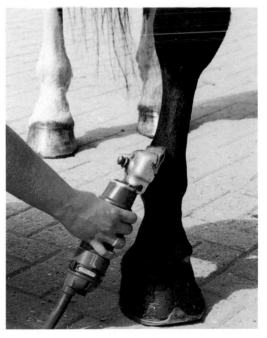

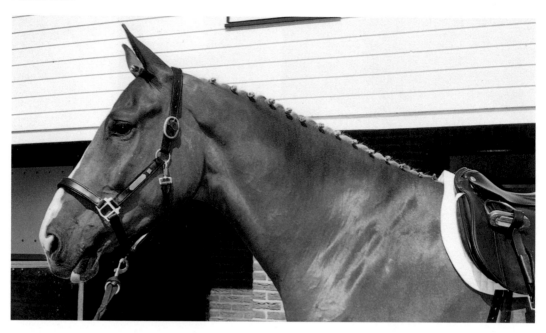

clipping a horse. These large scissors can be used for removing surplus hair in areas such as the throat and the outside of the ears. The mane can also be clipped using them, where the bridle comes behind the ears.

The whiskers around the eyes and muzzle can be made shorter but should never be cut right back because they are an important sensory aid for the horse.

Braided for the first time

PULLING COMB

The hairs of the mane can be pulled or plucked to length using a comb. The correct length is about a hand's breadth. Start by the ears and work towards the withers. If you pluck small tufts of hairs at a time, it does not hurt the horse.

Hair that is too long can be wound around the comb and pulled out with a short tug.

CLIPPERS

The hairs on the legs and at the side of the root of the tail can be cut with scissors, pulled with a comb, or trimmed with clippers. The bottom of the tail should reach to about half-way down the cannons. The hairs above the hoof can also be trimmed easily with clippers.

BRAIDING OR PLAITING

The mane will often have to be plaited for competition and showing. Before the mane is plaited, it must be thoroughly brushed. It is then moistened with a sponge to make the hair easier to work with.

The plaits are from three tufts of hair about 50mm (2in) wide. Fixing the plaits is an art best learned from someone who has already mastered it.

Short-clipped – hugged or roached – mane

CLIPPING

As autumn approaches, horses that are turned out a lot of the time start to get longer coats. However, with horses and ponies that work regularly there is the problem that these coats quickly get out of condition with sweating and there is the disadvantage that longer hair takes much longer to dry, increasing the chance of a horse becoming chilled. The solution is to clip the horse. This is best left until the winter coat has fully developed to prevent problems of shedding hairs.

There are a number of different manners in which a horse can be clipped. Riding horses are clipped differently from carriage horses and the particular style can be according to the rider's tastes. The most usual clip is the hunter clip which leaves only the hair beneath the saddle and under the legs.
The saddle area is not clipped because the stubble would prevent the saddle from sitting flat and might result in it slipping forwards. When a horse has been clipped, it needs rugging up with one thick blanket or two thin ones.

BLANKET AND TRACE CLIPS
The trace clip was formerly used for harness horses and only removes hair from the belly, between the thighs, and under the neck. The blanket clip leaves the hair of the loins and on the legs. This clip is used for horses that are kept out by day but brought in at night.

A Fjord Pony has a thick winter coat

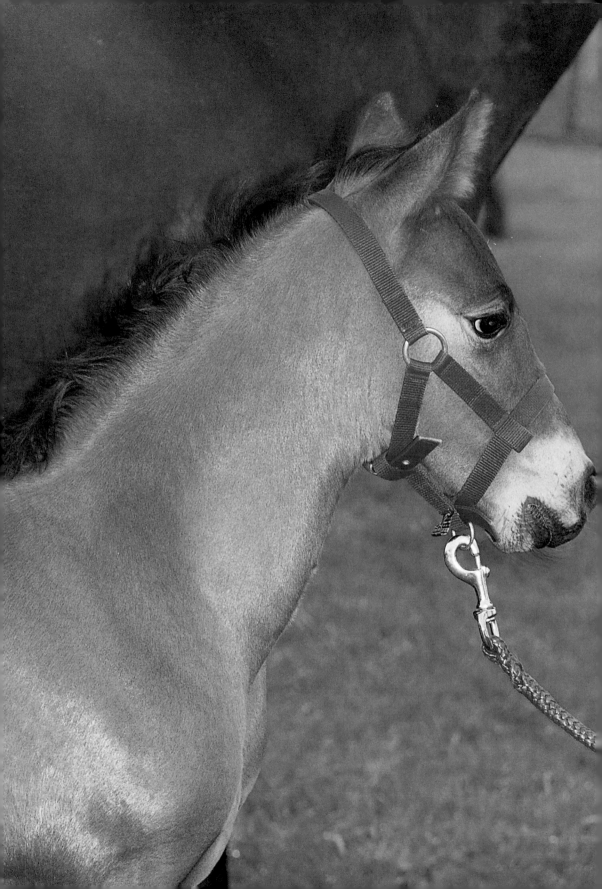

3 Riding

This chapter deals with training a horse, the basic principles of riding, and the necessary equipment. A first-class instructor and well-trained horse are essential for those learning to ride. Nobody can learn to ride from a book.

Training the young horse

Training starts when the horse is still a foal. The foal should learn to trust humans. It is therefore a good idea to put a head collar on a young foal and to take it for a walk. In this way it will soon learn to be led in-hand.

When a horse is two years old, a cautious start can be made with lungeing. The young horse is taught on the lunge to respond to the aids. It also becomes accustomed to the bridle, bit, and saddle.

Once a horse is three years old, it can be acclimatised to the weight of a rider (see *Backing*).

NOVICE HORSE
A novice horse is untrained or not yet fully trained.

IN HAND
The first step towards training a horse is to get it accustomed to being led. This starts while still a foal.
At first lead the foal following its mother,

Training a young horse

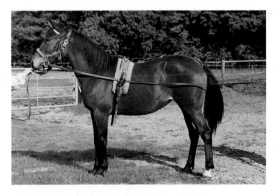

Training begins with the foal

Leading a foal

then move to lead it alongside the mare, and if this goes well, try to lead the foal a distance in front of its mother. When leading a foal in hand, always walk on its left alongside the shoulder as with adult horses.

YEARLING
Continue to lead yearlings regularly in hand. The young horse can become accustomed at this age to the bridle and the saddle. It is also sensible to introduce it to being groomed and having its hooves picked out.

Regular handling establishes trust and confidence. The horse becomes accustomed to its handler's voice and may even start to recognize certain commands, such as "ho!" and "walk on."

Until they are three, a horse should not be worked because they are still growing. Some breeds are ridden earlier but this has its consequences in the life expectancy.

Lungeing

Lungeing marks the start of the real training of a horse. When a horse is on the lunge, it is on a very long line known as the lunge rein, walking in circles around its handler. The advantage of lungeing is that the horse learns to react to the aids and to hear commands. The horse will only be introduced to the bit when it moves forward well. The lunge is also used to get the horse accustomed to the saddle. To start with, leave the saddle off and do not pull the lunge reins too tightly.

A second person is needed to help teach the horse to move in a circle and to react to the handler's voice.

Lungeing with the aid of a helper

Lunge rein

LUNGE REIN

A lunge rein is a long line (about 7.5m or 25ft) attached the center ring of a cavesson or outer ring of a mouthing bit that is held by the trainer.

The lunge rein is kept taut by driving the horse on, using a whip. The rein must not be allowed to twist and should be held neatly in the left hand with the horse moving from right to left (as viewed by the trainer). The whip is held in the right hand. When the horse moves in the opposite direction, the rein and whip hands change places.

FASTENING THE LUNGE TO THE MOUTHING BIT

It is important to attach the lunge rein the correct way. The rein should never solely be attached to the inner ring of the mouth bit because this will pull the bit from the horse's mouth.

It is better to hook the lunge rein under the chin strap and through the bridle to fasten it. Another possibility is to pass the lunge through the inner ring and to then attach it

The lunge rein is attached to the outer ring of the bit

Lungeing whip

Lungeing whip

Enclosed between lunge and whip

to the outer ring. The reins must not pass over the horse's head of course. Twist them together and fasten them to the chin strap.

LUNGEING WHIP

The lungeing whip or *chambrière* is about 2m (6ft 6in) long with a lash of about 2.5m (8ft) with a short knotted rope on the end to give the crack.

The purpose of the whip is not to hit the horse but to give it indications.

AIDS WITH THE WHIP

The whip is used to prevent the horse from moving inwards in the circle. The whip and the lunge rein between them keep the horse enclosed.

The whip is used solely to give indications to the horse and never to hit it. The horse must be able to trust the whip which should

point forwards at the height of the horse's quarters.

VOICE AIDS DURING LUNGEING

It is important that in addition to learning to respond to the lunge rein and whip, a horse should learn to respond to the voice. Vocal aids are no less important than the others during lungeing.

The horse needs to be able to learn from the commands what it is required to do. If it must slow down and stop, speak slowly with deliberately made commands and with a lower tone (h-o-o-h–h-o-o-oh). If the horse is to quicken its pace, the command must also sound lively and encouraging: (trot on, walk on). Always use the same commands with the same tone of voice for them.

BODY ROLLER

A body roller is a girth that passes around the horse's body with two small pads. On each side there are rings to attach side reins to. The body roller is used in the early stages of training on a lunge rein.

Body roller

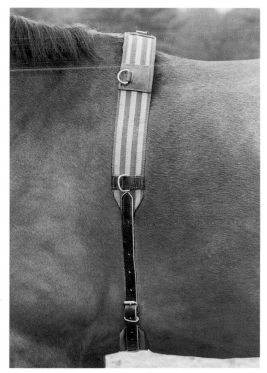

Lungeing cavesson

Backing a horse

LUNGEING CAVESSON

A cavesson looks like a sturdy halter or head collar but it has a special noseband with three rotating metal rings to which the lunge and side reins can be attached.

Backing a horse

The term "backing a horse" means getting a young horse used to having a saddle and rider on its back.

The horse gets used to having something on its back when it has a body roller attached during lungeing. A saddle can only be placed on the horse's back when it has become fully accustomed to the pressure of the body roller. This is best done in the comfort of familiar surroundings such as the horse's loose box and is best done by two people. One can talk to the horse and calm it, as the other puts the saddle on and somewhat later tightens the girth. Once the horse becomes accustomed to the saddle, it can be train on the lunge with the saddle. Subsequently you can cautiously begin to introduce the horse to the weight of a rider.

Riding first on the lunge

The horse must be at least three years old before this stage is reached. The first time, lie on your stomach across the saddle and continuously reward the horse by stroking it.

Only when the horse is fully accustomed to this can the horse be mounted for the first time. This is best done in a corner of the stables where the horse is prevented from bolting.

The basic riding principles are taught using the lunge rein. A young horse has to be gradually introduced to the bit because their mouths are still sensitive. The handler on the lunge rein allows the horse to quietly walk and trot while the rider cautiously draws up the reins. The rider reinforces the commands of the handler with the calves. This way the horse becomes accustomed to the leg aids for controlling forward movement. If the horse has learned to stop on the lunge to a voice command, the same command is used by the rider. This enables the reins to be used as little as possible.

It is a good idea when a newly backed horse is ridden off the lunge for the first time to do so in the company of a more experienced horse.

General riding

Riding well cannot be learned solely from books. A good instructor is absolutely essential. It is also quite impossible to teach a novice rider on a novice horse. To learn to ride, you must have access to a well-trained, experienced horse to enable you to develop the skills of riding.

CORRECT SEAT

A rider has the correct seat when he or she sits upright with shoulders relaxed, back and down. The elbows should not stick out while the upper arms hang loose and vertical, close to the body. The forearms should become extensions of the reins.

The hands are held about a hand's width above the mane with thumbs upwards and knuckles facing forward. The wrists should be relaxed and flexible so that you can feel the movements of the horse's mouth. A

The correct seat

Position of the hands

rider with a sensitive touch will trouble the horse far less than one with heavy hands. The reins should always be lightly tensioned. Relaxation is the most important aspect of a good seat and this also applies to the legs: the thighs and knee should rest relaxed against the saddle. The knee should not move around so that the lower leg can be correctly positioned. The lower legs are the most important aid for controlling forward movement. They hang loosely down immediately behind the girth. The ball of the foot rests in the stirrup with the heels pointed downwards. The toes are pointed straight ahead.

The length of the stirrup leathers play an important role in gaining the correct seat. For mounting, the leathers are adjusted to the length of an outstretched arm. The correct length for riding is then adjusted from the saddle. The stirrup iron should be level with the ankle when the leg hangs freely down. With the correct seat, an imaginary line can be drawn from the head through the hips to the ankles.

Some riding schools have mirrors in their school rings to help riders adjust their position.

WELL-BALANCED SEAT

A good seat is not a matter of the right position but of being able to maintain it, moving with the horse as it moves and maintain a comfortable balance. The legs and arms act as shock-absorbers so that the hands can be kept level and motionless to prevent tugging on the horse's mouth.

NATURAL AIDS

The natural aids are messages that a rider gives to a horse through their seat, legs, hands, and arms, to make their wishes known. In addition to the vocal aids, which will gradually be used less, there are also aids given by the legs, reins, and shifting the weight of the rider's body.

USING THE LEGS AS AIDS

The rider's legs control the hindquarters of the horse, forward movement, turning, and balance.

The inner leg is used to urge the horse on, to speed up, or to tighten the turn. The outer leg is used to control the hindquarters. By using both in unison, the horse is kept properly balanced.

The horse must learn quickly to react to little indications. To achieve this the riding whip can be used. If the horse does not react to the pressure of the calves, it is given a light tap with the whip on its shoulder.

The spurs are artificial aids to reinforce the leg aids but these should never be used by an inexperienced rider.

THE REINS AS AIDS

The rider maintains contact with the horse through the reins, which are attached to the bit. This should be with a light and flexible touch, with relaxed fingers, wrists, and elbows. By offering a little resistance, the rider signals that they wish to increase the tempo or to stop.

A horse's mouth is exceptionally sensitive. For this reason, you should never tug on the reins. The reins as aids are used in combination with the other aids that are given through the calves and the seat. If the rider wishes the horse to stop, they sit back in the saddle and give a little resistance via the reins.

SHIFTING THE WEIGHT

A rider can reinforce the aids given by the legs and reins by shifting their seat. By moving the weight onto the right leg so that the right-hand stirrup is more heavily laden and squeezing with that same leg, the horse gets a message to go to the right. The rider's weight in this way is an additional aid.

VOICE AID

See vocal aid under Lungeing.

A riding whip to reinforce the leg aids

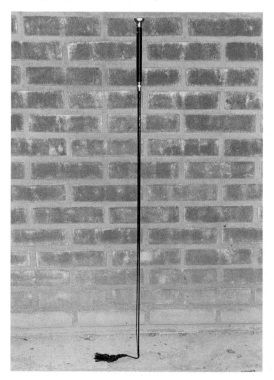

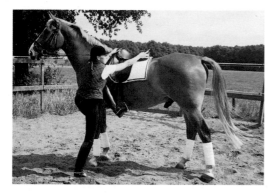

MOUNTING

Before mounting, check that the girth is properly adjusted and that the stirrups are hanging down. Stand on the left of the horse to mount. It used to be thought that while mounting the rider needed to be aware of the hindquarters so that they could avoid being kicked.

However, this overlooks the possibility of being bitten and meant that the horse tended to get a jab in the ribs which led to it not standing still.

It is better to stand at the front of the horse where you can watch both the forehand and quarters, with the reins in your left hand. Put your left foot in the stirrup, grasp the pommel or waist of the saddle with your right hand, and swing your right leg over the horse's back. Sit cautiously in the saddle – never land on it with a thump. Make sure that the point of the left foot does not jab the horse as you mount. Do not allow the horse to move off until you give it the signal.

DISMOUNTING

Before dismounting, first remove both feet from the stirrups. Hold the reins in the left hand and hold the horse's neck with this hand and the pommel of the saddle with the right hand as you swing your right leg over the horse's back. Bend forwards over the saddle and allow yourself to slide slowly to the ground.

Never keep one foot in a stirrup when dismounting because the horse could take fright and bolt with your foot trapped in the stirrup with you being hauled along behind the horse. Finally run the stirrups up and lift the reins over the horse's head.

swing the right leg over the horse's back...

and slide slowly off the horse

ACTION

The term action refers to the manner in which a horse moves its legs as it walks, trots, and canters, and also the way it balances itself as it moves. The action will vary with each of the gaits.

TEMPO

The term tempo for a horse's action refers to the number of hoof-beats that the legs

make. The walk is a four-beat gait because each hoof strikes the ground independently of the other three. The trot is a two-beat gait, with diagonally opposite legs striking the ground together.

WALK

The walk is a four-beat gait with the legs striking the ground in sequence: off hind, off fore, near hind, near fore. The walk is also a lateral gait, meaning that the legs on the same side move forward. By using the scat and legs aids with small indications through the reins you can keep in rhythm with the horse. If you want the horse to extend the walk, this is done by using leg aids behind the girth at the moment that a hind leg moves forwards. It is important to keep the steps in sequence and regular.

TROT

The trot is a two-beat gait, with the horse moving diagonally opposed legs forward together as the horse is suspended in the air. The sequence is: off hind and near fore legs – a moment of suspension – near hind and off fore legs. The aids for urging the horse forward are the same as with the walk except somewhat stronger. By using the seat and legs rhythmically, the rider can set the tempo. The rider can remain seated or rise with the trot.

SITTING TROT

With the sitting trot, the rider remains in the saddle. The legs are shortened and lengthened by bending to absorb the movements the horse makes. Inexperienced riders often find it difficult with the seated trot to maintain the correct seat. They get thrown from

left to right by the horse and vice versa. To prevent this, you imagine the rearward lift made in the rising trot but instead of rising from the saddle, you extend your upper body.

RISING TROT

With the rising trot, the rider comes out of the saddle at the moment the horse lifts one of its hind legs. At riding schools, pupils are taught to rise at the moment that the near hind leg is raised.
This is a rising trot to the "good" leg. It is easier to take the cue from the off fore leg: when this moves forward, the rider should rise to the trot.

CANTER

The canter is a three beat gait. To maintain a good balance in the turns, a horse can canter on the off or near legs. In the near-side canter, the legs move in the sequence:

use of the hands, legs, heels, and seat is very important.

The stride at each stage of the canter for an average horse is about 4m (13ft) long and the horse can reach a speed of 20 km per hour (12 m.p.h.).

EXERCISES FOR THE RIDER

To achieve the correct seat, a rider needs to be supple. There are a number of exercises that can be done before riding and during riding to relax and to warm up and loosen the muscles.

• Bend over to touch the toes. Start by touching the right foot with the right hand and repeat with left hand and foot. Between each movement remain upright in the saddle. Slightly more difficult is to touch the left foot with the right hand and vice versa. This exercise helps give a sense of balance and loosens the muscles.

• Lift the legs as high as possible and grasp the knees. Then lower the legs slowly. This loosens the muscles in both arms and legs.

Horse-back gymnastic exercises

off hind, near hind and off fore together, near, followed by a moment of suspension. The sequence is exactly opposite with the off-side canter. The horse's body is finely balanced during the canter and the rider should aid that balance by moving with the horse.

The upper body is kept upright while the legs flex with the movements. With each leap of the canter that the horse makes, the rider's legs bend and straighten. The impulsion to the canter is mainly given through the seat. The weight is transferred to the inner hip, applying pressure through the seat and the seat is then moved forwards.

The inner leg remains in position but the outer leg squeezes behind the girth. The heel urges the horse into the canter. The rider also moves the hands. The combined

• Lift both legs up above the horse's back and turn round fully in the saddle. This helps to develop both balance and co-ordination,

• Exercises with the arms can be done at the walk or trot. Make a knot in the reins so that they do not slide off, then lift the arms into the air and keep them there for several paces before lowering them. For variation, hold the arms out in front of you and behind.
A more difficult exercise is to swing the arms, either horizontally or vertically.

RIDING ON THE LEFT REIN OR OFFSIDE
Riding to the offside means that the left-hand side is facing the inside of the riding track.

RIDING ON THE RIGHT REIN OR NEAR-SIDE
Riding to the near-side means that the right-hand side is facing the inside of the riding track.

CHANGING REINS OR HANDS
A horse and rider change reins when the change is made in riding from the offside to near-side.

STOPPING
When stopping, the use of the weight through the seat is very important. By sitting back in the saddle with a straight back it is made clear to a horse that it must slow down. This is followed by gentle indications through the hands. When the horse stops, it should stand in balance on all four legs.

Riding to the left hand

Illustration of the schooling ring with the positions of letters A, F, B, M, C, H, E, & K.

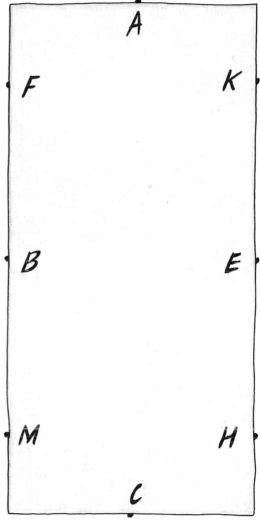

SCHOOLING RING

Schooling rings and dressage arenas consist of two short sides and two long ones. The dimensions are 20m x 40m or 20m x 60m (65ft x 130ft or 65ft x 197ft). Letters are fixed around the perimeter to denote specific positions. The side of the horse that is nearest the center of the arena is known as the near-side and the opposite side is known as the offside. In the same way, reference is made to the near-side and offside rein, near-side leg and offside leg etc.

Riding along two tracks

SCHOOLING TRACKS

The path alongside the fence or walls of the schooling ring is known as the outside track. About one and a half metres or five feet in from the edge of the ring is a second track, known as the inner track.

RIDING FIGURES

Many different figures can be ridden in the schooling ring. The most important ones are shown in the following illustration.
First decide which figure you intend to ride and from which position in the ring. It might be a straight line from A to C, straight along the center of the ring. Riding in a

straight line without the edge of the ring as a guide is actually quite difficult. The straight line is achieved by keeping even pressure on both reins while the impulsion aids are equally evenly applied.

Circles or *voltes* can be ridden at various parts of the school. The illustration shows a number of circles of different diameters ranging from 6–20m (20–65ft) and turns. It is important when riding turns to keep impelling the horse forward so that the tempo remains constant. The use of the correct aids ensures that the horse turns properly. A variation on the circle figures are serpentine figures which can incorporate different numbers of turns. The turns should all be executed with the same radii and the horse should always come back to same track.

SCHOOLING RULES
When there are other people riding in the schooling ring, certain rules have to be observed.
• If riders are not riding on the same rein then riders on the left or offside hand have priority. Pass "left to right."
• The outside track is the "main road" of the schooling ring. If you ride slowly here, you hold others up. If you wish to rest your horse a little on a long rein, then go to the inside track.
• Never ride too close to another horse.

Schooling figures:
1. *one broken line*
2. *change hands at F and H (across the diagonal)*
3. *large circle at B or E*
4. *large circle at A*
5. *small circle (half width of ring)*

6. *large figure of eight at A or C*
7. *small circle at E*
8. *change hands by riding a figure S*
9. *serpentine with five turns from A to C*
10. *serpentine with three turns from A to C*

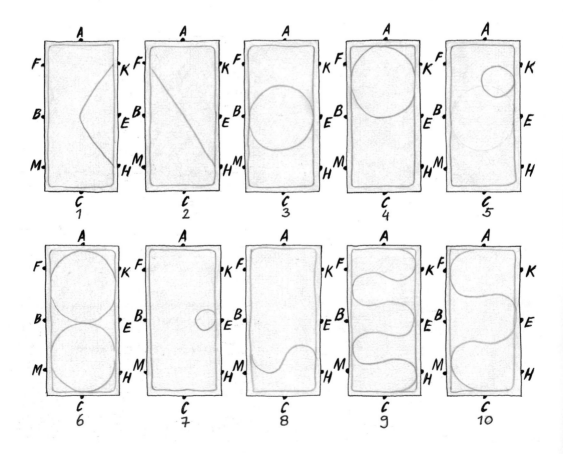

Tack and equipment

Tack

The tack includes bridle, saddle, reins, and anything else needed for the complete tacking up of a horse.

Bridle

The bridle ensures that the bit remains correctly positioned in a horse's mouth. It consists of a number of straps that are fastened around the horse's head.

Perhaps the best known is the snaffle bridle. The crownpiece or headpiece is placed behind the horse's ears. Cheek pieces and the throat latch are attached to the crown-piece. The noseband strap runs under the crownpiece and alongside the cheek piece to support the nose band or cavesson. A browband fits in front of the ears. The reins are attached to the bit.

SNAFFLE BIT AND CURB
A snaffle bit with curb has two cheek pieces each side – one for the bit and a second one for the curb.
The curb presses under the chin and against the neck to keep the head down. With a skilled rider, a bridle with a snaffle and curb refines the aids and it is a requirement for certain dressage categories.

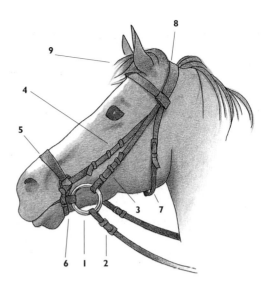

Bridle
1. snaffle bit
2. reins
3. cheek piece
4. nose band strap
5. drop nose band
6. chin strap
7. throat latch
8. headpiece
9. browband

Nose bands

DROP NOSE BAND
A drop, or training nose band is fastened under the bit and it ensures that the horse does not throw the mouth open or keep the lower jaw clenched.
A low nose band is always used with a snaffle bit.

HIGH NOSE BAND OR CAVESSON
The high nose band is fastened under the cheek pieces to the top of the bit. This type

Tack for a pony

Snaffle bit and curb

of strap is often used with a snaffle bit and curb chain.

Combined nose band

COMBINED NOSE BAND

The combined nose band incorporates the features of both the drop and high nose bands.

The bit is kept in position in the horse's mouth, ensuring that it functions correctly.

MEXICAN NOSE BAND

A Mexican nose band applies substantial pressure to the nose.

If the horse has a tendency to open its mouth, this nose band applies additional pressure to the nose.

Snaffles and other bits

SNAFFLE

A snaffle is a bit that has rings on both sides. The bit can be made as one or two mouthpieces.

The mouthpieces can also vary in thickness: the thicker the mouthpiece is, the more gentle is its action.

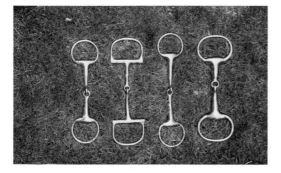

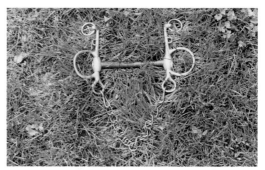

A rubber snaffle has a mouthpiece covered in rubber for a milder bit that is often used with horses that have sensitive mouths.

CURB

The best known bridle with curb is the combined snaffle with curb. The curb has a fixed mouthpiece with swivels on each side. The mouthpiece can be either straight or incorporate a tongue port.

Because the tongue is placed under the port in the mouthpiece, the bit presses far more on the sensitive parts of the horse's mouth.

The length of the swivel joints and of the

Curb

Hackamore

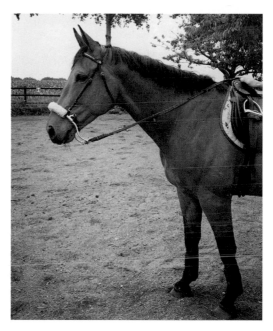

curb chain have a bearing on the severity of the bit.

PELHAM BIT

A Pelham bit can be used with either single or double reins.

With double reins, the lower rein has the more severe action and the upper rein a normal mild action.

HACKAMORE

The term is loosely but incorrectly applied to all bit-less bridles. The origin of the true hackamore is with the western riders. It works on the nerves in the nose and jaw and is becoming more widely used by show-jumping riders.

Dressage and showjumping reins

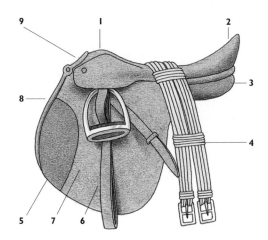

A general-purpose saddle
1. Pommel
2. Cantle
3. Saddle cushions
4. Girth straps
5. Stirrup iron
6. Stirrup leather
7. Saddle flap
8. Knee roll
9. Gullet

Reins

The reins are attached to the bit by means of buckles. The reins can be used to apply pressure to the sensitive parts of a horse's mouth in order to control it.

Dressage reins have an entirely smooth surface but showjumping reins are made with raised sections to provide a firmer grip.

PLUMB LINE

The plumb line is an imaginary line from the neck of the horse perpendicular with the ground. For bits to work correctly, it is important that a horse holds its head correctly.

The horse's nose and chin should be slightly in front of this imaginary line. If the head is too far forward, the horse is *above the bit* and if the head, nose, and chin are all behind the line, the horse is running *behind the bit*.

Saddle

The choice of the correct saddle is very important for riding a horse. The saddle must fit the horse but it must also be right for the rider. The measurements of the

General-purpose saddle, dressage saddle, and showjumping saddle

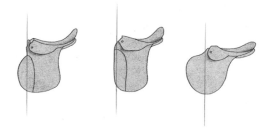

saddle should be appropriate for the rider's seat. The type of riding or equestrian sport that you will be doing is also an important consideration.

The most commonly used types of saddle are the general-purpose ones, dressage saddles, and showjumping saddles.

Horses in riding schools usually have general-purpose saddles. This type of saddle can be used for schooling and for hacking. The pads beneath the saddle rest to right and left of the horse's back. Between them is a hollow space beneath the tree of the saddle known as the gullet. Beneath the pads there are usually flaps to protect the saddle from sweat. The rear part of the saddle tree is the cantle and at the front, next to the withers, is the pommel. The girth billets to which the girth straps are attached are between the top flap (or knee roll) and bottom flap of the saddle. The stirrup leathers hang outside the knee roll and are attached to the stirrup bar under the skirt.

SIDE-SADDLE

In Medieval times, women sat astride a horse just as men did but "ladies of station" rode in a kind of chair in which they sat sideways on the horse.

The ladies' saddle or side-saddle is reputed

Lady's side-saddle

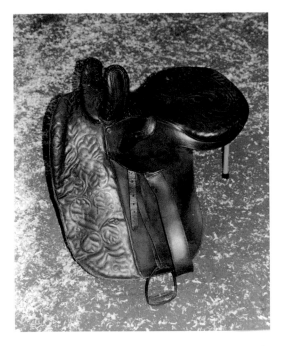

there is only one stirrup iron. The rider has to use her cane to replace the aids that would normally be given by the right-hand leg.

RACING SADDLE
See chapter 9: Racing and Harness racing.

SADDLE PADS (NUMNAH)
A saddle pad is always placed beneath the saddle. This protects the saddle from sweat but also protects the horse from abrasion by the saddle.

Numnahs are shaped like a saddle but other saddle pads are rectangular.

Girth straps

The girth straps keep the saddle in place. The girth straps are made of leather or webbing, and they are attached to the saddle between the knee roll and bottom flap.

to have been invented by Catharina de Medici in the sixteenth century. The side-saddle was widely used up to World War I. It fell out of use as riders changed to the Caprilli seat style of riding.

With a side-saddle, the rider has both her legs on the left-hand side of the horse and

Numnah

The girth strap buckles are fastened to the billet straps behind the knee roll

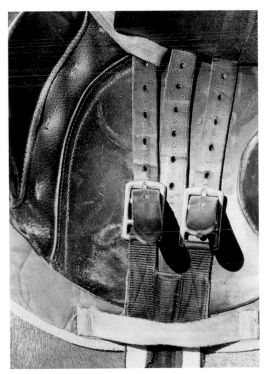

Girth straps

Tacking up

Tacking up is the process of putting the saddle on a horse, usually followed by putting the bridle on.

If a horse is a known to be difficult when it comes to putting a saddle on it, then it is best to replace the head collar with the bridle first because the bridle offers a great degree of control.

SADDLING UP

Make it a habit to brush the horse thoroughly before putting its saddle on, with special attention being given to its back and that part of the belly where the girth comes. Any

dirt beneath the saddle or the girth can hurt a horse. Saddling up is always done from the left of the horse. Place the saddle well forward against the withers and then push it backwards until it is in the correct position. In this way, the saddle does not lift any hairs.

The girth straps are passed under the horse's belly and buckled to the billets beneath the outer flap of the saddle.

ADJUSTING THE GIRTH

The girth should not be fastened too tightly at first because horses can react badly to having their girths tightened. Once the horse has walked a few paces, the girth can be adjusted or tightened. Some horses push their bellies out against the girth when it is first done up so the girth will need adjusting after riding for a little. It is usually sufficient to walk the horse in hand to get the belly to relax.

PUTTING THE BRIDLE ON

The reins are first put over the horse's head so that when the head collar is removed, you have some means of control. Once the head collar is off, the bit is fed into the horse's mouth as the cheek piece and head

Lay the reins over the head

Remove the head collar

Push the bit against the teeth

Pass the headpiece over the ears

piece are held in the right hand. Most horses open their mouths automatically when they feel the bit against their teeth. If the horse does not open its mouth, then press with thumb and forefinger against the mouth. The headpiece is then passed over the ears, bearing in mind that horse's ears are very sensitive, so care is required. Make sure the forelock is clear of the front strap of the headpiece and check that the headpiece is correctly fitted.

Finally fasten the throat latch and nose band. Check that the throat latch leaves sufficient play by placing the fist vertically under it. There should be sufficient room for two fingers placed on the flat beneath the nose band.

UNSADDLING

Unsaddling follows the reverse procedure to saddling up. Undo the girth straps on the left-hand side and pass them over the right-hand side of the saddle.

Do not remove the bridle until the saddle has been removed.

Horses are often wet with sweat beneath the saddle after a ride and once the bridle has been removed they often have an urge to roll. If the bridle is removed first there is a

Leave enough room for a fist under the throat latch

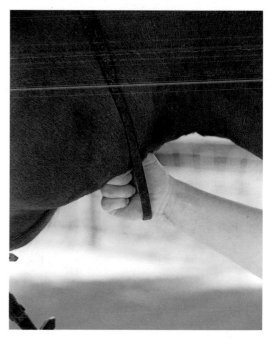

risk of the saddle being damaged if the horse decides to roll before the saddle has been removed.

137

REMOVING THE BRIDLE

Removing the bridle is done in the reverse sequence to putting it on. First place the rope of the head collar around the horse's neck to prevent it from bolting. The nose band and throat latch are then undone. The headpiece is then carefully removed over the ears and the bit is removed from the horse's mouth. The horse will usually open its mouth to let the bit fall out.

Breastplate

The breastplate or breast girth is an item of harness that is fastened across the horse's breast and fastened to the girth or saddle on both sides in order to keep the saddle in place.

Martingales and balancing reins

There are various reins and other items of tack that are designed to help control a horse or correct a fault. They should never be used severely and always fastened in the correct manner.

Breastplate

Martingale

MARTINGALE

A martingale is used to stop a horse bringing its head up so far that the rider loses contact with the bit. Provided the head is held correctly, the martingale should have no effect on the horse.

SIDE REINS

Side reins are short, adjustable straps that are attached to the bit or cavesson when a horse is being schooled on the lunge rein. They are intended to keep the horse's head in the correct position.

BALANCING OR DRAW REINS

Balancing reins are used to make a horse keep its head down. They are either fastened to the saddle or between the forelegs to

Side reins

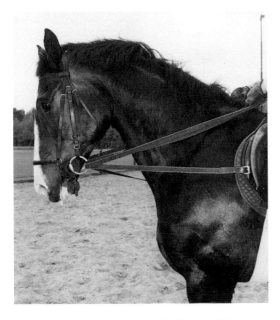

the girth and pass through the snaffle rings to the rider.

This aid can only be used by a very experienced rider. Used incorrectly, they can do great harm to a horse.

AUTOMATIC BALANCING REINS

An automatic balancing rein is only effective when a horse raises or lowers its head

Automatic balancing rein

too much. Provided a horse holds its head correctly, the automatic balancing rein has no effect on it.

Taking care of tack

In order to thoroughly clean a saddle and bridle, all the straps have to be taken apart and any dirt removed with a damp sponge. If water alone fails to remove the dirt, try rubbing a little lukewarm milk into the leather; this will quickly remove any stubborn dirt. When all the pieces of tack have been cleaned and surface water removed with a chamois leather, dry them as much as possible with a cloth.

The leather is now treated with saddle soap, which despite its name, is not for cleaning leather but for preserving it and keeping leather supple. The saddle soap is worked in thoroughly to both sides of the leather with a damp sponge. Some other leather preservers are too greasy and should certainly never be used on the outer surface. Once the saddle soap is thoroughly worked in, buff it up with a brush to a shine.

The frequency and thoroughness required for such major tack cleaning depends entirely on how regularly the tack is used. It is certainly a good idea to make it a habit to always remove dirt and sweat from the

Cleaning tack

saddle and bridle after a ride. The bit should always be rinsed off with water after use. Leather girths can be dealt with in the same way as the other tack but for webbing it is best to use green household soap in fairly tepid water. The buckles must be dried immediately.

Stirrup irons should be polished regularly with a metal cleaner.

Leg protection

BANDAGES
Bandages can be used to support the tendon and protect a horse's legs. It is important that they are correctly applied, since if they are too tight they can harm the horse by restricting the flow of blood, or if they are too loose they have no effect and could come loose, possibly leading to an accident.

BOOTS
Boots are made of leather or felt that is strengthened with leather. They are quick and easy to apply.
Make sure though that they fit the horse properly. Not every boot or tendon boot is suitable for every horse.

OVER-REACH BOOTS
Special boots made of rubber that protect the coronet band and pasterns are often worn by showjumping horses.

BRUSHING BOOTS
Some horses have a tendency to strike their own legs with their hooves while they are being ridden.

Bandages and boots

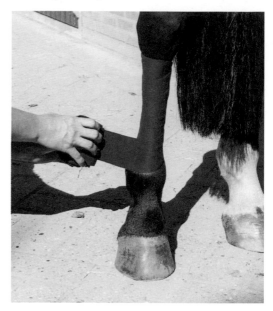

Removing a bandage

If the horse is wearing shoes the potential for injury is quite high and therefore such horses are best protected with special boots that protect them from being struck by their own shoes.

Boots and over-reach boots

Brushing boots

Brushing boots

Spurs

Other riding equipment

BELLY PROTECTOR
Horses that lift the legs high for jumping are usually given a belly protector.

FLY NET
A fly net keeps insects out of a horse's ears.

SPURS
Spurs are used to reinforce the leg aids and are worn on the heels of riding boots for use with horses that do not react to the calves. They should only be worn by very experienced riders who can keep their lower legs in the correct position while riding. There are both sharp spurs and blunt ones.

RIDING WHIP
A riding whip, cane, or crop is used to reinforce the aids given by the rider's legs. For hacking and jumping, a short whip is

usually used no longer than 750mm (about 30in). A longer whip of at least 1m (3ft 4in) is used for schooling horses and dressage so that the aids given by the heel can be reinforced in the correct place.

RIDING CLOTHES
Whatever clothes you prefer to wear for riding, they must meet certain basic requirements.

Arms and legs should be covered in order to protect them and no loose waving scarves should ever be worn.

Fly net

Belly protector

Riding breeches or jodhpurs must be a comfortable fit

Riding jacket and hat

Formal long-tailed riding jacket for dressage

Jackets must have sufficient room to be buttoned-up when mounted and done up. Flapping jackets, with a zip perhaps, can hurt both the rider and the horse. It is also sensible to pay heed to the weather. Neither profuse perspiration nor the shivers exactly enhance the pleasure of a ride.

JODHPURS OR RIDING BREECHES

Riding breeches need to fit very well so that there are no creases or folds on the insides of the thighs, knees, and heels that prevent the rider from having perfect contact.

Remember when buying breeches or jodhpurs that some competitions require a specific color.

RIDING JACKET

A riding jacket must provide sufficient freedom to move for the rider when all its buttons are done up. The rear of the jacket must have a vent to accommodate the high cantle of the saddle.

DRESSAGE JACKET

For top-level dressage trials, riders must wear long riding jackets with tails.

Boots are helped on with boot pullers...

and removed with a bootjack

BOOTS

Boots are available in leather and rubber. The boots must fit well and the shanks should come up to just below the knee. Leather boots are put on with the help of boot pullers and taken off by putting the heel in a bootjack.

RIDING HAT

A riding hat that will protect against a fall or being hit by low-hanging branches is essential. The hat must have a hard protective safety shell that will act as a helmet and have a chinstrap.

For eventing, where horses are ridden cross-

Riding gloves

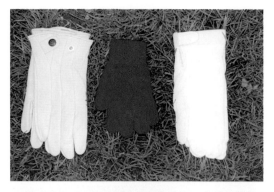

A stock

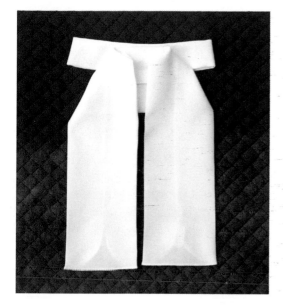

A stock

hat or bowler. These are usually kept in place by elastic or side combs.

GLOVES

Riding gloves need to be strong because they have to cope with a great deal of moisture during a ride, with horse sweat, and with dirt. They can be made of wool, cotton, or leather. For some competitions, the wearing of white gloves is required.

STOCK

A stock (or hunting tie) is worn for dressage instead of a tie by women competitors.

Rosettes

The prize winners in every form of equestrian sports from Pony Club games and gymkhanas to World Championships are awarded rosettes.

The colours can vary from country to country and from one organization to another. Generally the first prize is usually red, with blue for second prize but in the United States this order is reversed.

country over obstacles, a riding helmet is worn. Most stables make the wearing of a safety hat obligatory for all riders, but certainly for those under sixteen.

FORMAL HAT

When showing a horse and during dressage trials it is often required to wear a formal

Rosettes

4 Dressage

Dressage is one of the most important elements of equestrian sport. The general principles of dressage date back to the ancient Greeks of pre-history but modern dressage has its roots in the Renaissance. Frederico Grisone founded an equestrian academy in 1532 where horses were trained to perform complex and spectacular movements. The sport became immensely popular with the nobility throughout the continent of Europe and dressage developed from a kind of circus performance to dressage as we know it today. Dressage was first included at the Olympic Games in 1912.

The rider's task is to teach a horse to move as finely as possible. The training seeks to extend the natural movements and characteristics of the horse.

A horse that moves well, does so fully balanced or poised with its legs relaxed. It also creates the impression that it does everything of its own will. To achieve this, the horse must immediately respond to the aids that its rider gives.

Those who decide to take up dressage not only require the motivation to train their horse in the correct manner but must also have the discipline to improve their own riding ability and to be prepared to learn to ride to a far higher standard.

A wonderful sight

Left: on the bit

Impulsion

This chapter deals first with the terminology associated with dressage. This is followed with a description of the various dressage exercises to the high school level. There is also information about the Spanish Riding School with its famous high school airs. Finally, the chapter deals with formation dressage, team dressage, and other formation riding.

Terminology

ATHLETICISM IN A HORSE

A horse needs to be fully fit to be able to carry out the more difficult requirements of dressage. In addition to the necessary muscular strength and agility, the horse needs to be sufficiently well-schooled to execute difficult drills, making intelligence an essential requirement.

A horse that cannot understand the different figures will not be able to perform them. The physical and mental capabilities influence each other, so that a horse which understands an exercise but is not fit enough to carry it out is running a great risk of straining itself.

IMPULSION

Impulsion refers to the urge to move forward that a rider creates in a horse which is fully under control. It is only possible to impel a horse correctly if the right combination of impelling aids and help through the hands is achieved. The intention is not to speed the horse up but for the horse's hindquarters to exhibit a lively urge to move forward.

RIDING ON THE BIT
When a horse is said to ride on the bit, this is the result of good interaction between the aids being given to get the horse to move forward, and the sensitive use of the hands. The impulsion created by the calves can be felt by the rider through the bit. This impulsion should form a direct link, from the rider, through the hindlegs of the horse, and its back, and neck, returning through the bit to the rider's hands. One way to see and feel that a horse is on the bit is when with its neck muscles relaxed, and its neck curved upwards, it happily takes the bit with light pressure on the reins.

WORKING THROUGH
A horse is working through when it constantly is on the bit, relaxed, and moving its hindquarters correctly.
To get a horse working through properly, maintain constant contact through the reins which the horse can sense without pulling on the reins.

COLLECTED
In order to ensure a horse is properly balanced, the rider must distribute the weight correctly. The horse's forehand naturally bears more weight than the hindquarters. If a comparison is made with a table firmly standing on four legs, when a weight is placed to the front of the table – as the

Working through well

Collected

horse's head is – the point of balance will be moved forwards. When the rider's weight is then added, this leads to extra pressure on the forehand. By developing the back and hindquarter muscles, these can take part of the load off the forehand.

This is achieved by bringing the hindlegs under the horse's body to lighten the forehand. When the rider uses the seat and leg aids to get the horse to carry more of its weight on the hindquarters, we speak of the horse being collected. A horse must not be collected through over use of the reins, nor should the hindlegs be allowed to come too far forward to bear the weight, or the balance will be disturbed.

The object of collecting the horse is to improve the balance. It requires the quarters to dip slightly as the hindlegs shift under the weight, so that the forehand is light enough to be able to perform all kinds of exercises. This should all be achieved without giving an impression of a forced activity.

EXTENSION
Extension means that a horse is urged to take large strides with each step without changing to a faster gait. The horse can stretch its neck slightly in order to do so but it should remain calm, relaxed, and on the bit.

MEDIUM WALK, COLLECTED WALK, EXTENDED WALK, AND FREE WALK
Between the various elements of the dressage test, the horse can walk to rest and relax. A young horse is likely to get above the bit.

Extending

Once the horse is able to better understand the aids given by the rider, work can begin with the medium walk.

The reins are shortened slightly but the action should remain lively and regular. The hind hooves slightly overshoot the hoofprints from the front feet. The rider helps the horse to find the correct rhythm through seat and leg pressure. The hands move with the horse's head.

In the collected walk, the horse's paces are shorter than in the medium walk and it lifts its legs slightly higher. The neck is raised up and the head is carried slightly ahead of an

Extended walk

imaginary vertical line. Despite the shorter steps, the rider ensures that the action is smooth and not rushed.

In the extended walk, the paces are strong and as long as possible. The hindlegs clearly overshoot the hoofprints of the forelegs. The horse is allowed to carry its head slightly lower, without coming off the bit. The free walk is a relaxed, natural walk. The horse is permitted to bring its head and neck forwards and down.

See also: *Walk,* Chapter 4.

COLLECTED TROT, WORKING AND MEDIUM TROT, EXTENDED TROT

Some horses do not have the natural ability to trot in a steady rhythm and well-balanced with a rider on their back.

Medium trot

Extended trot

In such cases the first step is to achieve a slow trot. Before a start can be made with the collected trot, the horse needs to be balanced.

The collected trot, like the collected walk, should consist of short, raised steps. The hindlegs should be actively bent, the forehand light, and the neck arched upwards. The collected trot gives a light-footed impression. In between the collected trot and the medium trot, there is the working trot. Here too the balance is very important. The horse must be encouraged to make rhythmic springing steps. The quarters should be full of driving effort.

The next trot is the medium trot, with which the steps are longer and the horse may lower its head slightly. The head does not have to be carried so forward as in the collected and working trot. Finally. with the extended trot, the horse should try to cover as much ground as possible with each step. This needs strong impulsion from the horse. The horse may lengthen and lower its neck, but contact with the bit must be maintained. The steps should be a rhythmic as possible. See also: *Trot,* Chapter 4.

COLLECTED CANTER, WORKING AND MEDIUM CANTER, EXTENDED CANTER

Most horses have no difficulty whatsoever to canter. It is important though that the horse remains on the bit and can canter in a straight line. The head and neck should move with the leading foreleg.

When the horse is suspended in air, it is balanced, and the head, neck, and forehand rise upwards. To get the horse to break into a canter, the rider uses seat and legs to urge the horse at the right moment. To make sure the horse canters properly, the rider needs to reposition his or her seat.

In the collected canter, the horse holds its head up. Because the weight is transferred to the quarters, the shoulders are lithe and able to move freely. Each leap in the collected canter is relatively short but light-footed, and lively. All the legs are very active in the working canter. The horse springs lithely forwards with a powerful and extended action. Between the working canter and the extended canter, there is the medium canter.

The horse moves its hindquarters in large forward bounds. The head is permitted further above the bit than with the working and collective canters. The neck and head may also be carried somewhat lower.

Finally, in the extended canter, the horse gains as much ground as possible with each bound. The inside hind leg lands well under the body without disturbing either the rhythm or balance. The neck may be stretched out with the head lowered further, with the nose pointing forwards. See also: *Canter,* in Chapter 4.

DISUNITED CANTER

The disunited canter is when the forelegs canter left and the hindlegs to the right so that the horse crosses over.

Collected canter

Continued pressure while reining back

This canter occurs primarily with young horses that are not yet confident of their balance. It is a very uncomfortable gait for the rider and must immediately be corrected.

OVERTRACKING
When a horse places its hind leg in front of where the foreleg grounded, it is overtracking. With extended gaits, overtracking is essential.

TRANSITION
Transition is the change from a quicker to a slower gait and vice versa but there can also be a transition within the same gait when there is a change of tempo.
Transition exercises help to develop athletic hindquarters, such as from medium trot to extended trot and back.
To slow down, the aids are applied as though stopping and to quicken the pace, the rider urges with the calves and by giving with the hands on the reins. That is to say, the hands immediately move forward with the horse as it reacts to the leg aids.

Transitions and changes of tempo must be attractively performed, as a smooth flowing action in which the urge to move forward is never hindered. The gait to which a horse changes should be maintained until the next transition.

HALTING
When stopping, the hands first offer resistance and then relax while the horse is being pressed through the seat and calves.

This presses down on the quarters and these yield slightly so that the horse shortens its stride, stops, or moves backwards. With a half halt, the horse changes to a slower gait or a reduced tempo. With a complete halt, the horse is stopped.

HALF HALT

A half halt is an extremely important exercise. Dressage riders use the half halt as a means to "change gear" to move from one tempo to another, or to a new figure. With a half halt, the rider makes the forehand wait while the hind legs move under the body. This collects the horse, reducing weight on the forehand. The horse is now ready for a new exercise. The exercise also demands that the horse pays attention as it knows that something is expected of it. Well performed half halts are indispensable means of making clean transitions.

BENDING

A horse makes a right-hand or left-hand length bend when its neck and body are slightly curved to one side or the other. When only the head is held to either right or left, this is referred to as a head bend.

Dressage exercises

RIDING TURNS

When riding a turn, the horse looks in the direction in which it is going and its head and body are bent.

An example is when riding a circle or volte. The horse must make a length bend in order to be able to be ridden in a circle. The length bend should match the circle which

Riding a turn

Riding straight ahead

is being ridden. The quarters should follow the track made by the forehand. The rider too always looks in the direction of the turn and brings the weight on to the inner hip. The inner calf gives an impulse to maintain the tempo and to prevent the horse from coming inside the desired line.

The hindquarters must not swing out so the outer calf is moved backwards to keep the correct length bend through the circle. The rider holds his or her hands slightly forwards and in, but they must not touch the mane. Do not ride the same circle more than two or three times at a go. Alternate this exercise, for example, with riding a straight line, followed by more circles on the opposite hand.

RIDING IN A STRAIGHT LINE

Horses have a natural inclination to walk slightly askew because they have their preferred side just as we are right and left-handed.

To move in a straight line, the first requirement is for the reins to have even pressure on both sides. It is also important to maintain the impulsion aids.

Most horses will accept more pressure on the bit on their "leading" side, so the rider must urge this side on slightly more than the other, to get the horse to walk straight.

Every dressage rider hates having to ride exercises straight down the center of the dressage arena. The horse then has to walk

Standing still

straight without the benefit of the wall or fence to guide it.

STANDING STILL

When a horse stands still correctly, it does so quietly and squarely, with its weight born evenly on all four legs.

To stop the horse, the rider uses legs and seat to move weight to the quarters and provides pressure through the bit but the hands remain sensitive. The horse should react immediately but must never be abruptly halted. When standing still, the horse gently chews the bit, ready to move forwards or backwards.

REINING BACK

In order to move backwards, the rider first urges the horse to move forward but at the moment the horse lifts its hindleg to take a

Reining back

TURNING ON THE FOREHAND
A turn on the forehand is a quarter circle turn in two steps, with the size of the horse determining the dimension of the circle. The off foreleg steps around the near foreleg to complete the turn.

Leg aids applied on one side only ensure that the hindquarters move with the forehand.

A variation of the turn on the forehand, is a reverse turn on the forehand, which is useful for opening gates when out trekking. From standing still, the horse turns half way round on the forehand, using the near foreleg as a pivot.

This should ideally stay more or less in one spot. The near hindleg steps over the off hindleg as many times as is necessary to turn half way round.

FIGURES AND EXERCISES
In addition to the exercises dealt with in chapter four, such as changing hand, stopping and standing still, circles, and serpentines, there are other figures which are not restricted to high school dressage.

- Figure eight: consisting of two inter-linked

Riding figures

stride, the rider reins back in a similar way to halting.
When a horse is reined back, the legs move in diagonally opposite pairs: left fore and right hindlegs together and right fore and left hind. The feet should be lifted clearly off the ground and the hindlegs should remain in line with the forelegs.

TURNING ON THE HINDQUARTERS
When a horse turns on the hindquarters, it makes a quarter of a circle within two steps. The size of the circle is determined by the size of the horse. The off hindleg steps around the near hindleg to complete the movement.

A variation of turning on the hindquarters is when a horse makes a reverse turn. From the standing still position, the horse turns half-way round to left or right using its near hindleg to pivot on. This leg should more or less remain in one position until the turn is completed.

circles of equal size. The circles touch each other at the center of the arena (at X). When the rider reaches X on the first half circle he or she changes hand to ride a full circle back to the intersection where they change hands to complete the first circle.

- Half circle left, followed by half circle right: the rider starts from half-way along the short side of the arena to ride half a large circle. At the center of the arena, several steps straight ahead are taken before half a circle is then ridden on the opposite hand. The figure ridden is an S.

- Changing hands by riding an S: this exercise begins by riding a semi-circle that is half the size of the arena before changing hands by first taking a few steps straight ahead and then riding a second half circle.

There are many more possible figures of course, all of which can be executed at a walk, trot, or canter.

Lateral work

In order to move laterally (or side-step), the horse moves its front legs and hindlegs on different tracks to move forward sideways. Lateral work helps to make a horse flexible and nimble on its feet.

LEG YIELDING
Leg yielding is a lateral exercise in which the horse moves forwards and sideways as a result of leg pressure, looking slightly in the opposite direction to the one in which it is moving. Leg yielding is at the heart of all lateral work. The horse should ideally move parallel to the sides of the arena. The body should bend only slightly with the neck bent as little as possible without the head tilted. The movement should be smooth and consistent. The legs cross in front of each other and sideways. The rider uses the seat aid to urge the horse forwards and the calf to urge the horse laterally. The reins keep the head in position. The outer leg reinforces the movement to prevent the horse from moving in the wrong direction.

HALF PASS
A half pass is one of the first lateral movements that riders learn. The forehand is lightly moved inwards to bring the near hind and off forelegs in line with each other.

Shoulder in

This exercise demands less collection and bending of the body than shoulder in.

SHOULDER-IN

With a shoulder-in movement, the horse makes three tracks as it moves laterally, with the head bent away from the direction in which the horse is moving.

The hindquarters remain following the original track while the forehand is moved slightly inside, causing the body to bend lightly around the rider's inside leg. The outside hindleg and inside foreleg follow the same line. The inner foreleg crosses over the outer one.

Advanced dressage exercises

TRAVERS

The *travers* is a sideways movement with the horse's head to the wall and looking in the direction in which it moves. The horse makes four separate sets of hoofprints. The forehand of the horse remains on the main track but the hindquarters are brought inwards.

The horse's body bends around the rider's inside leg. The horse's outer legs cross in front of the inside legs. The angle should not be more than 30 degrees but is greater than with shoulder-in movements.

RENVERS

The *renvers* is a sideways movement in which the horse moves with its tail to the wall at an angle of not more than 30 degrees. The horse bends around the rider's outside leg. Like the *travers,* this exercise leaves four sets of hoofprints as the horse moves along the main track of the arena but this time with its head towards the inside of the arena.

APPUYEMENT OR HALF-PASS

Appuyement is an advanced lateral exercise in which the horse moves diagonally – usually from the main track towards the center line – with its body and head lightly bent in the direction of the movement. The outer legs cross in front of the inner legs and the forehand is directed forwards on the bit while the hindquarters yield to one-sided leg pressure. Although the exercise can be performed at a walk, trot, or canter, in dressage trials it is only ridden in a collected trot

Travers

Appuyement

156

and canter. When the exercise is correctly ridden, it appears as if the horse is gliding effortlessly across the arena. The horse keeps its body more or less parallel with the wall and lifts its legs up. The exercise becomes harder as the angle of the diagonal increases.

SCHALTEN
Schalten is a reining back exercise for advanced riders.

The horse moves forward a set number of steps and then the same number of steps back before continuing. The transition from backwards to forwards and vice versa has to be fluid, without faltering.

PIROUETTE
A pirouette is a full 360 degree turn. The forehand of the horse moves in a circle, while the hindquarters remain as near as possible on one spot. This exercise demands a high degree of co-ordination from horse and rider.

Because horses naturally turn around their middles, they need to be firmly collected to get them to pivot on their hindquarters. Once the weight is on the hindquarters, the forehand should complete the pirouette in one fluid motion. The score for this difficult maneuver is often doubled.

A semi or half pirouette is demanded for the Prix St. Georges, but from Intermédiare upwards complete pirouettes are performed. The number of permissible steps for a semi-

pirouette is three to four and six to eight for a full pirouette.

COUNTER CANTER
The counter canter requires a horse to canter around the arena, or in a circle, with the off foreleg leading. This exercise requires a great deal of agility on the part of a horse.

FLYING CHANGE
When a horse reacts to the aids given by the rider to change action while off the ground in a canter this is what the French dressage term calls *changement*.

During this flying change of canter, the horse should remain light-footed and maintain its impulsion. The flying change should always take place with the fore and hind legs simultaneously, so that if the forelegs change first and then the hindlegs or vice versa, this is not correct. A simple change of canter is a preparation for this exercise, with the horse breaking into a few paces of walk before the new canter. The horse should not trot during the transition and this should be smoothly done.

High school airs

ZIGZAG APPUYEMENT
Zigzag *appuyement* is a series of lateral half-pass paces on each side of the center line of the dressage arena in a set pattern of so many paces left, then the same

number right and so on. Zigzag appuyement are frequently ridden across the center line. The rider can, for example, make four paces to the left, change direction and make eight paces to the right, change direction again and make four paces to the left to regain the center line. The paces need of course to be even so that the ground covered is the same. For Grand Prix competitions, the required number of paces is three and six.

SERIES OF TRANSITIONS

A great number of transitions from one action to another and from one tempo to a different tempo can be executed during a top-level dressage test. This might be every fourth step, or every third, every other step, or even every step. To be able to perform such a test, a horse needs to have powerful springing strides. This gives longer in the air for each transition to be performed and for the horse to change legs.

The Prix St. Georges requires a change every third pace. At Grand Prix level, a series of fifteen changes are required every other step.

Passage

PASSAGE

Passage is a slow elevated trot, with the forehand being raised with the hindquarters being strongly collected. There is a clear moment of "floating" when the passage is performed which makes the horse appear to be in slow motion. The exercise is exciting to watch because of the tremendous impulsion from the hindquarters and the muscular energy that the horse exhibits.

Piaffe

PIAFFE

The *piaffe* is a spectacular elevated trot performed on the spot. The legs are diagonally lifted and put down in a springing trot without the horse moving position. The piaffe is one of the most difficult of the high school airs.

The horse must lift its four legs equally high, virtually jumping from one step the next. The hindquarters are strongly collected so that the horse almost appears to be sitting. At Intermédiaire level horse and rider are permitted to move seven or eight steps forward during its performance but at the more senior competitions, the standards are more rigorous.

Competing in dressage

The point of a dressage competition is to ascertain whether the rider has his or her horse under control and is able to perform the required elements of the test. The jury also takes note of how well presented horse and rider are with separate marks being awarded for turnout. This means that the horse has to be thoroughly groomed, its mane plaited, and the rider must wear the required clothing. Do not forget to make sure that the tack is thoroughly clean.

DRESSAGE CLASSES

The international F.E.I. dressage classes are B, l, M1, M2, Z1, Z2. In Britain the classes are graded Preliminary, Novice, Elementary, Medium, Advanced Medium, Advanced, Prix St. Georges. F.E.I. class L equates approximately with Medium, and Class M is roughly equivalent to Medium Advanced.

DRESSAGE ARENA

The lower dressage classes are performed in an arena of 20 x 40m (65ft 6in x 131ft). All other levels of competition are held in an arena 20 x 60 (65ft 6in x 197ft). Where dressage competitions are held in restricted indoor arenas, higher level tests can be performed in a 20 x 40m arena but the tests are adapted with more letters than usual. The left-hand side has letters F, P, B, R, and M, with K, V, E, S, and H on the right. On the A–C line, there are imaginary letters D, L, X, I, and G.

DRESSAGE TESTS

Dressage tests are divided into short exercises each of which is awarded a mark out of ten: excellent = 10, very good = 9, good = 8, fairly good = 7, satisfactory = 6, sufficient = 5, insufficient = 4, fairly bad = 3, bad = 2, very bad = 1, not performed = 0.

Lap of honor of the dressage arena

The manner in which the tests are performed is the most important consideration. The things which the jury considers are the cleanness and uniformity of the gaits, the impulsion, the general standard of riding, the attentiveness and confidence of the horse, the effectiveness of the aids, and the standard of presentation of horse and rider.

In classes B and L, a whip is permitted to be used. In classes M and Z, spurs are required but a whip is forbidden.

WARM-UP AREA

The organizers must provide competitors with an adequate warm-up area (F.E.I. rules demand a minimum of at least 525sq m (630sq yd) preferably 35m x 15m (115ft x 50ft). It is very important for a horse's muscles to be loosened up before a competition because only a horse that is warmed up will be agile enough to perform the exercises well. There is no need to practice the elements of the test or those which the horse finds most difficult. The intention is to loosen and exercise the muscles in the back and neck by trotting, riding turns and through other exercises. There is no point

Loosening up before entering the arena

whatever in tiring the horse before the competition.

DRESSAGE JURY

The officials who judge dressage trials are selected from an official list of those with the appropriate experience for the required level. Class Z1 and above have at least two but not more than three judges. International competitions are judged by five officials: two on the long sides at B and E, and three at C. The senior official is always at position C. This means there are least three viewpoints to judge the execution of the dressage tests. Contestants are given a report after the competition with the points awarded and with the general impression the horse and rider made on the jury.

SENIOR STEWARD

The schedule of the day's program and everything to do with the arena fall under the responsibility of the senior steward. The order in which they are to appear and the timings are very important to contestants so that they are neither too early nor late in loosening up their mounts.

PAYING RESPECT

The rider stops and stands still in front of the jury at C, with the reins and whip, if used, in the left hand. The right hand is lowered next to the thigh as the contestant bows the head. When there are more judges, the contestant is only required to pay respect to the senior official.

Correct wear for dressage

REQUIRED DRESS FOR DRESSAGE TRIALS

Unless dressed in the uniform of their association, riders must appear in the arena dressed in:

- a black or dark blue riding jacket or frock coat
- white, beige, or yellow riding breeches
- an appropriate white tie or stock
- a pair of white gloves
- black leather riding boots
- a cap, top hat, or bowler.

Military personnel and police officers may choose to wear riding habit or their uniform.

International competitions and regulations

INTERNATIONAL EQUESTRIAN FEDERATION (F.E.I.)

The International Equestrian Federation or F.E.I. is the international ruling body for equestrian sports. The F.E.I. was founded in 1921 with the aim of regulating equestrian sport but also to advance all aspects of competition with horses. Horses that are permitted to compete in international competition have F.E.I. passports and the Federation approves and controls competitions run by other organizations. They also require there to be veterinary checks of the horses taking part and ensure that there is sufficient stable space and exercise space for them.

PRIX ST. GEORGES

The Prix St. Georges is the least strenuous of the F.E.I. tests. The elements included

Competing in uniform

Kür to music

are medium, collected and extended gaits, lateral work, transition every third step, and a half pirouette from the canter.

F.E.I. INTERMEDIAIRE I

The F.E.I. Intermédiaire 1 is a dressage trial between the Prix St. Georges and Intermédiaire 2. The elements required include transition every second step and a full pirouette from the canter.

F.E.I. INTERMEDIAIRE 2

The F.E.I. Intermédiaire 2 is a dressage trial between the Intermédiaire 1 and the Grand Prix. The elements required include transition in the canter every other step and *piaffe* with a limited number of steps.

GRAND PRIX

The Grand Prix is the most advanced level of dressage trial under F.E.I. rules. The elements required include zigzag diagonal lateral figures, transition every step, *passage,* and *piaffe*.

KUR TO MUSIC

The test to music known as *kür* to music can be ridden at all levels of competition. The test includes a number of required elements but the rest of the program is free for the contestant to decide on. The music must suit the dressage figures and the manner in which they are ridden. There is a maximum time permitted for the *kür*.

High school

The high school of equitation refers to the classical equestrian arts and the teachings of the masters of the past. The literal high points of high school work are the elevated airs in which horses spring into the air. These are only practiced these days by the Spanish Riding School in Vienna.

SPANISH RIDING SCHOOL

The Spanish Riding School is located right in the center of Vienna, where it was established in 1729. The riding school and stables are a part of the Hofburg. It is the oldest school where equestrian arts are taught according to classical principles.

The Spanish Riding School ride solely Lipizzaner stallions. The stallions that are chosen for the school start training on the lunge and the long rein in their third year. They are not backed until they are four years old. Their training to the top levels of dressage lasts a further five years.

Elevated high school airs

LEVADE

With the *levade* the horse deeply bends its hindlegs, rears up with the forehand from the ground and remains still for a moment in the rearing position. The entire weight is borne on the hindlegs, with the forelegs being tucked in against the breast.

COURBETTE

The *courbette* starts off as the *levade* but the horse then makes a number of springs forwards on the hindlegs without its forelegs touching the ground.

CROUPADE

With the *croupade,* the horse rears up and then jumps vertically into the air with its forelegs tucked against its breast.

CAPRIOLE

The *capriole* is undoubtedly the most diffi-

Pas de deux

cult of the high school airs. The horse first rears up, bending its hindlegs very low. The horse then leaps into the air and when the body is horizontal, the rear legs kick out powerfully. The rider has no stirrups to assist them with the maneuver.

Team dressage

Taking part in team dressage is an opportunity to participate with others in a dressage competition. This team sport depends on the performance of the team collectively rather than an individual. Each team member needs to be sufficiently advanced of course to be able to ride the tests correctly. Teams consist of four or eight combinations of horse and rider.

CAPTAIN
Each team of four or eight has a leader who gives the commands during the dressage test.

COMMANDS
To get his team riding the dressage elements correctly, the captain uses a combination of warning instructions and commands to execute, rather like a drill sergeant.

The warning advises which exercise or figure is to be performed next.
The execution command is an agreed short crisp word.

OPEN AND CLOSED ORDER
In open order, the riders keep space between themselves. In closed order, the

Levade

Courbette

Capriole

riders are stirrup to stirrup alongside each other.

SINGLE FILE
When the team rides in single file, the riders usually hold a distance of about a metre or yard between themselves, unless other instructions are given. If the captain issued orders to ride two abreast, the leading rider slows down so that number two can come alongside them to the left, then number four comes alongside number three and so on.

CHANGING DIRECTION
Direction can be changed in column or in open and closed order. When the command is given "Head of column...left turn," the leading rider turns left followed by all the others. If the command, "Column... left turn," is given, all the riders turn left together.

Formation dressage

A formation dressage team normally consists of 12, 16, or 24 riders, who collectively ride dressage figures, usually to music. The uniformity of the formation is very important. The foundation of the formations is a column, two abreast, with the horses' heads close together and the riders stirrup to stirrup and maintaining this distance throughout.

COLUMNS AND SECTIONS
During formation dressage, the basic column of twos may divide in two. The two sections may themselves also further split into smaller groups. The number of figures that can be ridden by the different sections is therefore very varied, offering spectators a fine display.

Figures in formation

There is enormous scope for variation with formation dressage.

• Making an entrance: this can be done traditionally, with all the riders lined up in front of the jury, but the group can appear in a V-formation, divided into two sections, or in a diagonal line.
• Changing hand can be performed by pairs or in sections, in trios, down the middle, or diagonally.
• Decorative figures can be made with names like herringbone, hour-glass, butterflies, clover-leaf, and tourniquet.

HERRINGBONE OR CUPS
A column of twos forms along the center line of the arena. All the riders to the left ride a small circle to the left while those on the right do likewise to the right. Each pair meets up again at the center line to continue to the next figure.

Formation dressage

Formation dressage

HOUR GLASS
The team rides in single file towards the center of the arena but splits half way down the arena. The first rider heads for the left-hand corner, the second to the right-hand corner and so on. The riders pass each other on the short side of the arena and head back to the center of the arena where they cross over each other. The movement is repeated on the opposite side of the arena so that the shape of an hour glass is performed.

One of the most spectacular examples of formation dressage is the Musical Ride of the Royal Canadian Mounted Police. On black horses specially bred for the Mounties, and carrying light lances tipped with pennants, 24 red-coated riders perform such figures as the Maltese Cross, the Maze, the Dome and Salute, a demonstration of lance exercises, and an exciting final charge to the far end of the area.

5 Showjumping

Showjumping is a relative newcomer to equestrian sport. Being able to jump was certainly important for cavalry exercises and for clearing obstacles while hunting. The first official jumping competition was held in Dublin in 1864 but the sport did not become accepted by the Olympic Games until 1912. The foundations of the sport were laid by Frederico Caprilli (1868–1907). This Italian equestrian expert introduced a new seat in which the rider moved with the horse. This is now known as the forward seat.

Most horses in the wild or when running free will happily jump, and are naturally good jumpers. Jumping is more difficult for them when they have to take the weight on their back into account in order to get the right balance. This is why horse and rider have to work as a team together. The rider has to ensure that his or her weight is as little hindrance to the horse as possible. The rider must also be able to read the fence so that the horse can be put at it in the right way. Some riders have a better eye for fences than others and one horse is better at exactly when to take off than another. The natural instinct for jumping can be further developed through a lot of jumping experience.

This chapter deals with the most widely used terms in showjumping and in jumping competitions.

Teamwork between horse and rider

Left: the forward seat

A swish cane is short and convenient

Showjumping

SHOWINGJUMPING EQUIPMENT
There are a number of items of equipment and tack that are specially developed for use in showjumping.

Jumping saddle – this allows the rider to sit more forward and with shorter stirrup leathers than with a general purpose saddle. Jumping saddles usually have a spring tree, deeper knee roll and a higher cantle.

Swish cane – this is short and convenient. The rider lets it hang alongside the shoulder where it causes no problem for the horse during the jump. Whips used for competition should not exceed 750mm (30in).

PROTECTING SHOWJUMPING HORSES
The purpose of tendon boots and knee boots are to prevent a horse from injuring itself on a fence or by kicking itself with a hoof.

Tendon boots are made of leather, foam rubber, plastic, or felt. They protect the cannons, pasterns, and tendons of the lower leg.

Knee boots protect the horse from kicks by its own hooves.

Showjumpers have a tendency to catch their pasterns against fences. To prevent injury, leather rings are fixed around the coronary band. Over-reach boots also protect the

Showjumper

specific size for them, though their conformation is important. They must have long, sound cannons and tendons.

The hindquarters must be rounded, strong, and muscular, with sound joints because this is where the jumping power comes from. A very short back is not preferred for a jumping horse because this makes it more difficult to jump a fence. The horse has to be supremely fit. Those in the know reckon that half the problems encountered when jumping are of a physical origin.

A muscle pain or strain can lead to all kinds of difficulties, even when there is nothing external to be seen.

foot, coronary band, and forelegs from being kicked by the hindlegs. Horses are most likely to kick themselves on heavy and soft ground. Leather boots are strapped to the legs but rubber ones can be pulled over the hoof so that they protect the coronary band, pasterns, and hocks.

SHOWJUMPER

Good showjumpers can be a very wide assortment of breeds and there is not a

FORWARD SEAT

A horse has to be able to achieve balance as effortlessly as possible when jumping. This means that the rider needs to keep his or her weight as far as possible in the same position without grasping at the reins.

Riders can only give the aids correctly when they are wholly balanced. The forward seat is the correct position for a rider during a

Pivoting

jump. For this, the stirrups are set two or three holes shorter so that the knees come tighter in to the saddle. The rider moves his or her upper body slightly forwards and transfers the weight through the upper legs and knees to the stirrups. The stirrup irons are placed under the ball of the foot. It is important for the heels to stay well down to keep the lower leg in position. The upper arms should hang down relaxed, with the forearms forming an extension of the reins. This posture reduces the burden on the horse's back and makes it easier for a horse to balance itself.

PIVOTING

When a horse is in mid-jump, it pivots, bringing its head and neck down, and by arching its back, to form an overall curve.

A spread with parallel rails is the ideal obstacle to school a horse over to ensure it pivots correctly. The shorter the spread, the quicker a horse must pivot.

THE HORSE'S TECHNIQUE

A jump is really just an extended leap at the canter. Getting that extension is the trick of successful jumping. The technique of a jumping horse can be subdivided into foreleg, hindleg, and head/neck technique. The forelegs must be lifted up high out of the way and tucked under the belly. Some horses let their lower legs hang down which means that they need to jump higher to clear the jump.

A very widespread fault is for horses to tuck their hind legs under. At the apex of the jump, a horse needs to stretch itself out and if a horse forgets this by keeping its hindlegs tucked under, it has insufficient room to clear the obstacle. The movement of the head and neck by the horse during a jump are responsible for assuming the correct shape of the back.

The jump

APPROACH

A fence should be taken at a steady tempo and rhythm. The leg aids ensure impulsion so that the horse does not stop at the obstacle. Try to approach the fence as squarely on as possible so that the horse is well balanced for the jump. The type of

The right approach is crucial

fence will determine the speed at which you approach it. Wider spreads demand a higher speed. At the moment that the horse is just about to reach the take off point, the rider brings the hands forward to give the horse room.

TAKE OFF

The horse initially lowers its head and neck to judge the correct distance and then when it jumps, the head and neck are raised as the forelegs are tucked back under the body. Next, the body is raised, the neck shortened and the hindlegs push off against the ground to achieve take off.

During take off, the rider shifts his or her weight forward, following the horse's movements, while maintaining very light contact with the bit, and with the hands moving with the horse's head. This is the most difficult stage of the jump.

The rider must assume the jumping position at precisely the moment the horse leaves the ground. If too early, the forehand will be overburdened and the horse will lose its balance; if too late, the rider will be behind the action and contact will be entirely lost with the bit.

MOMENT OF SUSPENSION

During the moment of suspension, all four legs of the horse are clear of the ground and it is apparently suspended in the air. The withers are the highest point of the horse at this moment.

Before the descent begins, the horse has rapidly to bring its forelegs back into position.

Moment of suspension

The suspension demands so much co-ordination of all the muscles that the rider cannot possibly play any role. Any pressure on the reins will prevent the horse from stretching its neck, leaving it insufficient room at the shoulders in which to tuck up its forelegs.

The rider prepares for the landing during the brief moment of flight. It is important that the rider keeps looking ahead throughout the jump. If the rider looks down, he or she will react too late at every stage of the jump.

LANDING

The horse stretches the forelegs out as it lands and as they touch down, it brings its head up to regain balance and to prepare itself for the shock as the hindquarters land. The hindlegs touch down more or less in the hoof-prints of the forelegs as the canter is continued. The rider has to make sure not to fall backwards in the saddle during the landing.

When the hindlegs touch down, the rider

must give forward impulsion aids immediately. The horse transfers its weight from its forehand to the quarters in readiness for the next fence. Even if you are only jumping one fence, it is best to let the horse carry through after the jump.

Simple jumping exercises

WALK AND TROT OVER POLES ON THE GROUND

Exercises over poles or rails laid on the ground are an excellent preparation for true jumping. The rider learns to time the precise moment that the jump begins and develops a sense of rhythm and balance. The horse learns to accept more readily the rider's aids, even when confronted with an obstacle. The horse becomes more supple and learns to extend its stride. A novice horse can be exercised at a walk and then when it has developed, at the trot. Make sure that the rails cannot roll away by fixing them with pegs.

Impulsion aids after the jump keep the horse moving

Cavalletti

CAVALLETTI

Cavalletti (the singular is cavalletto) are low hurdles formed of rails resting on low supports that are between 150–300mm

Cavalletti

173

Cavalletti

can be set at different heights. They have lost popularity because people forgot to peg them down. It is not advisable to pile cavalletto on top of each other because the fence is then too dangerous.

SCHOOLING OVER CAVALLETTI

An excellent way to teach a horse to assess distances and to remain balanced with a rider on its back, is to set four to six cavalletti at set distances from each other. Depending on the size and length of the action of the horse, set the cavalletti at 1–1.4m (39–55in) apart. If the horse or rider are inexperienced, it is best to start with one cavalletto and gradually increase the number.

CROSS HURDLES

It is important to bring a horse square on to a jump. To practice this and to help point out the center of the fence, cross hurdles can be used. Lay one end of a rail on the upright, with the other end on the ground and repeat with another rail from the other upright to form a cross. The horse will naturally choose to jump the lowest part of the hurdle.

(6–12in) high. The supports are often in the form of a cross. By turning them, cavalletti

Schooling over cavalletti

COMBINATION EXERCISES

Once a horse is sufficiently experienced that it can jump combination fences, it can be schooled over a simple series of obstacles not more than 500-800cm (20–32in) high. The object of the exercise is to train the horse to make a correct approach and to adjust its gallop between the fences. In this way, the horse can be introduced to a variety of obstacles.

In addition to low fences, rails can be laid on the ground to teach the horse to recover its balance and to always take off and land with two legs. The fences can be arranged in a serpentine form to practice turning and changing hand.

Fences

SINGLE FENCES

The two most important forms of single fence are the spread, such as the oxer, and the high fence.

COMBINATION FENCES

Obstacles which consist of more than one fence are known as combination fences. A

Single fence

triple fence is regarded as one obstacle but the horse has to make three jumps.

Combination fences have letters to indicate their constituent parts. If a horse refuses at one of the elements, the entire combination has to be jumped again.

HIGH FENCES

A tall fence is a single fence. High fences are far more trouble for a horse because it is far more difficult to assess distance for a tall fence. Generally a horse needs to be very collected for a tall fence and ridden slowly.

Combination fences

Combination fences

Wall

Horse's eye view of a combination

Spread

The take off point is much closer to the obstacle than with spreads because the horse has to gain more height. There are numerous types of high fence from single rails to a wall.

HIGH JUMP

The high jump is an upright fence that can usually be adjusted for height or have additional elements added to increase its height. It is the equine equivalent of the

High jump

school high jump. It is used much less in competition than previously.

WALL

The wall is a tall jump made up of blocks. The difficulty is increased with this type of fence by not being able to see the landing place.

SPREAD

The spread fence extends horizontally so that a horse not only has to gain height to clear the fence but must jump sufficient distance too. Examples of spreads are the various types of oxer and triple bars.

JOKER

A joker is a difficult but not an unsporting fence. There is no set manner in which to construct a joker but it will usually look different from the other fences by having, for instance, a crooked tree trunk as part of its construction. These fences are often

Straight oxer

Triple bar

indicated by a joker card and in certain competitions with cumulative scoring, clearing a joker fence can double the score for the previous fence.

OXER

An oxer is a spread fence which forces the horse to clear a certain height and distance. If the front and rear rails are at the same height, then the fence is a straight oxer but if the rear bar is higher then it is a progres-

sive or ramped oxer. Fences which are progressive on the take off or landing side are easier for horses to jump than parallel bars which force a horse to have to maintain height as well as length. Even if an oxer consists of a number of elements, it is still a single fence that has to be jumped at one go.

TRIPLE BAR

A triple bar is a fence in which the rails or bars get progressively higher.

Water jump

Clearing the water jump

material, preferably white, so that a judge can see whether a horse has left a hoof print. The plank must be at the water's edge and firmly fixed to the ground.

GROUND-LINE

A ground-line is a clear marking at ground level that can be seen by the horse and rider. It is important that a high jump fence has a clear ground-line because about 4m (13ft) from the jump, a horse can only see part of the jump. A ground-line makes it easier for a horse to judge the height and where to take off.

Fence with ground-line

The jump has to be cleared at one go. A variation on the triple bar is the hog's back which has first and third rails that are parallel but the second rail is higher, forming the apex of the jump.

WATER JUMP

The water jump forms a part of the showjumping course. The water spread is not usually wider than 2–4m (6ft 6in–13ft) and about 100–150mm (4–6in deep).

A water jump may only be included in a course if it can be sunken into the ground so that its top is level with the ground. The way in which a horse reacts to water is an important factor with the water jump, because if a horse fails to clear the jump, it lands in the water.

There may be a rail, low wall, or hedge on the take-off side but it must not be higher than 500mm (20in). The landing side must be marked by a plank of wood or similar

Jumping as a competitive sport

CONCOURS HIPPIQUE

A showjumping competition is internationally known as a *Concours Hippique*. Riders and horses compete by jumping the same course with a number of fences.

LEVEL OF COMPETITION

Showjumping competitions are held at every level from local gymkhanas and Pony Club events to international. There are competitions at all levels, so that a rider may progress from elementary levels to the major regional shows and then on to national and international events if they have the talent and the right horse. The standard of the courses is adapted to the level of competition.

ROUND

A round is a completed ride from start to finish of the course.

When all the competitors have completed their rounds, a winning classification may have been decided.

SIZE OF THE RING

To meet F.E.I. rules, an outdoor showjumping ring must cover an area not less than 3,200sq m (3,840sq yd). The shortest side must be not less than 40m (44yd). Pony jumping competitions can be held in a ring covering an area of at least 2,400sq m (2,880sq yd).

Showjumping ring

Practice jumping

An indoor jumping arena should measure at least 1,200sq m (1,440sq yd) and have a minimum width of 20m (65ft).

be at least 15m (50ft) wide and measure not less than 400sq m (480sq yd). A practice ring must contain a minimum of one straight fence and one spread.

SIZE OF THE WARM-UP
AND PRACTICE RING

An open air practice ring must measure at least 15m x 35m (50ft x 115ft).

A warm-up/practice ring for a *Concours Hippique* and for indoor competitions must

WARMING-UP AND PRACTICE JUMPING

It essential that a horse is warmed-up and "ridden in" by putting it over a number of jumps before a competition. A horse that is cold will be too stiff and uneasy to perform

The next competitor can start after the bell

well. The rider should check the order of jumping beforehand so that the warm-up exercises can be started at the right moment. Take care not to over-tire your horse. The objective is for your horse to be supple and jumping freely, so that the pair of you can enter the competition with confidence.

THE BELL

The bell is used to signal messages to competitors such as:
- the next competitor to be ready to enter the ring
- to give the start signal
- to stop the competitor
- to give the competitor permission to restart after an interruption
- to disqualify the competitor (long ring).

If a competitor fails to obey a bell signal to stop, they can be disqualified. Failing to wait for the bell after an interruption can also lead to disqualification.

FLAGS

A straight fence must have one red and one white flag on the wings of the obstacle. A spread must have a minimum of two red and two white flags.

The competitor is always required to jump to their right of the white flag and to the left of the red flag.

TIMING

The clock starts timing the round from the moment the horse and rider pass the start line until they cross the finish line.

JUMP OFF

If more than one rider has a clear round or are tied on the same number of faults, all the competitors that are level must jump off over a course that is usually shorter but can have one or two additional fences.

The rider with the fewest faults in the fastest time is the winner.

COURSE

The course is the route the rider must take from the starting line to the finishing flag.

Raising the height for a jump off

Fence No. 5

The fences in the course are numbered in the order in which they must be jumped, with the exception of certain competitions in which the participants can take any route they choose.

WALKING THE COURSE

Participants in a showjumping competition get one opportunity to walk the course (in the appropriate clothing) in order to familiarize themselves with its layout. It is not permitted to wear stable clothing in the ring. The competitors may closely examine the fences and decide how best to jump them. With cumulative points courses, the rider also has to decide which fences are most likely to score points, given the ability

of their horse. The riders also examine the condition of the ground over which the course is ridden, and the size of the different fences.

COURSE BUILDER

The course builder builds a course that is appealing to both the competitors and the public. The fences must be positioned to give horses a fair chance of jumping a clear round. Good course builders know precisely how horses jump and what difficulties they encounter when they jump. In designing and constructing the course, the course builder must bear in mind the level of the competitors and ensure that the degree of difficulty is appropriate for the experience of the entrants. A half hour before the start of jumping, the course builder displays a plan of the course as near as possible to the entrance to the arena, with all the relevant details about the course. The judges are also given a copy of the plan.

HORS CONCOURS

Hors concours means non-competitor. A

Walking the course

Course builder

combination that is *hors concours* may not be considered for a prize, nor may the points from the competition count towards any other class or championship. Regardless of how well horse and rider have performed, non-competitors are also not permitted to take part in a jump off.

JUDGES

Showjumping competitions in which no more than 120 rounds will be ridden must have three judges. If there will be more than 120 rounds in one day, there must be four judges and in excess of 200 rounds, there have to be five. If there is a water jump, there has to be one additional judge. If the number of rounds will not exceed 50, two judges are sufficient.

PAYING RESPECT

Every participant in a showjumping competition is required to pay respect to the judges. Raising the riding whip and bowing the head are regarded as respectful. In these days of equality and safety hats with chin straps, both men and women do not remove their hats.

Regulation clothing

REGULATION CLOTHING FOR SHOWJUMPING

Horse and rider are required to be neatly turned out for the day ahead. Members of associations with their own uniforms should wear the association uniform when they compete and for walking the course. Otherwise, women riders should wear black or blue riding jackets with a white stock. The men wear scarlet jackets with a white tie.

In international competitions, the colour of the jacket is determined by the rider's nationality. Irish riders wear green jackets. A blue or black riding hat is mandatory. Whips are permitted but must not exceed 750cm (29$^1/_2$ in). Riders are permitted to wear spurs at all levels of showjumping provided that the points face downwards and outwards. Furthermore, riding boots, breeches, and shirt are all required apparel. If the weather is exceptionally hot, the judges may decide that a riding jacket is not required. Competitors may never enter the ring wearing a sleeveless blouse, pullover, or polo-shirt. When the weather is poor, the judges may permit a raincoat to be worn.

The course builder's staff rebuild the fence

Four faults

The ground rail has not been knocked down

Military or police competitors are permitted to wear their uniforms. For children's jumping competitions, the clothing should be appropriate, practical, and simple.

JUMPING FAULTS

Jumping faults are recorded if a part of a fence is dislodged or a horse puts a foot in the water jump.

A dislodged rail or element is only counted if its removal reduces the height or the spread of an obstacle. If the bottom rail of a high jump is dislodged, it does not accumulate faults.

GOING THE WRONG WAY

If a competitor jumps fences in the wrong sequence, they have "gone the wrong way." To rectify the mistake, participants have to re-jump the course from the point at which the mistake was made. If they fail to do so, they will be disqualified.

FALL

A fall is any time that horse and rider are parted from each other during the round. In some competitions, this leads to automatic disqualification. Where this is not the case, the next fence has to be jumped within 60 seconds. Penalty points or faults are always given for a fall.

EXCEEDING THE TIME LIMIT

A competitor who exceeds the time limit for the round will accrue penalties according to the rules of the competition.

There is also a maximum permitted time, and if this is exceeded, the horse and rider are automatically disqualified.

Disobedience by the horse

REFUSAL

A horse refuses a jump if it stops instead of jumping the obstacle, regardless of whether the fence was down or even moved.

The rules of the International Equestrian Federation (F.E.I.) disqualify a combination of horse and rider if the horse refuses a fence three times.

A combination fence at a classic showjumping competition

RUN OUT

A horse runs out if it fails to jump between the flags, escapes an element of the obstacle, or fails to pass through a required part of the course.

RESISTANCE

A horse resists when it refuses to move forwards.

RAPPING AND OTHER BANNED TECHNIQUES

Various techniques which encourage horses to jump higher, by for instance getting the horse to rap its legs against a bar during practice, are not permitted for participants in showjumping competitions.

If it is discovered that a entrant has been using such techniques, that rider will be disbarred from all competition for at least 24 hours.

PENALTY POINTS OR FAULTS

The faults made during a round are converted into penalty points. Most competitions are run according to the International Equestrian Federation (F.E.I.) rules with the following penalties given.

First disobedience or refusal = 3 penalty points, a second refusal = 6, disqualification at the third refusal. One fence down, or one or more feet in the water = 4 penalty points, a fall = 8 points, exceeding the time limit = 1/4 point for each second over time.

During a jump-off, each second over time is one penalty point. If the maximum time limit is exceeded, horse and rider are disqualified.

Showjumping competitions

CLASSIC SHOWJUMPING

A classic showjumping competition is designed to test the ability of horse and rider over fences.

If more than one rider has a clear round or share the same number of faults, the outcome is decided by one, or at most two jump offs.

During the jump off, the fastest time with the lowest faults or penalties wins.

HUNTER TRIALS

Hunter trials are principally about speed and maneuverability. Speed is an overriding factor in the design of such courses. Any jumping faults are added to the time as penalty seconds.

A refusal

The wall during a puissance competition

Basket with rosettes

PUISSANCE

Puissance competitions consist of a number of rounds in which the riders must go clear to proceed to the next. After each round, the obstacles are raised in height and made generally more difficult. The wall can reach 2.25m (7ft4½in) by the end of the competition. The fourth round usually brings a result. When there are riders on the same number of points after four rounds, the prize money is divided between them.

Special showjumping competitions

SPECIAL SHOWJUMPING COMPETITIONS

A progressive competition takes place over a course with six, eight, or ten fences that get progressively more difficult. The degree of difficulty is not due solely to the height and spread of the obstacles, but also to the course layout. Points are awarded for each fence cleared: one point for fence one, two for two, three for three and so on, with a maximum of 21, 36, or 55 points available.

AMERICAN COMPETITIONS

Showjumping competitions on American lines are jumped against the clock over a moderately difficult course. A contestant's round terminates with the first fault of any nature (knocking off a rail, a fall, or refusal).

TEAM RELAY JUMPING

Teams of two or three riders participate collectively in this sport. Depending on the competition program, the team members may stand in for each other. A member of the team who has completed a round cannot ride again.

FREE CHOICE COMPETITIONS

A special type of progressive competition is that which awards different points for fences cleared depending on their degree of difficulty.

A contestant gets a set time – from 60 to 90 seconds – to jump whichever fences they choose in whatever order. Each fence may be jumped twice.

CHOOSE YOUR OWN ROUTE

A different form of free choice competition is one where all fences (a maximum of eight) are to be jumped but the rider may decide the order in which to jump them.
Each fence may only be jumped once.

OUT AND BACK

The course consists of six fences which can be jumped in both directions. Riders have to complete the course twice, once from fence one to six, then from fence six to one.

PRESENTATION COMPETITIONS

There are competitions in which contestants are also judged on the following points.

• Turnout and riding style: the horse and rider are carefully appraised for the quality of their turnout, condition of the tack, and the way in which the course was walked, the manner in which horse and rider entered the ring, stopped, and paid respects. Horse and rider are also judged on a walk and trot over a distance of 25m (82ft).

- The way in which the course is ridden.

- The rider's seat and bearing.

- The jumping itself.

HORSE TRIALS AND COMBINED TRAINING

Combined training competitions are a test of basic equitation skills, including relatively simple showjumping and dressage. They are an initial route into either showjumping, dressage, or eventing.

This discipline has in Britain replaced the *Prix Caprilli* trials under F.E.I. rules, although these competitions are still held elsewhere in Europe.

Also a prize winner

6   Driving

A fine looking carriage headed by one, or a pair of horses, is a nostalgic sight. Yet the role of the working horse in the past was anything but romantic. Horses pulled guns and other military wagons, worked hard on the land, and were responsible for the carriage of goods and of people. The power of the horse played an important role in the conquest of continents, the development of agriculture, and travel by people. Even when the motor replaced horses, its power continued to be expressed as horsepower. Driving a horse in harness with a carriage or trap is nowadays mainly done for leisure and pleasure. A flourishing branch of equestrian sport has developed with exciting competitions.

Driving in harness is also known by the name of the size of the teams of horses, such as two-in-hand, and four-in-hand. The driver uses the reins, the whip, and the voice to control the horse, or horses.
Horse driving competitions are divided into three disciplines.

- Driving trials.

- Private driving classes.

- Recreational driving.

This chapter deals with the harness and other equipment, driving technique, driving trials, driving classes, recreational driving, and the rules of the road.

The harness for a driving horse

A good knowledge of the specialized harness required for driving is essential. There are two main types of harness: breast collar, and full, or head collar. Harness must be a good fit for the horse to prevent pressure sores. Breast collars can be adapted by buckles to fit a horse but full collars must be made to measure.

Horse driving is mainly done for recreation these days

Breast collar

The harness for a driving horse takes in every part of the horse's body. The neck and breast are encircled by the breast band with the traces attached and the neck strap with rings for the reins. At the back and belly is the girth with the saddle at the top, with a clip for correcting reins if required, the back strap, and the straps on both sides for fastening the shafts. At the quarters, there is the breeching with loin strap and crupper or tail strap. The reins run from the bridle to the hands of the driver.

BREAST
The breast collar consists of the following parts.

• The neck strap which is fastened around the neck by buckles and is adjustable to the horse. The neck strap also adjusts the required position of the breast band. The neck strap has to be broad enough not to cut into the horse's mane.

• The breast band, which is made of double-thickness leather. The seam should always be on the underside. The width and strength of the breast band needs to be suitable for the anticipated load that the horse will have to draw.

• The traces, which are connected to both sides of the breast band. These can be made of leather or rope.

Breast collar

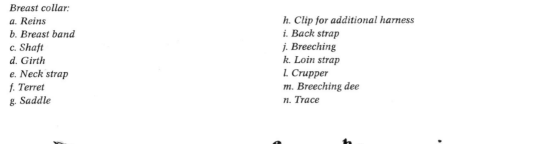

Breast collar:
a. Reins
b. Breast band
c. Shaft
d. Girth
e. Neck strap
f. Terret
g. Saddle

h. Clip for additional harness
i. Back strap
j. Breeching
k. Loin strap
l. Crupper
m. Breeching dee
n. Trace

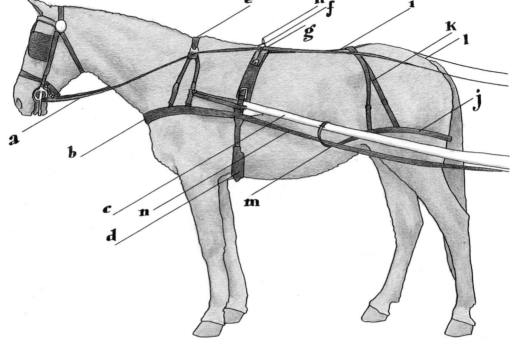

• Terrets or movable rings to hold the reins in place.

WITHERS AND BACK
The following items of harness are located at the withers.

• A clip for attaching additional harness such as additional reins to hold the horse's head in position.

• The saddle with two harness pads.

• Terrets on either side of the saddle through which the reins pass to keep them in place. They must be roomy enough to not hinder the reins.

• Tugs on both sides to prevent the traces being overrun. These can be made of leather or rope.

• The girth which is sometimes comprised of an inner and outer girth strap.

• The back strap and crupper or tail strap which are fastened to rings at the rear of the saddle.

• The breeching, which is a broad strap around the horse's hindquarters.

At the ends of the breeching, there are straps, or breeching dees, that prevent the shafts rising up or the carriage or trap from overrunning.

• Loin straps, which keep the breeching at the correct height.

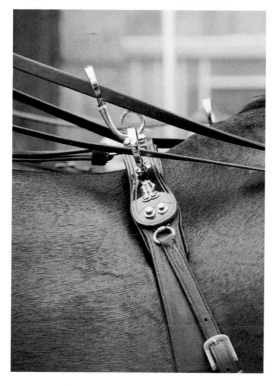

FULL COLLAR

With a full collar, the harness is principally located around the neck and breast at the front, and around the withers and belly. The collar lies around the neck and shoulders of the horse. The full collar is not adjustable and they therefore have to be individually made for each horse. The collar is padded like a cushion and it has to be fitted over the horse's head. The collar is fastened by means of the hames to which hames straps are attached. At the lowest part of the collar are the bottom hames strap and the hame tug. The uppermost fastening is the top hame strap. This strap is the weakest link in the full collar harness and needs regular checking and care because the result of it breaking does not bear thinking about!

Four-wheeled carriages that have shafts that turn are usually attached to stretcher rings rather than breeching dees to prevent the shafts from coming free.

REINS

There are two reins for a single driving horse, the left and right reins. The total length of each rein when fastened needs to

Full collar harness

193

Four-in-hand reins

Finger loop

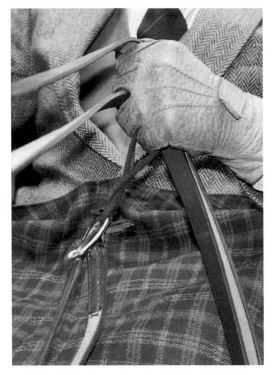

Release catch

be at least 4.3m (about 14ft). There is a finger loop at the end of the left-hand rein and an oval hole or clasp at the end of the right-hand rein.

The reins should be smooth, without any rings or other attachments. Additional reins are used for driving two or more horses but they are of different lengths. The inner reins are longer than the outer reins.

FINGER LOOP

Put your little finger through the finger loop at the end of the left-hand rein, where the left- and right-hand reins are buckled together. The finger loop prevents the loose ends of the reins from dangling to the ground.

RELEASE CATCH

A release catch enables a pin to be simply removed to release the horse from the vehicle in an emergency situation.

Bridle or head collar

The bridle for a driving horse has a few additional features to those worn by riding horses. In addition to the headpiece, throat-latch, nose-band, and cheek-pieces, there are also blinkers, rosettes, and adapted bits, such as Liverpool and Buxton bars. A chin chain is often used, that strengthens the lever action of the bit.

BLINKERS

The purpose of blinkers is to prevent a horse taking fright from unexpected things close behind it on the ground which would endanger the carriage and those seated in it. They do not disturb the forward vision.

Blinkers should fit so that they do not touch the eye and they need to be firmly fixed. About two-thirds of the blinker should be beneath the level of the eye.

BLINKERSTAYS

Blinkerstays prevent the blinkers from flapping about due to the wind or rush of

Bridle:
a. Headpiece
b. Browband
c. Rosette
d. Blinkerstay
e. Blinker
f. Throat-latch
g. Cheek-piece
h. Nose-band
i. Liverpool bit
j. Chin chain
k. Reins

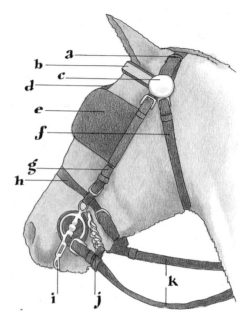

Bridle

Blinkers

air. Flapping blinkers will make a horse anxious. The other end of the blinkerstays is attached to the browband. They are made of very stiff leather or reinforced with metal wire.

ROSETTES

Where the browband is attached to the head collar, there are usually decorative plates or rosettes. It is thought that the origins of the

rosettes may have been amulets that were attached to the horse – which was a prized and most valuable possession – to ward off evil spirits.

NOSE-BAND
The nose-band should fit well on the inside of the cheek-pieces of the head collar. They prevent the cheek-pieces from being pulled backwards when the reins are taught. The nose-band is correctly fitted when two fingers can be placed beneath it.

HARNESS BRASSES
Some head collars for teams of horses have decorative harness brasses at the front so that the team has a similar appearance when seen from the front.

Bits

In addition to the snaffle bit that is particularly used for training young horses, driving horses are usually fitted with a bar type bit. This type of bit has a lever action with a swivel. The proportion by which the swivel

is above the bar determines the extent of the lever action. The effect is stronger the greater this proportion is, requiring greater sensitivity on the part of the driver.

The angle of the swivel lever to the mouthing piece should be 45 degrees.

LIVERPOOL BIT
A Liverpool bit has two or three connections for the reins so that the extent of the action of the bit can be adjusted.

BUXTON BIT
With teams of two or more horses in tandem or line behind each other, the rear horse will often be fitted with a Buxton bar. The bar with a Buxton has a bridge with two levers connected to each other.
The bridge prevents the reins from the forward horses working too severely on the bit.

HARNESSING
With a single horse, the harness is put on from the left. With a team of two, the left-hand horse is harnessed as normal and the right-hand horse is harnessed from the right.

Full collar harness with false martingale

With a breast collar, take the breast band in both hands with the neck strap uppermost. Place the neck strap over the neck and adjust. The breast band is properly fitted if there is room for the breadth of a hand above the breastbone.

A full collar is placed over the horse's head upside down, with the narrow end downwards. Once past the ears, the collar is turned around. The full collar fits correctly when there is room for a fist between the collar and the horse's body.

The harness is then placed on the withers and the girth is fastened lightly. With a full collar, a false martingale is attached between the forelegs to the girth. The harness should be about a width of a hand back from the withers. The back strap is then loosely passed over the back and connected to the crupper or tail strap. Once the tail is in place, the back strap can be adjusted and fastened.

The loin strap is fastened to the back strap and the breeching can be checked by placing the width of a hand between the harness and the buttocks. Once this is done, the traces can be attached and then finally,

Buxton bar

the reins are passed through the eyelets or terrets and attached to the bit.

When the headpiece is put on, it is important to ensure that the links of the chin chain do not get twisted up in the groove under the chin.

HITCHING UP

Place the horse in front of the vehicle and have a helper pull it towards the horse but with the shafts raised slightly so that there is no risk of them catching the horse. The shafts are then lowered and fastened to the tugs and dee loops. The loops must always be in front of the hooks that prevent the shafts from overrunning. The final step is the attachment of the traces and breeching. The breeching should always be horizontal. Once everything is in place, the girth can be tightened.

UNHITCHING

Unhitching is dealt with in much the same way as in hitching up but in reverse order. Once the horse is free from the vehicle, check to see if the harness has rubbed and for any wounds before grooming.

MAINTAINING THE HARNESS

It is sensible to clean the harness thoroughly after use with a wet sponge to remove any dirt and sweat. The salts in sweat harden leather. Once every two weeks, the harness should be treated with saddle soap which requires all the parts of the harness to be taken apart. Once the saddle soap has been thoroughly worked in, let the harness dry thoroughly. The drying process should never be speeded up by putting the harness in the sun or near any heater. The leather would dry too quickly and crack. Smear the clean harness with a little wax and polish until it shines. Patent leather should not be treated with wax. Instead, polish with a dry cloth.

HARNESS RACK

A harness rack on wheels makes it easy to hang the harness up in the correct order and it can be wheeled to the horse the next time the horse is to be harnessed. When a team of horses has to be harnessed and unharnessed it can become quite a chore to keep everything in the correct place. One rack is needed for each main part of the overall harness: one for the collar, one for the saddle and girth pieces, and another for the headpiece. Although the whip is not part of

Unhitching

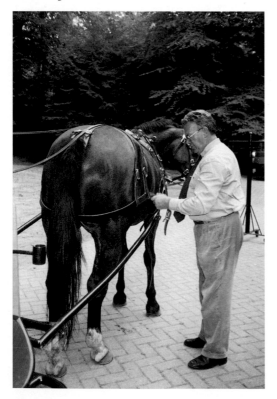

Harness rack

the harness, it is important not to forget to hang this up properly on a special rack so that it remain straight and in good condition.

Horse driving technique

PRACTICE RIG
A practice rig can be used to learn how to hold the reins without them being attached to a horse and bit.

Holding the reins

STANDARD GRIP
Both reins are held in the left hand with their smooth side uppermost. The left-hand rein is passed over the knuckle of the index finger and the right-hand rein is held between the second and third fingers. The bottom two fingers grasp both reins. The left hand is held with a slightly bent wrist in the center of the body with the forearm horizontal. The whip is held in the right hand pointing downwards, slightly forwards and to the left. This is the position the driver should return to.

TWO-HANDED GRIP
Two-handed grips are normally reserved for competitive driving under rigorous circumstances. A two-handed grip which has the characteristics of the standard grip brings the right hand in front of the left hand. The bottom three fingers grasp the rein. The thumb and index finger of the right hand lie bent on the left-hand rein and point to the horse's left shoulder.

Practice rig

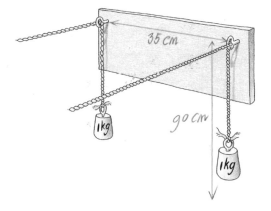

Standard grip

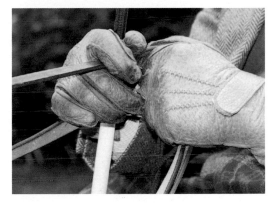
Two-handed variant of standard grip

Both hands are held straight in front of the body, with the forearms horizontal and the hands brought in slightly towards the body. The elbows rest against the body.
The whip is held between the thumb and index finger.

DRIVING TRIALS AND DRESSAGE GRIP
The true two-handed grip can be adapted from the two-handed variant of the standard grip. The right hand takes the right-hand rein about 100mm (4in) away from the left hand and is relaxed.
The left hand holds the left-hand rein with the bottom three fingers. The two reins must be held an even distance apart so that the horse continues to move straight ahead.

PREPARING TO DRIVE
Before climbing in to the vehicle, place the left foot on the step with head turned towards the horse. Keep watching the horse as you step up into position. The horse must be prevented from moving off until you give the appropriate aids by voice and or whip.

Preparing to climb aboard

variation of the standard grip but a little in front of the left hand and grasps the reins. The left hand is then moved forward and this movement can be repeated as often as is necessary. It is also possible to change hand over hand by placing the left hand in front of the right hand and so on.

STOPPING

The grip for stopping starts from the two-handed variation of the standard grip but the right hand holds the reins about 250mm (10in) in front of the left hand. The right hand then pulls backwards and the left hand moves vertically upwards to make room for the right hand. The reins are lengthened by pulling the reins forward a little at a time with the right hand from the left. The right hand then returns to the two-handed variation of the standard grip. For an emergency stop, the driver can apply force by holding the left-hand over the right hand but this is only for really dangerous situations.

MOVING OFF

To move off, the horse must be on the bit. The rider applies slight easing of the reins

TAKING THE REINS

The length of the reins should be such that you should not need to alter your hands once seated in the vehicle. Light contact with the horse's mouth should be maintained from before entering the vehicle until preparing to move off.

SHORTENING THE REINS

To slow down, the reins have to be shortened. This is always done a little at a time. The right hand is placed in the two-handed

and the horse will move. If it does not respond to the voice a slight indication can be given with the whip. The purpose of the whip is to give an indication to the horse, not to hit it.

AIDS WITH THE WHIP
Although its use should be sparing, the whip is an indispensable tool for carriage driving. The following aids are provided with the whip.

• Signal to move off or to pick up tempo. When the whip is used to give impulsion, the reins must also be eased.

• Aid to collect the horse, which is the same as the impulse-giving aid but without any easing of the reins. Sometimes slight resistance on the reins is necessary, for instance, when changing from a free trot into a more collected trot.

• A punishment, together with strong application of the reins to prevent a horse from going too fast or bolting. The driver must only ever use the whip to punish at the precise moment that a horse is disobedient.

Indicating with the whip

If punishment is given after the event, the horse will not understand and the punishment will not correct the fault.

TURNING

In order to turn, the hands are placed in the two-handed variation of the standard grip.

The driver has to bear in mind his or her position in the vehicle as the rein is shortened, on the side to be turned, in order to maintain contact with the horse's mouth. The shortening is done a little at a time by sliding the right hand in front of the left as for shortening the reins.

Once the turn is completed, the hands return to the two-handed grip and the reins are lengthened.

SINGLE-HANDED (ACHENBACH) GRIP

The best known method of driving is sometimes named after the German, Benno von Achenbach, who developed it. This method retains the reins solely in the left

hand and turns are made by easing the hand to the right or left. Instead of applying pressure on the outer reins, the turn is achieved by yielding on the inner reins. The right hand remains free at all times to indicate direction using the whip.

Driving competitions

It is possible to compete in driving competitions with a single horse, a tandem (two horses one behind the other), a pair, or four-in-hand (a team of four horses).

REQUIRED CLOTHING FOR DRIVING TRIALS

During the dressage and obstacle phases of driving trials, men are required to wear dark suits with a tie. Either a bowler or top hat should also be worn.

Women are required to wear a suit or neat blouse and appropriate long skirt, and they too should wear a hat to match their outfit. Both men and women are required to wear gloves and covering for their laps. The lap apron should fit closely over the thighs of the seated driver. The apron ensures that the reins and gloves do not cause dirt to spatter on their clothes. Participants may also wear riding clothes or the uniform of their association.

During the marathon stage, less formal clothing is permitted. Participants and their grooms, however, are still required to wear hats or caps.

Well presented

Some drivers and their passengers go to great trouble to dress in style, often adapting their dress to the specific period or original purpose of their vehicle.

PAYING RESPECT

Contestants stop their vehicle in front of the judges to pay their respects.
The men lift their hats, the women bow their heads.

HORSE DRIVING TRIALS

The impetus for horse driving trials came from British carriage driving enthusiasts who wanted to continue the tradition of the former mail coaches that ran between the provinces and London.
The coaches departed from the head post office in London. Before departure, the horses, harness, and coaches were thoroughly inspected to make sure nothing would prevent them from maintaining their schedule.
Someone accompanied the coach to make sure that the timetable was strictly adhered to.

The women bow their heads

The coaches drove through a great variety of landscape. The going was more difficult in hilly country than on the flat. Sometimes the coachman had to find a way around a collapsed bridge or a tree that had fallen across the road. This set the coach behind on its schedule and a great deal of effort was required to catch up. A coachman had to be skilled and resourceful to get his coach to its journey's end. Today's trials consist of
a. presentation and dressage
b. the marathon
c. the obstacle course.

PRESENTATION

In the presentation stage of the competition, the judges assess the total impression of the horses, driver, the grooms, the harness, and the vehicle. The team remains stationary in the ring while they are judged.

DRESSAGE

The degree of difficulty of the dressage trial is in accordance with the level of the competition and of the anticipated level of experience and training of the entrants. The dressage trial is driven over a ring of at least

Mail coach

30m x 60m (100ft x 200ft) for single horses and pairs, and at least 40m x 80m (130ft x 260ft) for tandems and four-in-hands. The exercise lasts about twelve minutes. The test is intended to assess the calmness, consistency of action, and impulsion of the horses, together with the proficiency and style of the driver. With teams of horses, the way the horses work together is also assessed. Each driving test starts and ends with greeting or paying respect to the judges. Classes 1 to 2 may be judged by just one judge but with Class 3 it is preferred to have at least three judges. If there is more than one judge, the others are divided on the short side between B and E. The senior judge always sits at C. If a participant cannot complete the dressage test because of equipment failure, they are disqualified from the entire competition.

MARATHON

The marathon is a cross country test that includes skill elements and obstacles. The distance is 27km (17 miles) divided into five sections (A –E) of different distances and at different speeds. Section A (10km or 6 miles) is taken at the trot at an average speed of 15 km/h (9 mph). Section B

Start of the dressage test

The marathon

(1200m or 1300 yd) is walked at 7 km/h (4¹/₄ mph). Section C (5km or 3 miles) is a fast trot at a speed of 20 km/h (12¹/₂mph). Section D is as section B and section E as section A. There are always natural hazards on the trotting sections and section E includes specially constructed obstacles to negotiate. This stage is the most spectacular part of the competition for the spectators, drivers, and their grooms, and is the toughest part of the competition. The grooms sit at the rear of the vehicle and spring into action if a team gets into difficulties.
They also help to provide counterbalance through the corners.

OBSTACLES IN THE MARATHON

An obstacle has a maximum of six gates, marked A–F with red and white tape. The

The grooms are at the back of the vehicle

Water obstacle

Water obstacle

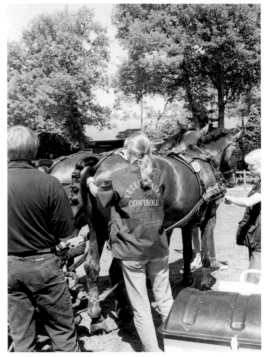

Veterinary check

contestant must enter and leave the gates in alphabetical order and pass between the red and white tapes, keeping the red tape on the right. A contestant is disqualified if he or she takes longer than the maximum five minutes to negotiate an obstacle, has to unhitch one or more horses, seeks help from outside the team's entourage, takes a gate in the wrong direction, or exhibits bad temper.

VETERINARY CONTROL
A minimum of two veterinary controls are required during the marathon. The first is held before the start of section A or at the end of section B. The second control is always done at the finish.

BUCKBOARD JUDGE
A judge travels with each participant, seated next to the driver. The judge checks the times and observes the correctness of the required gait for the section.

OBSTACLE JUDGES
Each obstacle in section E has a judge to record the time that the competitor takes to negotiate the obstacle and to observe any faults.

OBSTACLE COURSE
The obstacle course is designed to test the obedience of the horse or horses and skill of the driver. The course is 500–800m (546–874yd) long and consists of 20 gates through which the competitors and their horse and vehicle must pass. The gates are formed from plastic cones with a ball on

Buckboard judge

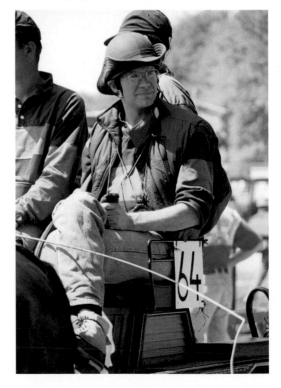

top that is easily knocked off if the cone receives the lightest of knocks. The distance between the cones is set 300–600mm (1–2ft) wider than the track of the vehicle. The course has to be completed within the set time. If more than one driver has a faultless round, an eliminating round is driven to decide first place. The competitors are given the opportunity to familiarize themselves with the course before taking part.

TRACK OR AXLE WIDTH
The track width or axle width is the distance between the rear wheels of the vehicle.

PASSENGERS ON THE VEHICLE
Rules are laid down for those who are permitted to ride on the vehicle during the various parts of the driving trials.
During the dressage and finale obstacle stage:
single horse, pair, or tandem –
- 1 competitor
- 1 groom
four horse team –
- 1 competitor
- 2 grooms.

During the marathon:
single horse or tandem –
- 1 competitor
- 1 groom

Driving skill test

Four-in-hand: one competitor, two grooms

A pair of horses –
- 1 competitor
- 1 groom
(a second groom is permitted)
four horse team –
- 1 competitor
- 2 grooms.

Passengers are not permitted. If a competitor carries a passenger, they will be disqualified.

CLASSES
Competition is divided into different classes or categories:
- single pony
- single horse
- pairs of ponies
- pairs of horses
- tandem ponies
- tandem horses
- four-in-hand ponies
- four-in-hand horses.

LEVEL OF COMPETITION
Young and inexperienced drivers can compete at a local level in special classes for them.

Progression to higher levels of competition is possible for drivers who are successful at the novice and junior levels.

FINAL PLACINGS
The final placing in the driving trial is arrived at by working out the penalties received in the dressage, marathon, and driving skill or obstacle stages.

The competitor with the fewest penalties is the winner.

A number of equestrian organizations hold dressage trials combined with driving skill competitions which give drivers the opportunity to get competition experience.
Competitors who reach the required standard can proceed from these local competitions to the full driving trials at senior level.

Private driving competitions

Private driving competitions principally focus their attention on the driving horse or horses.
The horses are particularly judged on their action and in particular their trot.

Driving for fun

People also drive horses just for fun. There are associations that organize tours in groups, often dressed in period costume or clothing appropriate to the original use of the vehicle they are driving. Such events are full of nostalgia.

CARRIAGES

Roughly speaking, there are two types of vehicles: two-wheeled and four-wheeled. The best-known type of two-wheeled vehicle is the gig, widely used for training horses. A gig will not swing the wrong way when reversing and is more stable in sharp corners.

Private driving trials

Driving for fun

Four-wheeled carriages or carts include the phaetons used for the marathon and formal landaus.

Regardless of the type of cart or carriage, certain parts are found on many different types.

- The buckboard, on which the driver sits.
- The shell, on which the driver rests his or her feet.
- The front mudguard that protects the driver from being spattered with mud.
- The shafts or poles – two shafts either side of a horse, or pole between a pair or team of horses.
- The central axis
- The front axle with four-wheeled vehicles.
- The pivot, with four-wheeled carts and carriages, linking the front axle with the rest of the vehicle.
- The rear or sole axle and chassis.
- The rear step
- The backboard or main part of the cart or carriage in which the passengers are conveyed. This is known as a compartment if the carriage has a roof.

Presentation standard vehicles are used for the driving skill and dressage stages of the driving trials. Two- or four-wheeled vehicles can be used with a single horse or tandem but four-wheels have to be used with pairs and teams. A marathon vehicle

A German hunting wagon (right) and a French wagonette (left)

needs to be compact, with a small turning-circle.

For private driving competitions, a light vehicle is used to show the horse off. Carriages and carts have to comply with highway requirements when used on the road, including the need for rear red reflectors. The same vehicle must be used for both the dressage and driving skill (obstacle) stage of a driving trial. Contestants are permitted to use a different vehicle for the marathon stage.

RIGS

The term rig is used here to encompass the horse or horses, their appropriate harness, hitched up to a vehicle to form an overall whole in keeping with each other. The driver and any grooms or passengers are not part of the rig but should also dress in appropriate style for the rig.

There are six main types of rig: the traditional English rig, the country rig, the recreational rig, and American, Hungarian, and Russian rigs.

• The traditional English rig emphasises functionality, simplicity, and tradition. The two- or four-wheeled vehicle should be in proportion to the size of the horse or horses. The rig can comprise of a brake/wagonette or a phaeton with a light full-collar harness. The driver is dressed formally, often in grey, with a coachman's apron and driving gloves. A feature of the English rig is the arched whip.

Recreation rig

• The country rig has its origins in Germany. The emphasis is on tidiness and safety. With lighter rigs, such as the Friesian gig or German hunting wagon, a breast collar harness is worn. The driver's clothing is frequently redolent of the country area from which the rig and driver originate. Country rigs use a lopped whip.

• Recreation rigs as the name implies are not so formal. However the turnout of the

rig should appear smart and well-cared for. Marathon and training vehicles fit in this category.

Rules of the road for carriage driving

Driven horses are slow moving traffic. Here are a few points that must be borne in mind when driving a horse and cart on a road.

CHANGING LANES
Slow moving traffic does not need to change lanes unless markings on the road require it. The driver may change lanes in order to turn into another road but should not do so to turn into a drive or gateway.

CHANGING DIRECTION
The driver must give a clear advance indication of the intention to change direction. Certain signals with the whip are used to indicate left or right turns.

SIGNALS WITH HAND AND WHIP
• Slowing down: the right arm is stuck out and waved slowly up and down.
• Stopping: the right arm is held up with the whip pointing straight upwards.
• Turning left: the right arm holds the whip above the head, indicating to the left.
• Turning right: the right arm is stuck out to indicate right.
• Straight ahead: the right arm points forwards.

A clover-leaf trio presented at a show

Turning right

LIGHTING

Horse-drawn vehicles must have lights just as motor-vehicles, from a half hour after sunset to a half hour before sunrise. Two bright lanterns should be placed at the same height at the extreme right and left of the front of the vehicle and a red light on the rear with two red reflectors. It is also advisable to attach a red warning triangle on the back of the horse-drawn vehicle.

COACHING LICENCE

In Britain, unlike some other European countries, and in North America no licence or qualification is required before driving a horse on the public highway. Children may drive a single horse or a team on the road from any age and about the only thing that a driver in charge of a horse or horses can be prosecuted for in Britain, is being drunk.

In many jurisdictions in North America it is an offence under the Traffic Code to "race or drive furiously any horse or other animal" on the highway or its verges – the penalty: summonses, and the imposition of fines.

LOAD OF A HORSE-DRAWN VEHICLE

There are a number of matters to be borne in mind before taking a horse out for a drive, just as there are with riding a horse. It is important to drive gently and at a steady pace, changing from walk to trot quite regularly. By letting the horse walk for a while after a quarter of an hour trotting, it is more able to complete a longer run. Do not take too much additional weight with you, whether passengers or goods. The general rules of thumb for the load a horse can pull are as follows.

- On paved roads, most horses can draw three times their own body weight.

- On rough tracks, sandy soil, and other such terrain, twice the horse's weight is a better yardstick.

- On hilly or mountainous terrain the absolute maximum is once the horse's own weight.

Finally, if making a lengthy trip, it is important to stop regularly to give the horse a rest. Change to a walk some distance from the resting place (about half a mile or one kilometre) so that the horse or horses have the chance to rest a little before they stop.

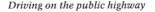

Driving on the public highway

7 Western riding

Western riding is a matter of calmness and simplicity

The cattle industry grew rapidly in North America during the nineteenth century. This was the world of the true cowboys on the ranches who tended, branded, and drove the cattle to market under tough conditions. This was how the western style of riding was born.

The relatively few men who did this work required agile, maneuverable horses with a quiet nature, that were willing to work. These men had to ride these horses with one hand because their other one was needed for working.

These American cattle herders often covered great distances, so they developed a safe, comfortable style of riding. The demands of their work, and the sport the cowboys indulged in when free to play, are the basis of present-day western riding.

Western riding has nothing to do with rodeo. Rodeo is all about excitement and sensation, while western riding is a matter of calmness and simplicity. One essential for this style is a relaxed horse. The careful selection by the cowboys of their horses has shown that three breeds are best suited to western riding: the Quarter horse, the Paint horse, and the Appaloosa.

Western riding has become a very popular

Left: stopping to the cry of "Whoa!"

branch of equestrian sport with many enthusiastic riders. For those who wish to compete, there is a choice from showing horses in hand, dressage-style reining competitions, and competitions that test the abilities of a working horse.

The western rider

A good western rider sits naturally in the saddle and gives light aids to the horse. The western horse is ridden with a loose rein. The rider only gives gentle and yielding contact with the mouth if a horse needs correcting. Western style riders typically stop with the voice command, "Whoa!"

THE WESTERN SEAT
With the correct western seat, a vertical line can be drawn from the ear, through the shoulder, and hip, to the heel. The length of

The western seat

The head is held erect

Riding a senior horse

Riding a junior horse

the stirrup leathers is an important component of thc correct western seat. The angle of the upper leg (from hip to knee) should be the same as that of the lower leg (knee to ankle). The feet should be in a line directly under the body. The ball of the feet rest in the stirrup with the heels pushed down. The feet should be parallel with the horse's body.

The calves hang loosely next to the horse and are only used to drive the horse on if really necessary. The upper leg and knee rest relaxed against the saddle.

The rider sits up straight with relaxed shoulders that point downwards and backwards. The upper arms hang loosely next to the body. The head is held erect to keep a good look-out, not staring at the ground or the horse's neck.

RIDING A JUNIOR HORSE
When riding a junior or inexperienced horse, the reins are held over each other with both hands. The hands are held just above the saddle horn.

RIDING A SENIOR HORSE
A senior or experienced horse is ridden with

only one hand on the reins. Either the right or left hand can be used but most people ride with the reins held in their left hand because they are right-handed, leaving the "good hand" free to open gates etc. The cowboys used their right hand for their lariat or lasso. In the slower exercises of western riding, the hand that holds the reins is held just in front or just above the saddle horn.

The free hand is held close to the hand with the reins or hangs loose beside the hip. With the faster exercises, the reins are held above the saddle horn and the free hand is held either close to the stomach or next to the horse's neck. The loose ends of the reins hang on the side of the hand with which the rider holds the reins.

Gaits

WALK

The walk should be slow, clean, and regular. To start the horse walking when standing still, light pressure of the calves is used. Once the horse walks, the pressure is taken off. The reins are held as loose as possible and only tightened if strictly necessary.

JOG

The jog is a gentle, relaxed trot, which keeps the horse active without over-tiring it. It is mandatory to sit for the trot in competition, press the calves against the horse and hold the hands freely.

Jog

TROT

Once the tempo of the jog increases, this is known as a trot. The cowboys used the trot as a means to cover ground quickly – the trot is less tiring for a horse than the lope. They rode light in the saddle, resting in the stirrups, and with a hand on the saddle-horn, to maintain their balance. To change from the jog to the trot, urge the horse forward with both calves pressing forwards and bring both hands forwards at the same time.

LOPE

The lope is a gentle canter which consists of

Walk

Trot

a sequence of consecutive jumps. The outer calf only urges the horse on if necessary. To change from the jog to the lope, press the outside leg against the horse.

NECK REINING

With neck reining, the horse is trained to react to the touch of the reins on its neck. To let the horse know which way to turn, the flat of the rein is laid against the right or left of the neck.

Neck reining

During a turn, the inner rein is yielded and the outer rein is laid against the neck. If the horse is being ridden with one hand, the finger between the reins can lightly push the outer rein away. This should not be necessary on a well-trained horse but it is a useful aid while learning neck reining.

The aid given through neck reining is reinforced by leg aids. If the horse is to turn right, the left-hand rein is laid against the neck and the left-hand leg applies a little pressure while the right-hand leg yields. This gives the horse the chance to go right. The horse should not drop its inside shoulder. Both shoulders should remain level in comparison with the back. The back is allowed to bend slightly.

CANTERING IN CIRCLES

When cantering in circles, the outer leg is lengthened which puts more pressure on the stirrup iron and automatically causes the rider to move the weight to the side. In competitions, the speed at which large and small circles can be ridden can be a deciding factor. To go faster, move the hands forwards.

ROLLBACK

A rollback is an abrupt stop from a canter with a 180 degree turn, immediately cantering back the way the rider came. It is important that each stage of the maneuver is done quickly.

SLIDING STOP

In a sliding stop, a horse stops from a fairly fast canter with the back legs dug into the

ground while the front legs continue. It is best to practice this stop from a gentle pace at first. The rider sits back in the saddle and moves the upper body backwards as they shout "Whoa!"

The legs are moved away from the horse so that it has room for its hindquarters to move

Sliding stop

forwards. If the horse does not react to these two aids, both reins are grasped to stop the horse. The exercise is then repeated so that the horse understands the intention of the aids for the sliding stop. The horse needs to be relaxed to make a good sliding stop.

When the horse is tense, it lifts its head at speed so that the back and hindquarters cannot perform the stop correctly. When training a horse to do the sliding stop, the tail is often plaited or bandaged to prevent the horse from damaging its tail.

SPIN

In a spin, as the name suggests, a horse turns around almost in a pirouette with the inside hindleg remaining in the same place while the outer hindleg is moving forwards. The spin is achieved by a combination of neck reining and the appropriate seat and leg aids.

To learn how to execute the spin, the horse is ridden in circles with the inner hand away from the neck and the outer rein pressed

Plaited tail

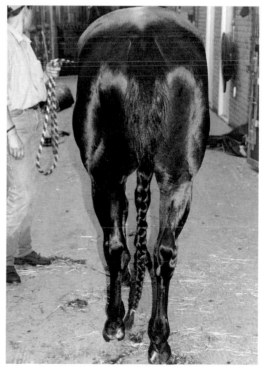

against the neck. The circle is then made tighter by giving light pressure with the outer leg and yielding with the inner leg so that the leg does not prevent the horse from turning tighter. While working towards the spin, teach the horse to bend with it and to bring its inside hind leg beneath itself so that the outside hindleg does the work. The outside leg must keep moving forward while the inside leg stands still.

In the early stage of learning the sliding

Teaching the spin

Riding the trail

stop, the horse will have learned to stop to a vocal command. During the spin, "Whoa!" is used but this time it refers solely to the inside hindleg. The other forward urging aids such as the reins, calves, and seat, remain active.

It is best to use both hands while learning to ride the spin in order to give the horse as much support as possible. At first, it is important to turn slowly but in a steady

The spin

The spin

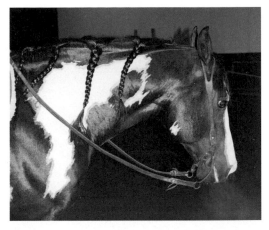

rhythm. The tempo can then be gradually increased. The intention is to get the horse to turn as flexibly as possible. This exercise requires considerable strength and agility on the part of the hindquarters.

It is also important to make sure to start with that the horse does not become dizzy from going round and round. It is sensible to stop after a couple of turns.

TRAIL RIDING
The western riding name for trekking in the great outdoors. Riding trail is also a form of western riding competition.

Browband bridle

Crownpiece, browband, cheek-piece, and throat latch

Riding equipment

HEADSTALL

The headstall is the bridle. There are two main types of western bridle: browband and split ear bridles. These bridles usually have no nose band.

REINS

There are two separate reins.

O-ring snaffle

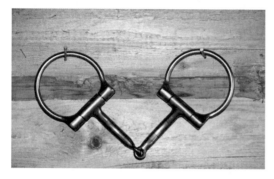

The reins

SNAFFLE

The snaffle bit used for western riding is usually somewhat slimmer than the usual snaffle bits and is made of sweet iron that rusts very quickly.

Since horses like the taste of rust, this is not a problem. There are O-ring and D-ring snaffles, describing the snaffle rings.

SCISSORS BIT

The scissors bit has rings to give a scissors action on both sides. The lever effect has a strong action on the mouth. A sensitive rider will be aware of this but the bit must not be allowed to cause unnecessary pain.

BOSAL BRIDLE

A bosal is a bitless bridle that works on the nerves in the nose and jaw.

The bosal is particularly used with four-year-old horses which have tender mouths because their teeth are still developing. Normal bits can lead to resistance during training so a bosal is used instead.

A bosal always has a leading rope attached which is always attached to the saddlehorn with a bowline.

Scissors bit

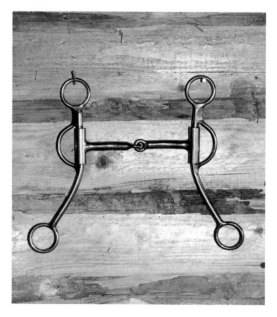

LEADING ROPE

A leading rope (or lead rope in western parlance) is used for walking a horse in hand. For in hand showing classes, the leading rope is usually a leading rein of leather attached to a chain. The chain should not be touched during showing.

BOWLINE

To tie a bowline, make a loop over the saddle horn, repeat this and then pass the loose end of the leading rope through the loops.

WESTERN SADDLE

Some of the terminology for a western saddle differs from the names given to European saddles.

1. Fork, 2. Tie strap, 3. Front rigging dee, 4. Tie strap, 5. Fender, 6. Stirrup leather, 7. Stirrup, 8. Stirrup tread, 9. Front cinch, 10. Cinch connecting strap, 11. Back cinch, 12. Saddle strings, 13. Rear rigging dee, 14. Skirt, 15. Back jockey, 16. Cantle, 17. Seat, 18. Seat jockey, 19. Horn

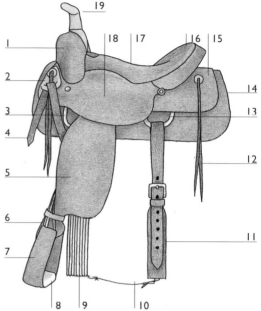

Bosal with leading rope

Bosal

Showing halter with leading rope

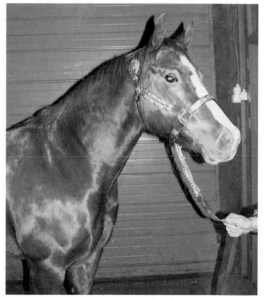

The loop goes around the saddlehorn...

This is repeated...

Pull the end through the loops to tie

Parts of the saddle

FORK
The fork is the front part of the saddle.

HORN
The horn is the prominent part at the front of the saddle where the pommel is in European saddles. The saddlehorn is usually made of untanned leather and is used as a tool for hitching a rope to when working cattle. There are competition elements in which the horn must not be touched.

FENDER
The fender acts as both stirrup leather and sweat guard.

STIRRUP
Stirrup is the same with a western saddle and European saddle.

TIE STRAP
The leather strap to which the girth (or cinch) is attached is called the tie strap.

TIE STRAP HOLDER
The excess length of tie strap is passed through the tie strap holder.

Fork

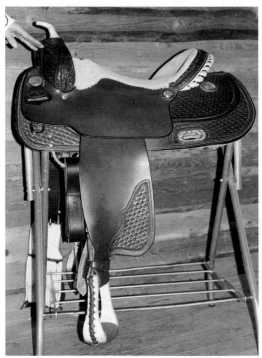

Horn

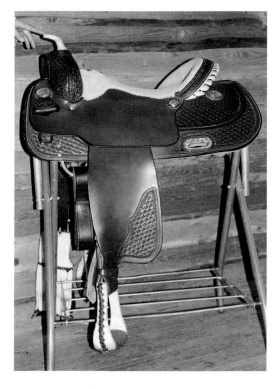

Stirrup

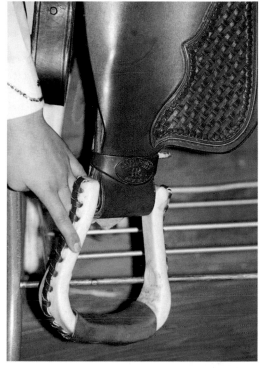

Fender

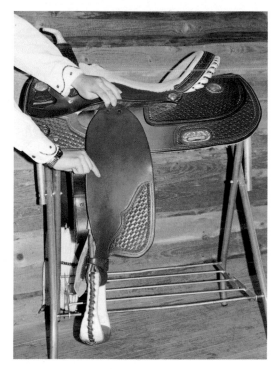

Tie strap

Tie strap holder

Rigging dee

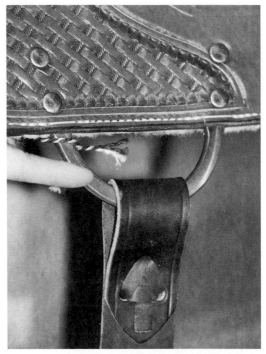

Saddle with cinch and back cinch

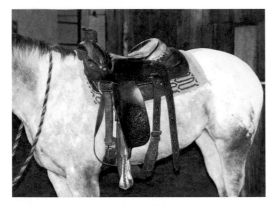

Seat

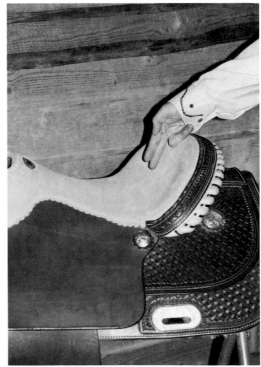

CINCH
The cinch is the girth.

BACK CINCH
The back cinch is a second, rear girth which is specifically used for working cow horses and for cutting. The second girth prevents the saddle from riding up.

RIGGING DEE
The rigging dee is the D-ring that attaches the tie strap to the saddle.

Cantle

Saddle strings

Back jockey and skirt

SEAT
The seat is the obvious part of the saddle. This is often made of suede because of the better grip it gives the rider.

CANTLE
The cantle, as with a European saddle, is the rear part of the saddle tree.

BACK JOCKEY AND SKIRT
The saddle rests on the back jockey and skirt. Western saddles have no padding.

SADDLE STRINGS
Saddle strings can be used to fasten items to the saddle.

Types of western saddles

There are several types of western saddles that have been developed for specific uses.

RANCH OR PLEASURE SADDLE
The ranch or pleasure saddle is suitable for general riding. There is also a special equitation saddle for show use. Both these types of saddle have hand-tooled leather and are often decorated with sterling silver.

CUTTING SADDLE
The cutting saddle can be recognized by the flat seat and high saddlehorn.

ROPING SADDLE
A roping saddle is used for real ranch work. It has a stronger saddlehorn than other saddles and is generally heavier and more robust than the others.

Ranch or pleasure saddle

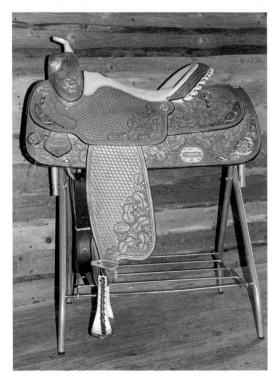

Roping saddle

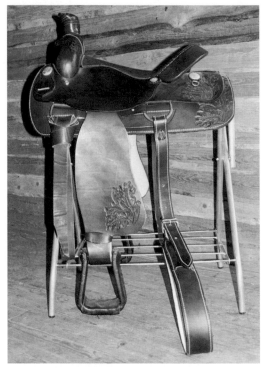

Cutting saddle

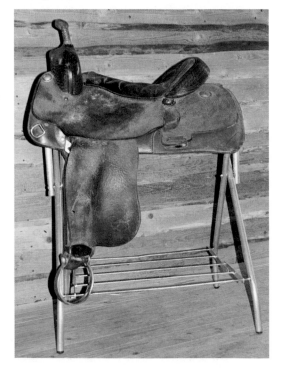

A saddle pad under a western saddle

SADDLE PAD

A saddle pad is a blanket that goes under the saddle. Because western saddles have no padding, the pad has to provide some springing between the saddle and the horse and prevent rubbing sores.

Types of stirrup

FLAT BOTTOM

The flat bottom stirrup is used for reining and speed contests. The flat bottom stirrup is kept under the ball of the foot.

Flat bottom

Spurs

Oxbow

Sliding shoes

OXBOW

The oxbow is the type of stirrup used for working with cattle. The oxbow is held against the edge of the heel.

SPURS

Although spurs are not required to be worn for competitions, most western riders wear them. Good western riders never or rarely use them.

SLIDING SHOES

A horse performing sliding stops is shod with slippers – smooth-bottomed shoes wider and somewhat larger than ordinary horseshoes.

Clothing

The basic clothing for western riding are jeans with external double-seams, cowboy boots, and a Stetson. The jeans do not have internal double-seams to prevent friction while riding.

For showing horses on the halter, women wear a smart jacket and stylish trousers. No spurs are worn when leading horses in hand for showing. For most of the reining events,

Basic western riding clothing

women wear close fitting clothes such as a body stocking.

The men wear a jacket and tie for showing horses and for reining competitions they wear a long-sleeved shirt with a collar, jeans, cowboy boots, and a Stetson. There are also hunter under saddle classes for which conventional British hunting clothes are worn. When cutting or riding working horses both the men and women usually wear chaps.

CHAPS

Chaps are leather leg protectors. There are working chaps and show-ring chaps. Working or ranch chaps are usually broader and normally have no fringe at the side. Show chaps can usually be fastened all the way down but working chaps usually have just a couple of straps. It is not mandatory to wear chaps for competition but most riders wear them for cutting and working cow horse trials.

Western riding competitions

The different types of western riding competition are designed to show off the all-round

Competition dress for a man

Competition dress for a woman

strengths of the western horse. There are three main disciplines in western competitions:
- reining
- speed games
- working.

In addition to this there are showing classes in which horses are led in hand on a halter. Almost all the disciplines are divided into junior for horses up to five years old and senior for horses of six years old and above. Where there are too few entrants for separate classes, entrants can participate in the same "all ages" class.

Ranch-work chaps

Show-ring chaps

Junior horse

Clubs and societies can of course arrange all manner of their own competitions based either on Western riding disciplines or on the Western horses themselves: quarter horse, Appaloosa, paint etc.

These categories will usually be divided into classes by age and experience. Riders and handlers under the age of eighteen may participate in junior classes regardless of their level of experience.

JUNIOR HORSE
A junior horse is one that is not older than five years. During competition, junior horses are ridden with a bosal bridle or snaffle bit.
Riders of junior horses are allowed to use both hands on the reins.

SENIOR HORSE
A senior horse is one of six years old or above. During competition, horses are ridden with a scissors bit. Riders are only allowed to use one hand on the reins.

Senior horse

JUDGES

Competitors are assessed by one judge who has a ring steward to note the adjudication. Contestants may only ask questions through the ring steward during the judging to prevent any pressure being applied on the judge.

RING STEWARD

See Judges above.

DOUBLE-POINTED SHOW

For some competitions, the organizers can decide to appoint a two-person jury. The contestants are judged twice and there are also two sets of prizes.

GREETING

Riders are required to greet the judges except in speed events. The point at which the greeting should be made varies from one type of event to another. It is always required on entering the ring but some classes require a greeting at the beginning and end of the test. The head is nodded in acknowledgement of the judges.

LINE-UP

Contestants are often required to line up next to each other at the beginning or end of a competition.

Competition elements

Showing classes in-hand

Horses in halter classes are shown in-hand with a leather head collar and leading rein or rope. The leading rope has a chain with a leather strap attached. Competitors must not touch the chain while they are in the show ring.

Halter competitions are divided into showing and showmanship classes.

HALTER SHOW

In a halter show competition, the judges assess the horses. Horses that are shown in halter show classes meet the conformation-

Line-up

Leather halter

Halter show

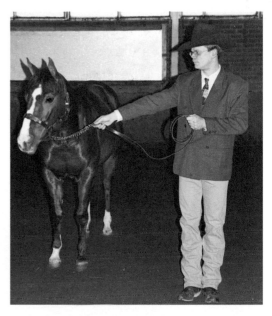

The judge in position 1, the contestant at 4.
The judge at position 2, the contestant at 1.
The judge at position 3, the contestant at 4.
The judge at position 4, the contestant at 1.

al requirements for a western horse but they are usually too cumbersome, and too excessively built to perform well as working horses. Halter horses are shown for their looks. Halter shows are divided into classes by breed, age, and gender.

The horses are assessed by conformation, balance, style, and beauty.

The horses at a halter show stand behind each other and the judges walk around them. The handler holds the leading rope in the right hand with the end of it rolled up in their left hand. When the horses are standing still, it is important that they stand square. If they do not, it is permitted to move the legs with the hand, even when the judge is assessing the horse. If the horse is standing correctly, the handler stretches both arms towards the horse with the thumbs pointing upwards. The place where the handler must stand is prescribed as follows.

2	h	3
	o	
	r	
	s	
1	e	4

If the judge moves position, the contestant must also change position. This happens in three stages: at the front, at the side, to finish.

SHOWMANSHIP CLASSES

Showmanship when leading a horse is a competition for the young and amateurs. Handlers are assessed on their ability to produce and show a horse, present it well prepared, and handle it to show off the horse to good advantage. The contestants all line up, standing on the left of their

Showmanship competition

231

horses. Everyone waits for a signal to move off at a walk or trot. The contestants are judged from the first moment they enter the ring, so the time in the line-up also counts. Once given the signal, the handlers move off at a brisk pace. The hands are held as if carrying an imaginary tray. When the horses are halted for inspection, the contestants may take their time. It is important to get the horse standing properly square. The horse may not be touched in this class. Once the horse is standing correctly, the participant bends the arms lightly towards the horse with hands together. The same rules apply for the correct position as with showing on a halter. When the judge has seen enough, they indicate to the contestant. When returning to position, the contestant must look at the judge every third step.

Horsemanship trials

The choice of western riding competitions for equestrian skills is from: western pleasure riding, western horsemanship, western riding, trail riding, reining, and hunter classes.

WESTERN PLEASURE

It is important that the horse shows that it enjoys being ridden for this contest. The riders all ride together in the ring. They must demonstrate the walk, jog, and lope from the right and the left. At the end of the test, riders are asked to rein back. The calm manner of the horse, and quick reaction to the aids given by the rider when transitions are made is assessed. Penalty points are given for riding too fast and for the wrong gait.

Western horsemanship

REVERSE

When the command "reverse" is given during western pleasure contests, the riders must make an immediate 180 degree turn. The command can be given during the walk or jog.

WESTERN HORSEMANSHIP

Western horsemanship is a competition in which the riding capabilities of the competitor are assessed. There are two parts to the competition: an individual test and a collective one. During the individual phase, the rider must complete a course that has been made known to them. This includes elements that enable the judges to thoroughly examine the riding ability of the competitor. This includes walk, jog, and lope in a straight line and in circles, or figures such as a figure eight. The course has to be completed within 30 seconds. Once the time is up, the rider and horse must leave the ring. If the test has not been completed, this will cost the competitor points but not a disqualification. The finalists from the first round are requested to ride again as a group to ride a test collectively. This requires them to show their horses walking, jogging, and loping.

The judges pay attention to the seat of the rider, their confidence, and the manner in which they communicate with their horse.

WESTERN RIDING

Western riding trials require a range of different exercises to be ridden on a pre determined course that is designed to assess the proficiency of the horse. Sometimes the course passes over a length of timber at an angle and just high enough to affect the horse's action. Jumping the log or baulk is not permitted. The test may include cantering through a series of pylons so that the leading leg keeps changing. The test will want to see walk, jog, and lope. The closing part of the test will be a halt from the canter and then reining back in a straight line.

The judges look to see if the horse reacts without resistance to the rider's indications and if the horse is relaxed and graceful.

TRAIL COMPETITION

This is not what it sounds, but a horsemanship contest held in a show ring with various obstacles to represent the kinds of things that can be encountered in the wild. There are three compulsory obstacles in the trail competition: the opening and shutting of a gate, reining back through a course made of logs, and riding over four log or baulks of timber. Other obstacles are permitted, provided they are fixed, not higher than 450mm (18in), and do not present any danger to horse or rider.

Examples are logs which have to be crossed sideways, turning around within a wooden square, a ditch, or a wooden bridge. The horse's confidence in the rider plays a major role in the trail competition. The horse is judged by its obedience, intelligence, and the ease and good grace with which it tackles the course. Bonus marks are awarded for combinations that complete the course at a reasonable speed but not if speed is at the cost of correctness. The horse must always take care where it places its feet and must not touch an obstacle.

Western riding competition

Trail competition

REINING

The most spectacular riding event under the western riding umbrella is reining. Reining competition calls for the rider to demonstrate total control over the horse's every movement. The horse and rider must complete one of the 10 prescribed routines laid down by the American Quarter Horse Association. during which the horse is assessed for neatness, maneuverability, obedience, quiet nature, but also speed. The test includes sliding stops, spins, rollbacks, changes of canter, and control of speed when cantering in small circles. The combination must also rein back a number of paces. Each combination starts with 70 points. The judges deduct points for any element that is poorly ridden and gives extra points for a well ridden element. A fine, fluid stop will always win extra points. The judges deduct points if the horse for example opens its mouth too far or holds its head too high during a sliding stop, if the stop is not fluid, or regular, or the horse fails to react to a change of pace or gait. The combination is disqualified if they fail to follow the correct course.

REINING TRIAL OF THE AQHA (AMERICAN QUARTER HORSE ASSOCIATION)

The following example shows some of the types of exercise that can be included in a reining trial under AQHA rules. The length of the course is indicated on the long side of the ring by pylons.

1. Start in the center of the ring; start to the right hand and ride a small circle at a gentle pace, followed by a large, quickly ridden circle.
2. Change canter in the center of the ring.
3. Ride a small circle on the left hand at a gentle pace, followed by a large, quickly ridden circle.
4. Change canter in the center of the ring.
5. Canter past the furthest pylon on the short side of the ring and make a rollback to the left.
6. Canter to the opposite short side and make a rollback to the right.
7. Canter to the center of the ring and make a sliding stop.
8. Rein back to the center of the ring.
9. Make four right-hand spins.
10. Make four left-hand spins.
11. Stand still.
12. Drop the reins to show that the test has concluded.

FREESTYLE REINING

In addition to reining, there is also freestyle reining. One of the attractive elements of this competition is that the competitors are usually dressed in western-style clothing and the tests are ridden to music. With freestyle reining, each competitor can choose their own routine. There are compulsory elements that must be included but the order is a matter of free choice. The test must be longer than one minute but may not exceed four minutes.

Changing canter

Freestyle reining

with the mouth. The horse's head should be in line with an imaginary upright or just ahead of it. The general appearance should be relaxed. The horse should have extended, smooth action in each gait. The horse will be required to:
- walk
- jog (trot)
- extended jog (extended trot)
- canter
- rein back
- stand still.

Speed games

Western riding also includes a number of horse-back games ridden at speed. This is not surprising considering the quality of the Quarter horse. The Quarter horse is the fastest horse over a quarter of a mile distance.

BARREL RACE
One of the most exciting games is the barrel race.
Three barrels are placed in a triangle and the riders have to ride a ring around each barrel. The rider can choose whether to start with the right-hand or left-hand barrels. The third

VERSATILE HORSE
Versatile horse competitions consist of elements from western pleasure, western horsemanship, western riding, trail, and reining.

HUNTER CLASSES
Hunter classes are ridden in English hunting style with clothing and harness in the English manner. The most commonly ridden class is "hunter under saddle."

HUNTER UNDER SADDLE
For hunter under saddle classes, the stirrups are shortened and the rider sits well forward. The hands are kept in front of the saddle with the knuckles upwards. Light contact is maintained through the reins

Hunter under saddle

Barrel race

barrel stands at the end of the ring and this is encircled last of the three. The run is timed from the moment the horse's nose crosses the start line to the moment it crosses the finish line. The fastest time wins. The competitors are permitted to touch the barrel but get a five seconds penalty for knocking them over. If the course is not correctly ridden, the rider is disqualified.

POLE BENDING
Pole bending is a game that tests the speed and maneuverability of a horse. Six poles stand in a straight line about 7m (23ft) apart. The riders and their horses first race to the far end of the poles, they then return, zigzagging through the poles, turn and ride around the poles once more, finally galloping hard back to the finish. Every pole that horse and rider knock over gets a five second penalty. Riders are disqualified if they do not complete the course correctly.

TEAM PENNING
This team game is based on the work of a cowboy. Teams of three have to move three calves from a herd of calves across the ring to a holding pen. This has to be done within 90 seconds and the time begins once the

Pole bending

Team penning

first horse puts its nose over the starting line. The clock stops when the three calves are in the pen and the gate has been closed. This game is used by many riders to give their horses experience of working with cattle.

Working classes

Working classes for western riding means working with cattle. To be suitable for the work, a horse must be capable in reining tests and also possess cow sense. It is very important that horse and rider instinctively understand each other. The two principal disciplines are working cow horse and cutting competitions.

COW SENSE
The natural ability of a horse to judge what cattle are going to do is termed "cow sense." The horse needs to be capable of thinking and moving more quickly than a cow.
Horses need to have cow sense for both working cow horse and cutting competitions.

Cow sense

WORKING COW HORSE

During working cow horse contests, the horse must demonstrate its ability to carry out the duties of a working ranch horse. There are two parts to working cow horse contests: dry work (without cattle), which consists of reining tests, and working with cattle.

DRY WORK

In dry work contests, horse and rider have to complete a routine over a set course, with reasonable speed, as with reining competitions. The judges are looking for the precision and willingness to work of the horse.

FENCE WORK

Fence work is done with a cow in the ring. Firstly, the horse must control the cow on the short side of the ring and then the horse must drive the cow at least twice along the longer side of the ring. This entails the horse turning the animal in the direction of the wall or stopping it before the short side is reached. Finally, the horse has to drive the cow to the center of the ring and circle round it once in each direction. The judges assess this element on cow sense, good behavior on the part of the horse, and maneuverability. The horse must demonstrate total control over the cow. Penalties are given, for example, for over-aggressive han-

dling of the cow, and for the inability to keep the cow under control at the end of the ring.

CUTTING

For cutting competitions, the horse and rider must select a cow from a herd that is brought into the ring. Once the rider has chosen the cow to cut, the horse and rider must separate the animal as quickly as possible from the other cattle and drive it to the center of the ring. The horse's task is to prevent the cow from rejoining the herd. It is important that the horse stays at the correct distance from the cow. The test lasts for 150 seconds, starting from the moment

Cutting

that the horse and rider separate the cow from the herd. If the cow is not active enough, or it turns away from the horse, the rider is permitted to choose another cow. This can be done a maximum of three times during the same trial. If the horse turns away from the cow, penalty points will be given. Penalties are also incurred if the cow escapes from the horse or if the rider gives the horse directions or instructions. The horse must be able to work unaided.

HERDHOLDERS

During the cutting contest, the herdholders keep the herd together in the ring.

TURNBACK MEN

The turnback men have the task of ensuring that the cow does not stray beyond the center of the ring.

DUMMY COW

Stuffed or mechanical dummy cows are often used to train cow horses. These must be able to turn quickly to left and right so that the horse can learn to keep the correct distance form the cow.

Grooming the western horse

For horses that are shown in halter classes, the manes needs to be no longer than the breadth of a hand so that the neck can be clearly seen. The mane can be plaited to achieve this result and a special plait that is used for showing western horses is the "stallion plait." The riding competitions are generally performed with horses with long manes, although these are usually plaited during training to protect them. The day before a competition, the tails of horses that are to be shown in halter classes usually have their tails bandaged. The bandage is

removed just before entering the show ring so that the upper part of the tail remains tightly compact, displaying the horse's quarters well.

Hooves are sometimes painted black for both showing and western pleasure classes. Horses with white markings are cleaned with a whitening agent that is sprayed on dirty patches. After leaving it to soak in, the patch is then thoroughly brushed.

Stallion plaits

Blacked hooves

8 Other equestrian sports

It must already be apparent that horse-riding is a many-sided activity. In this chapter, a number of other sports and recreational pastimes are described from the equestrian world. Once a rider has become confident with riding and jumping, it is likely they will want to spread their wings. Some will be attracted by the challenge of the tougher side of the sporting scene that eventing offers, while others will prefer trekking on horseback through glorious countryside. Whether or not you want to become a competitor or remain a spectator, you will be enjoying and involved in equestrian sport.

This chapter deals with horse trials (eventing), racing, harness racing, endurance riding, hunting and point-to-point, polo, trick riding, hacking, and finally trekking on horseback.

Racing and trotting

Horse racing and trotting – officially known as harness racing – have a special place among equestrian sports. For the owners and trainers, horse racing is a serious business, requiring a great deal of money to train, feed, groom, stable, and transport racehorses. Betting is closely associated with both forms of horse racing. Placing a bet on a particular horse makes a person very eager to support that horse and increases the excitement for the spectators.

Harness racing

Races with horses trotting or pacing at speed are enormously popular in North America and most of the countries of Europe. The sport has existed in Europe since the sixteenth century where horses were raced over short distances during annual horse fairs to see which was the fastest trotting horse. Since then, harness racing with a driver seated on a lightweight

Left: horse racing and harness racing occupy a special place in equestrian sport

Trotting race

sulky has become a major international sport attracting large numbers of spectators.

HARNESS RACE

In harness races, horses draw sulkies at a fast trot or pace along a race track. The maximum number of combinations permitted in a harness race is sixteen. The names of the horses and the drivers are notified in the race card which is also the source of information for betting on the horses. Harness races are usually held over a distance of 1,600–3,400m (1,760–3,740yd). These days the pace or lateral trot is preferred to the normal diagonal trot. Horses may not break into a canter or gallop in harness races.

Flowers for the winner

SULKY
A sulky is a very lightweight two-wheeled rig, usually made of metal, with pneumatic tires.

DRIVER
The driver sits behind the horse on the sulky with – (usually) his – legs supported on either side of the shafts. The colors worn by the driver appear on the race card, e.g. green, orange color, edging and lettering white.

SHORT COURSE RACING
Short course races are mainly held in the summer months over a distance of 300m (330yd) where they are often part of summer fetes and festivals.

MONTE
Monté races are trotting races ridden under saddle. The main center for Monté races is France. Horses race over distances ranging from 1,600–2,600m (1,760–2,860yd).

ROLLING START
Some harness races, where all the horses race over the same distance, have a rolling start that gives each horse a fair chance. A vehicle is used with a special starting gate that drives around the course as the horses get up to speed. For the start, the wings of the gate are folded away, and the vehicle leaves the track.

Training a trotting horse

Other set distance races are started by means of a flag.

STARTING TAPES
With races that are started without a moving starting gate and in which the horses race over different distances, starting tapes are used. Those horses that have the most prize money start with a handicap that is expressed in a certain number of extra metres to race. Once all the horses are in position, the tapes shoot up out of the way and the race is under way.

Training rig

WINNINGS

The winnings is the amount of prize money that a horse has won.

FINISH

Because races can result in very close finishes, the judges are helped by special cameras that takes a picture as the first horse crosses the line. This is known as a photo finish. With harness racing, unlike other horse racing, the photo may also show if a horse has broken into a canter – which is not permitted.

DEAD HEAT

Where the photograph cannot separate the winning horses, the collective prize money for first and second place (and third if three

Can't see back

horses dead heat) is divided by the two (or three) horses.

PACER

A pacer is a horse that has a lateral trot rather than the normal diagonal trot. A pacer lands left fore and left hind legs followed by right fore and right hind legs. Some countries have special races for pacers but in the United States, pacers are now more popular than trotting horses.

BREAKER

A horse that breaks from the trot into a canter is known as a breaker. A horse that breaks trot must move to the outside and lose ground making it virtually impossible to win. Some races disqualify breaking horses.

TRAINING TROTTING HORSES

Trotting horses are trained six days in the week. Four of those days are spent trotting a distance of about 14km (8³/₄miles). The other two days are used for trotting really fast. During the speed work, a trotter will normally cover about 4km (2¹/₂miles) at a fast trot.

TRAINING RIG OR JOGGING CART

For training harness horses, a training rig is used that is heavier than a sulky. The training rig is carefully balanced so that the horse does not feel the rise and fall action of the shafts.

CAN'T SEE BACK

Some horses wear woollen rolls that act as blinkers on either sides of their heads. These are known as "can't see backs" and their purpose is to prevent the horse from seeing other horses immediately behind it. This prevents horses that become restless or lose concentration when they are aware of other horses close behind. Some race horses wear blinker hoods.

Horse racing

The small Suffolk town of Newmarket in England has long been the world center of thoroughbred horse racing. Kentucky, in the United States, is the North American center of thoroughbred breeding and racing. In common with Ireland, both areas have phosphate-rich soil providing green meadows ideal for raising horses, and grassy downs or well-tended tracks for training race horses. The progeny of Newmarket and Kentucky studs are exported all over the world.

FLAT RACING

Thoroughbred horses are galloped over a "flat" course – that is one without hurdles or fences – with the jockey crouched forward and out of the saddle. This makes it easier for the horse to carry the jockey. In North America thoroughbreds race on groomed dirt or grass courses, over increments of a mile (the furlong: 220 yd). In Europe, most races are run over grass tracks at distances between 1,000–3,600m (1,100– 3,960 yd). The result declares the distance between the placed horses (by a nose, half a length, two lengths).

JOCKEY

The jockey rides a horse in a race in a special way. Crouched forward to reduce wind resistance and with the weight carried forward, the jockey seeks to make it as easy as possible for the horse to carry the load.
The colors of the owner's silks that the jockey wears are indicated in the race card.

RACING SADDLE

Racing saddles are little more than a place to hang the stirrup irons (made of aluminium). Most weigh little more than a pound (less than 500g).

WEIGHING OUT AND WEIGHING IN

Jockeys are weighed before and after a race,

A length ahead

complete with their saddle and clothing. If the weight before the start is too light, weights are added to the saddle. The winning and placed jockeys are weighed again after the race to ensure that the weight is the same as before the start. Very small differences in weight are permitted.

STARTING STALLS

For flat races, horses are placed in special gates known as starting stalls which when released give every horse the opportunity to start in a straight line. After the start, the stalls are removed from the track.

STEEPLECHASE

A steeplechase is a race over hurdles or

A race

Jockeys

A jockey sits crouched forward

fences. These are usually not difficult obstacles but they are taken at speed. The larger fences are usually made of soft conifer hedging. Jump racing is also known as National Hunt racing.

Racing saddle

Weighing in

Starting stalls

HANDICAP RACE

In a handicap race, horses that have won more races are given extra weight so that all the horses are theoretically given an even chance of winning.

Betting on horses

Placing a bet on a horse increases the level of excitement in a race.

Win – gambles on the winning horse.

Place – bets on a horse coming in second.

Show – wagers that the horse will come third.

There are other combinations of bet possible: across the board, double, trifecta or forecast.

Betting with stakeholders or bookmakers was not always above board. The parimutuel system was invented in France in 1865. Betting receipts go into common pool from which, after a sum for administration is deducted, winning wagers are paid.

OUTSIDER

An outsider is a horse that is not expected to win and which offers long odds. If the horse wins, a bet on the horse will pay out much

Training race horses

more than if the favorite horse wins.

SCRATCHED

A horse is scratched when it is withdrawn from the race.

Horse trials or eventing

Eventing

Horse trials or eventing (short for three-day event) are an all-round test of horse and rider. The form of competition has its origins in military equitation. Cavalrymen demanded horses that were calm and obedient on parade, brave and capable in the field, and fit enough to be able to perform their normal duties the following day. The first day or even two of a horse trial is taken up by a dressage test (which means that most "three-day events" are in fact four days), the following day is a test of speed and endurance with the steeplechase section as its high point. On the final day, competitors must complete a showjumping course.

DRESSAGE FOR EVENTING

The dressage test expects a consistent, obedient, and precisely performed test with the horse moving crisply forward with a fine but extensive action. This is easier said than done since the eventing horse must be fully fit and bursting with energy for the endurance stage of the trial and for it to show the supple athleticism required to perform the details of a dressage test demands absolute obedience and submissive.

SPEED AND ENDURANCE TEST

The speed and endurance test starts with a course along roads and tracks that is completed at a quick trot or gentle canter (stage A). The second stage (B) is the steeplechase in which the horses must jump a series of fences at speed. The course varies from 2–4km (1¼–2½ miles) usually consisting of brush fences. The horses must complete the course in a certain time to avoid incurring penalties but there is no value in going faster than necessary because no additional points are awarded for faster times. There is a second road and track section (stage C) after the steeplechase that is intended to give the horse the chance to get its breath back after the steeplechase. The two road and track sections together are between 10–20km (6¼–12½ miles). The rider has to complete the distance in a set time and may even run or walk alongside the horse to spare it if necessary. There is no advantage in completing the section more quickly. These two road and track sections can be regarded as warming up and cooling off before and after the steeplechase. On completion of stage C there is a compulsory halt of ten minutes during which the horse is checked by a vet. Only horses passed as fit enough are allowed to participate in the final cross country section stage (D).

CROSS COUNTRY

The cross country section of horse trials includes natural obstacles such as hedges, ditches, walls, and banks. None of the obstacles may be higher than 1.2m (47in). Many of them can be jumped in several ways, with the most difficult option costing the least time. The difficulty of the obstacles does not stem from their height, but the way in which they are sited, how they are combined, and the drop on the landing side. The cross-country stage is usually about 7km (4 1/2 miles). There is a maximum time for completion of the cross country stage but no advantage to be gained by arriving early. Late finishing does incur penalties.

Eventing

Many contestants protect the legs and breasts of their horses by smearing them with petroleum jelly or udder ointment.

OBSTACLES IN A CROSS COUNTRY COURSE

The fences and obstacles in the cross country are different to the fences in a show-jumping ring. The course is set out by a course builder but natural materials are mainly used that are suitable for the surroundings.

• The coffin is a classic obstacle, with a fence at the bottom of a slope, followed by a ditch and then immediately an upward slope with a further fence or hedge. The name enough is off-putting but considerable courage is required to take this combination.

• Ditches with running water can disturb inexperienced horses so it is important that the rider approaches them confidently.

• Banks need a turn of speed to reach the top but then balance must be achieved at the top prior to the descent.

• Water jumps: apart from the fact that every horse reacts differently to water, these need to be ridden fairly energetically but under control, since if too much water is splashed in its eyes, the horse will be unable to see the jump out of the water.

SHOWJUMPING AT HORSE TRIALS

During the showjumping, the horse must prove that despite the effort of the previous day, it is sufficiently fit to complete the showjumping course. Before that though, it has to pass a fitness check by a vet on the morning of the final stage of the horse trial.

CLOTHING FOR THE SPEED AND ENDURANCE PHASE

Safety helmets are mandatory for the cross-country phase of eventing and body protection is often required too. Most competitors wear a long-sleeved sweater of their club or society.

Combined training trials

Combined training trials bring together the elements of dressage, showjumping, and cross country in one day. The severity of the different components is much less than with eventing and these competitions are an opportunity for riders and horses to qualify to take part in the more challenging senior trials.

Some combined training trials are spread over two days, with the dressage and show-jumping on day one and a short speed and endurance section with road work and cross country on the second day.

Endurance riding (long distance)

Endurance riding and competitive trail riding can cover a course of between 15 and 100 miles (25–160km) in a day through the countryside. For competitive trail riding, a minimum speed is determined for the route which is usually about 7–8 mph (11–13 kph). These competitions are ridden under rigorous veterinary control, which takes place before the start, during the mandatory rest periods, at the finish, and after the event, to ensure that the horses are not over-worked.

The right equipment is even more important with endurance riding than other equestrian sports. The rider is in the saddle for a long time.

Endurance riding

A perfectly fitting saddle is essential for both the rider and horse. New saddles are quite unsuitable because they can crack and rub. The rider's clothing too needs to be chosen for its comfort. Clothing that is too tight, heavy, or stiff is not good for an endurance rider.

For really long distance rides, it is best to have people waiting along the route to look after the rider and the horse so that the rider can get a rest and is better able to complete the ride.

ENDURANCE HORSE

An endurance or competitive trail horse is one that has an easy, economical action with a minimum risk of injuries. It must also have the heart to keep going when the going is difficult or heavy and be capable of recovering quickly.

Good endurance horses are usually between 15.3–15.8hh (1.55–1.6m) and often much smaller.

TRAINING ENDURANCE HORSES

A suitable horse needs to be five years old before starting the special training.

Hunting

It is important to get the horse accustomed to everything it may encounter, such as wading through water, travelling over different surfaces, and confidence in the dark. Only when this is successful can the training proper begin to build up the horse's stamina by gradually making the horse work harder (but not longer).

Once the horse has developed sufficient stamina, the training continues with rides over longer distances.

Hunting

Hunting with hounds is traditionally rooted in hunting wild game (mainly deer) and foxes who are pursued by hounds, followed by riders on horses. Hunting in France is mainly in pursuit of edible game but in Britain and Ireland, the majority of hunts have pursued the fox with a smaller number of deer hound packs.

DRAG HUNT

Many countries have seen the drag hunt replace the hunting of wild animals. The riders and hounds follow a scent laid by a scent layer or runner.

SCENT LAYER

A scent layer, who can be a runner or a person dragging a scent behind a horse, lays a scent over all sorts of obstacles so that the hunt has as natural a chase as possible and the riders have the sport of taking fences in the same way they would if hunting a fox or deer.

MEET

The place where the huntsmen, the hounds, and those who want to follow the hounds come together before the start of the hunt is known as the meet.

MASTER

The Master of foxhounds or of staghounds has overall leadership of the hunt and the master's instructions are final in all things.

HUNTSMAN

The Huntsman or Kennel-huntsman if the Master hunts his own pack, is responsible for the hounds and their control during the hunt. Only the Huntsman may use the hunting horn to encourage or recall the hounds. He also carries a long whip, known as a hunting crop. Different notes and calls on the horn are used to communicate with the hounds over a distance. The hunting crop is used to control the dogs at closer quarters.

WHIPPERS-IN

The Whippers-in are hunt servants, like the Huntsman (unless he is also the Master). They assist the Huntsman with the control of the pack and also have long hunting crops.

HUNTING HORN

The hunting horn is used by the Huntsman during the hunt to send signals to the pack of hounds and to call off the hunt.

HUNTING CROP

A hunting crop is a whip with a long lash that is used by the Huntsman and Whippers-in to control the pack of hounds.

KILL

At the end of drag hunts, the hounds are rewarded by "the kill" by being given pieces of tripe which quickly disappears.

RIBBONS

A young or inexperienced horse that has not hunted before wears a green ribbon in its tail and must remain well back in the hunt until it has shown itself to be calm enough to hunt. Horses that have a tendency to be aggressive towards others are required to wear a red ribbon in their tails to warn riders to steer clear of them.

Polo

Polo originated over two thousand years ago in ancient Persia and was introduced to England by cavalry officers returning from service on the north-west frontier of India. Polo ponies must have a quick turn of speed and be able to turn and stop quickly. There are four players in a polo team, with numbers one and two being attackers, number three attacks and defends, and number four is the back, who defends the goal. Each player has a personal handicap from two to ten. There are goal posts at each end of the polo field and the objective is to hit the ball between the posts. The teams change ends when a goal has been scored. The polo field is 300ft x 200ft (272m x

The Huntsman with the Whippers-in

Polo

Polo pony

Polo bridle

182m). Each player needs more than one pony for a match.

POLO EQUIPMENT

The polo ball is not larger than $3^1/_2$in (88mm) in diameter and weighs no more than 134g ($4^3/_4$oz) The polo mallet has a long bamboo handle and a hard wooden hammer head. The ball is hit with the side of the mallet.

Players are required to wear helmets with chin-straps, and also wear special polo boots and knee protection. The polo ponies must be bandaged to protect their legs. The ponies' tails arc plaited so that mallets cannot become entangled in them. Polo ponies often have calkins in their shoes to give them extra grip.

CHUKKA

A polo match consists of six *chukkas*, or periods of play of $7^1/_2$minutes. There is a break of 3 minutes between each *chukka* to change ponies.

Trick riding

Trick riding is gymnastics on horseback. The suitable horse for trick riding is one that is consistent and relaxed on the lunge rein.

The horse must also have a well-rounded firm back and, of course, a good and reliable temperament. Trick riding is a team sport in which the group effort is rewarded.

A trick riding team has twelve members. Apart from a lunge rein and whip, trick riding has specialized equipment.

Polo equipment

TRICK RIDING GIRTH

A girth for trick riding has two hand grips on it. A blanket is laid under the girth. The girth sometimes has leather loops on both sides to act as stirrups.

BALANCING REINS WITH RUBBER RINGS

Balancing reins ensure that the horse does not throw its head in the air and also keeps its back level. Balancing reins are attached to the trick riding girth.

TRICK RIDING COMPETITIONS

During trick riding competitions there are both required and free elements that are performed. The exercises can be performed by one, two, or more members of the team. The jury awards marks for the mount and dismount, and for the way in which the exercises are linked together, as well as marks for the exercises themselves. Marks are also awarded for the general impression of the performance in which the presentation, way the horse is lunged, pace at which the elements are performed, and the cooperation between team members is all taken into consideration. The points awarded range from one to ten, with ten being the top score. No points are awarded for exercises that are not performed. The starting point for all exercises is the mount and dismount.

• Mounting for normal seat: the rider runs alongside the horse's shoulder and catches hold of the hand grip on the girth. The rider then continues to run alongside the horse and vaults onto the back of the horse, bringing the outside leg over the back.
• Dismounting: from the conventional seat, the rider rocks forwards and then backwards in one fluid motion so that he is clear of the horse, before closing the legs and jumping to the ground on the near side of the horse. A female rider lifts her outer leg over the horse's neck, brings her legs together, and jumps to the ground on the near side.

Hacking

Every rider likes to ride in the countryside for a change for themselves and their horse. Hacking in relative freedom is quite different from the restriction of the schooling ring. Most horses behave differently away from the stables, can easily become scared

Avoid paved roads as much as possible

of anything unexpected, and are above all usually more high spirited. Inexperienced riders should always ride with someone else when they first ride away from the safety of the school ring.

Horses in a group are usually calmer, and are always easier to handle. Find out what the weather will be before setting out because at the very least, it is a nuisance to be caught miles from home by a hail storm. There are other problems in winter, such as slippery roads and tracks. This can be overcome by fitting gripping studs to the shoes.

TEMPO DURING A RIDE

There are various ways of hacking: some prefer a gentle walking pace during which they can enjoy the countryside while others want the thrill of going faster. The right tempo depends on a number of different factors including the fitness and stamina of the horse, and the type of ground you are covering. For instance, galloping in loose sand is extremely tiring for a horse A horse will obviously tire less quickly on level going than over hilly ground.

Walking on a paved road

It is sensible to avoid paved roads as much as possible. It will be impossible to avoid them altogether though but never canter on a hard road surface and only trot if it is really essential to do so. Horse's legs are not fitted with shock absorbers.

OVERTAXING
The foremost rule for hacking is never to overtax your horse. By overtaxing is meant not demanding too much of it. There should be regular changes of pace between walk, trot, and canter, to give the horse an opportunity to recover.

URINATING DURING A RIDE
Sometimes a horse will slightly arch its back in order to spread its legs. This can mean that the horse wants to urinate.

It is best to stop and stand in the stirrups with your upper body forward in order to relieve pressure on the horse's back. In this way, a horse can urinate more readily. If the horse is unable to fully discharge its urine it can suffer from colic from the painful cramp that results from being unable to empty its bladder.

BRIDLEWAYS
Most open countryside and woodland is not freely accessible for riders and horses to ride wherever they wish. Where riding is

Galloping along a beach

Bridleway

- Never ride too close to another horse. Many horses cannot stand this and may kick out.
- If one of the riders in a group dismounts, the others must stop and wait until the rider has remounted and is ready to ride on.
- If you come up behind another rider or riders who you wish to pass, change to a walk and after letting them know you are there, ask if you may pass. Horses coming the opposite way are also passed at a walk. If you pass horses at a trot or canter, there is a chance that the other horses will want to join in, because horses are herd animals.
- If you are riding at the head of a group, check behind you regularly to ensure that the other riders can keep up with you.
- If a group of riders has to cross a road, make sure that you all cross together. Do not cross one at a time because this delays the traffic and a waiting horse could become spooked.

OTHER CONSIDERATIONS
When using the public highway, you must take other road users into consideration.

Some landowners issue riding permits

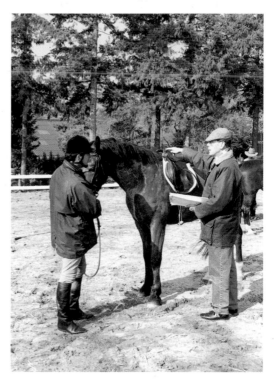

permitted, there will be specially marked bridleways. Even when riding through fields is allowed, it is only reasonable to ride around crops. Some riding areas are only available to permit holders.

RIDING PERMITS
Riding permits are sometimes issued by the owners of large estates, by water companies, forestry concerns and other landowners to regulate riding on their land. The permits are normally issued on condition that the horse and rider only ride on the routes indicated by signs and on the understanding that paths may be restricted at any time because of soil erosion, heavy rain, or for any other reason that the landowner chooses.

Permits usually have to be purchased for a modest amount of money.

RIDER ETIQUETTE
To reduce the risk of an accident, there are rules for the behavior of riders which should be adhered to. These rules are in the interests of the safety of the rider themselves and also to prevent accidents to any other riders who are met during a ride.

Never ride too close to another horse

Cross a road next to each other

Do not pass pedestrians or cyclists at a gallop.

Whenever you have to open a gate to continue on a bridleway or on someone else's land with permission, make sure that you close the gate behind you.

When the ground is wet take care to limit damage to fields and unpaved tracks and do not canter across such ground.

When you come across animals, change to a walk and keep as far away from them as possible to avoid frightening them. Other horses in a field can be so pleased to see another horse galloping that they go straight through a fence or hedge.

Make sure that you are covered for third party insurance risks so that if despite your care you cause damage or injury, you will be covered.

OBSTACLES IN YOUR WAY
All manner of obstacles can be encountered while riding in the countryside. It could be a steep slope which the horse has to

climb or descend, or wading through water. To descend a steep slope, your horse must go as straight as possible so that if it does slip, you should still reach the bottom safely. A horse that goes sideways down a slope is in danger of over-balancing.

To climb a hill, it is easier for the horse to zigzag.

Another obstacle is streaming water. Always wade across at an angle into the current. If you dismount to lead your horse through water, make sure that you walk next to the horse so that it will not leap on you if it is suddenly frightened. A frightened horse always bolts straight ahead.

Before riding a horse into unknown water, it is best to check first if the bottom is soft. Do not assume with deep water that every horse can swim for there are horses that cannot and they would be in grave danger.

If your horse has shown that it loves water and you decide to swim with it, make sure that you are beside or behind it because if

you get ahead of your horse, it may come on top of you. When you come to a closed gate, put your horse alongside the gate facing the catch so that with the reins and whip in one hand, you can lean over to open the gate. Make sure it will not close on you as you urge your horse through the opening – and do not forget to close the gate after you. If your horse is a bit restless, or the catch is very awkward, it is best to dismount.

RULES OF THE ROAD
Most riders will have to ride at least some distance along roads to reach open country-side. A horse and rider are traffic and must observe the Highway Code.

• Riders must observe any road signs that are intended for general road users.

• Horses should keep to the left, facing oncoming traffic.

• Horses are not permitted on motorways and footpaths.

• Riders must show a white light to the

Descending

Take a zigzag route to the top

front and a red light to the rear from half an hour after sunset to half an hour before sunrise. This is also required when visibility is otherwise reduced through mist or other weather conditions. (The safest manner is to fix a lantern to the right-hand stirrup iron or riding boot.)

• Where there is a verge on the right-hand side of the road that is wider than on the left, horses may use the right-hand verge.

REFLECTIVE CLOTHING
It is best to avoid riding in the dark or when visibility is reduced. If it is necessary to ride after lighting-up time, make sure that you and your horse are truly visible.
In addition to the lantern, there are also reflective jackets, armbands, and straps that you can wear and fasten to your horse. These aids have been shown to work extremely well.

Other road users can immediately see the movement of the horse's legs but however carefully you have equipped yourself and your horse, remember that drivers have a different viewpoint than your own.
They can be blinded by the headlights of an oncoming motorist or by the setting sun.

CLOTHING FOR HACKING
Comfortable and loose fitting clothing can be worn for hacking but for longer rides, proper riding breeches and boots are advisable. Trainers or gym shoes are not at all suitable because there is no heel to grip with, which means the foot can slide through the stirrup irons. If you fell from your horse in such a situation, you could remain hanging from the stirrup. It is also sensible to wear a hard hat.

TAKING A BREATHER
During longer rides, the horse will need to take a rest from time to time. Make sure that your horse is rubbed down because a sweating horse can easily get chilled if not dried off. Try to keep your horse out of the wind and if there is no shelter, turn the horse's hindquarters to the wind. The tail offers a little shelter for the body.

Check the bottom first

Riders must keep as close as possible to the verge

During a longer rest, remove the saddle. For such rides, it is a good idea to leave a halter on under the bridle, so that the bridle can be removed. Do not tie a horse by its reins since these are not strong enough to stop a horse.

Take care in letting your horse drink. Too much water at once can cause colic.

Loose fitting clothing is best

Trekking on horseback

Treks lasting for a few days require careful preparation. You will need to take everything that you need for the number of days you will be away and with the extra baggage, it is a good idea to take a second horse as a pack horse.

Various organizations throughout Europe and North America organize treks and trekking holidays, sometimes including the provision of the horses. Do not forget that you will have to take care of the horse during the trek.

PREPARING FOR A TREK

If you intend to take your own horse then it will need to have been ridden at least twice each week at a walk and in a gentle trot for three hours at a time. This training is best done out of doors. A week before departure, the horse will need to have new shoes fitted.

Take good maps and a compass. Check all the tack carefully because there is nothing more annoying than to have to pull out of your trek because a piece of tack has broken.

DURING THE TREK

It is necessary to let the horse drink from time to time. A horse can go longer without food than water. When you stop for a rest, the horse can graze. It makes a pleasant change for the horse as well as for you if you dismount and lead your horse occasionally. When you do, loosen the girths but do not forget to tighten them again when you remount. Check the shoes regularly to make sure they are not loose and check the hooves for any stones that might have become trapped.

If the horse is kept in a stable overnight, make sure the walls are strong enough. If the horse kicks the wall, it should not be possible for it to penetrate the wall and get its leg stuck. Remove nails and any other sharp objects from the wall which might injure the horse. Check that the fodder is of good quality.

9 Illness and disorders

If you keep a horse, or before you buy a horse, it is important to know when something is wrong with it. It is also sensible to know what the characteristics are of a healthy horse.
• A healthy horse should be alert and takes interest in its surroundings.
• The normal body temperature varies between 37–38°C.
• The warmth of a horse's body is evenly distributed throughout its body. Only the ears and the bottoms of the legs feel cooler to the touch.
• The flesh of the mucus membrane in the nose, mouth, and eyes should be pale pink and the mucus membrane should be moist.
• Horses have a well-developed sense of taste. If a horse leaves its food, check that it is not moldy. Horses are very fussy about their food.
• A horse's breathing should be quiet and regular. A horse should breath in and out about nine to fifteen times per minute.
• Horses produce droppings freely – usually in a large quantity at the same time. Depending on their fodder, the droppings can be green to dark brown. The droppings should remain firm.
• The hair should lie smooth and shine.
• A healthy horse walks with an even step.

The following symptoms can indicate that a horse is not well.
• The horse looks dejected, with its head drooping, the ears do not move, and it

A healthy horse has a shiny coat

Left: a healthy horse looks alert

shows no interest in its surroundings.
• The body temperature is high.
• The body temperature is uneven, with the ears and lower legs feeling extremely cold or very hot.
• The color of the eye and of the mucus membrane in the nose is very pale, dark-red, or yellow, and the mucus membrane is dry.
• The horse has lost its appetite.
• The breathing is irregular, faltering, or difficult and is accompanied by noticeable movement of the nostrils and chest wall.
• There is a rattle or whistle when the horse breathes.
• The horse has a short, dry cough.
• The droppings are small, hard, and dark or loose to watery.
• The horse keeps lying down and getting up again (colic).
• The coat hairs are raised up and dull.
• It is difficult to get the horse to move and its action is uncertain, wobbly, or painful.

There are many possible causes of the symptoms outlined above. This chapter deals with a number of things you can watch out for to judge if there is something wrong with a horse. The most common illness and defects are then described.
The chapter also includes information on basic treatment and medication for a horse. If in any doubt, or if the horse does not speedily recover, consult a vet.

What must you watch out for?

BODY TEMPERATURE
The temperature of a resting horse in its stall or at pasture is between 37.8–38.4°C (100–101°F). The temperature of foals ranges from 37.5–39°C (99.5–102.2°F). If a horse has a temperature higher than 38.9°C (102°F), it is ill.
If the temperature is very high (above 40°C) or exceptionally low (35°C or below), then a vet is needed urgently.

TAKING A TEMPERATURE
The temperature can be taken with an anal thermometer. This is smeared with petroleum jelly and inserted in an upwards direction into the anus. The thermometer should be turned as it is inserted. Stand next to the

Taking a horse's temperature

horse as you insert the thermometer. With restless animals, or ones that kick, it is sensible to get someone to help you keep the horse steady by holding up one of its forelegs. Take the thermometer out of the anus after three minutes and read the temperature.

HEART BEAT
The heart of a resting horse beats between thirty to forty beats per minute. The pulse becomes faster when the horse has a temperature and if the heart beats faster than eighty beats per minute, the horse is seriously ill.
The pulse is taken by pressing the index finger and middle finger against the artery at the back of the jaw.

BREATHING
Horses, on average, breathe in and out about twelve times each minute when they are resting. Mares breathe more frequently than colts and stallions, and foals breathe more frequently than adult horses. The breathing can be checked by laying the palm of your hand on the flanks of the horse where you can feel the rise and fall of the breathing. Another way is to carefully watch the nostrils.

Checking the pulse

Checking the breathing

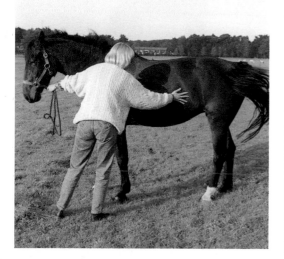

OTHER INDICATIONS

Other signs that a horse may be unwell are if it sweats profusely, has a swelling of the body, or moves differently from normal.

Even when the horse sweats more than usual when working, there might be something wrong.

Whenever in doubt, consult a vet. It is better to call the vet out three times for nothing than once too late!

Skin ailments

Skin ailments are troublesome and can take a great deal of time and care on the part of the horse owner to heal them. Horses that are not clipped but kept in a stable during the winter run a high risk of getting parasites such as lice and mites. In summer, problems with warble flies and horse flies are more common. The most frequently occurring skin problems are described below.

MANGE

The inflammation caused by tiny mites can cause a horse's legs to itch so much that they keep stamping and biting their legs. It can be so bad that they bang their legs against boards and poles, which can cause them to injure themselves. The places where

Skin problems on the back

Gall

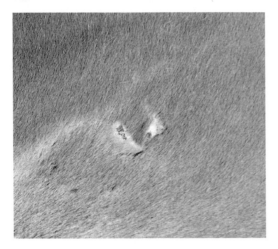

the itching mites infest the leg become bald and scabby. The problem is caused by a mite that otherwise does no harm to the horse. It can be easily treated with salves and ointments from the vet.

SADDLE SORES AND GALLS

Saddle sores and galls are caused by pressure or rubbing and are almost entirely due to ill-fitting saddles and tack. A growing horse needs a new or adapted saddle once a year.

Well fitting saddles can also cause galls however, when the saddle padding becomes ridged. Straps and the girth can also create galls if they rub or the tack is not clean. The pressure on the horse's body blocks the blood flow to that part of the body, resulting in the gall.

If the gall is quickly discovered, it causes no more harm than a slight skin irritation. If not dealt with soon though, the galls can become open sores that are liable to become infected. A horse with galls must be rested to give the places a chance to heal. Cold water on them speeds the healing process. A vet can use antiseptic treatments to cure the ailment.

SUNBURN

Some horses have unpigmented skin that easily becomes sun burned. This can cause hair to fall out and blistering of the skin. The skin dies off and large layers of skin can fall off. If caught soon enough, cod-liver oil ointment can prevent the skin damage. Horses that are susceptible to the sun should be brought indoors when it is very sunny.

LICE

Horses that are kept indoors in winter which grow long winter coats can be troubled with lice. It manifests itself by the horse rubbing and licking itself. To check if it is lice check around the root of the tail and in the mane.

The nits – yellowish white eggs of the lice – can be found stuck to the underside of the hairs. A vet can provide a treatment which has to be repeated a number of times.

MUD FEVER AND CRACKED HEELS

Mud fever and cracked heels affect the pasterns and heels of horses. The conditions can be caused by wounds, bacteria, allergy to certain fodder such as clover, penetration of damp (from muddy meadows but also diarrhea making the legs moist).

Mud fever

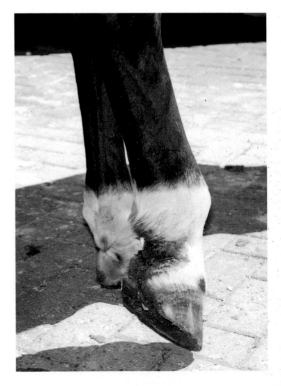

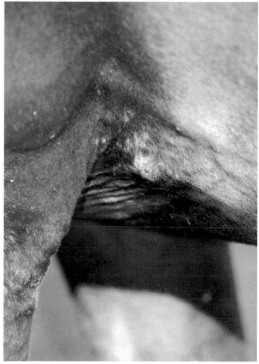

With mud fever, the white skin on the lower legs is affected. The legs swell up and suppurate until they form a scab. Cracked heels begin with peeling of skin that leaves painful grooves in the skin.

The treatment of the various causes of this group of conditions varies and it is best to consult a vet. In any event, these conditions need prompt treatment to prevent them from spreading. In a severe case, it can lead to blood poisoning.

To prevent the illness, make sure the legs are dried properly and then smear with some petroleum jelly.

RINGWORM

Ringworm is a highly contagious fungal infection of the skin caught from another horse that has ringworm or is a carrier without bearing the symptoms. The infection can be transferred through the horse being stabled in a stall with the infection or through a grooming brush.

The hairs stand up in small round areas and then they start to fall out. The infection spreads outwards in ring form. An infected horse must be isolated from others. The infection can be passed to humans so great care is needed.

An illness that is often confused with ringworm is treptotrichosis but this is not a fungal complaint but a bacterial infection. It makes itself known through tufts of hair that become stuck together by a greyish white discharge. If the hairs are pulled out, round or oval bloody patches are left which are painful if touched. The patches occur mainly on the back where it has remained moist beneath the saddle, around the groin, withers, and neck.

SWEET ITCH

The cause of sweet itch is an allergy to the saliva of midges that bite the horse affecting the tail and mane. The skin in these places becomes red and raised. The horse starts to rub and bite itself which can cause bleeding and injuries.

Shetland, Icelandic, and Fjord Ponies seem

Sweet itch on a tail

emerges to prevent it changing into an insect and affecting more horses.

WARTS
Warts can cause a great deal of trouble to horses. Present day treatments are very effective provided the wart has not got too big.

A vet can prescribe the correct treatment but if the wart does not respond it may need to be removed surgically. Chestnuts (castors) may look like warts but they are a harmless horny outgrowth on horse's legs that do not require treatment.

Wounds

Wounds in horses can be divided into abrasions, splits and tears, cuts, and puncture wounds. Abrasions are always surface wounds. Splits and tears, cuts, and puncture wounds can be superficial or deep, and they may or may not involve blood vessels.

A surface abrasion

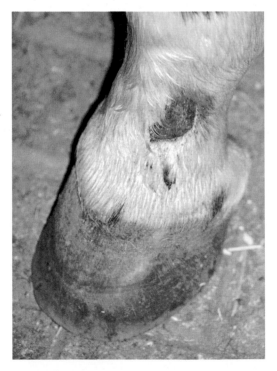

to be the most likely breeds to suffer from this eczema-like complaint. The affected places need to be treated with a lotion prescribed by a vet. Because the flies are only active in the twilight, it is best not to allow horses that are troubled by sweet itch out around dawn and sunset.

If the problem cannot be cured, it may be necessary to sell the horse to someone who lives near the sea, where the flies do not seem to be a problem. This is a difficult decision but it is the best for your horse.

WARBLE FLIES
Sometimes small yellow markings can be seen on horses. These are the eggs of the warble fly. The insect lays its eggs in the hair of a horse. The emerging larvae bore into the skin of the horse where they get larger. This leaves hard swellings beneath the skin. The swelling should never be pressed until the grub has emerged.

This can be speeded up by using hot compresses. Kill the grub immediately it

A deep wound with new skin starting to form

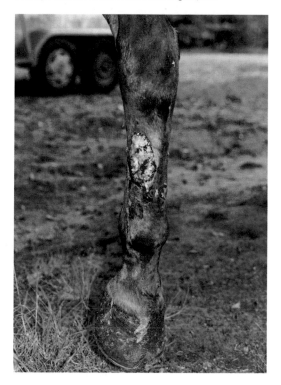

Tetanus injection

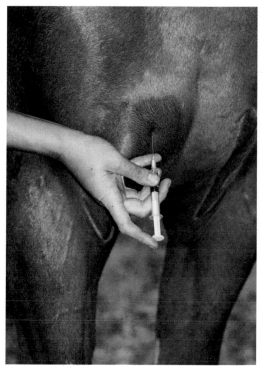

Surface wounds (the skin is not penetrated) can be dealt with by cleaning them and then spraying with an antiseptic spray (blue spray). With wounds where the outer skin has gone or is badly penetrated, it is best to telephone the vet. Never spray antiseptic into a wound! This will not only kill off any bacteria but will also kill the tissue cells that will then feed new bacteria. Even washing with tap water can damage the tissue cells.

If a wound is bleeding badly, the best treatment while waiting for the vet is to bind a damp cloth over the wound as tightly as possible. If the horse has been regularly injected against tetanus, the nature of the wound may determine whether a booster is required.

TETANUS

The greatest danger to a horse from a wound is tetanus. A deeply penetrating wound forms an ideal feeding medium for the bacteria that cause tetanus. Such a wound is not ventilated, forming a perfect environment for the bacteria to flourish. The bacteria produce a toxin that finds its

way through the nervous system to the spinal cord, severely affecting the nervous system. The symptoms are: the head is pushed forwards with flared nostrils, fore and hind legs are splayed, the tail is held up, and the horse cannot move. In severe cases, the horse cannot open its mouth because the jaw muscles are severely cramped. This symptom gives tetanus its common name of lockjaw. The only chance of saving the animal is rapid specialist treatment. To prevent tetanus, a horse should have regular tetanus inoculations. If the horse is seriously injured, the vet will need to give it a booster jab straight away.

Lameness

When a horse starts to favor one leg by putting its weight on another, its action is not consistent and we say it is lame. A horse can suddenly become lame through getting a stone, nail, or other sharp object in its hoof. A horse can go lame through problems with its legs or hooves, or through muscular strains or stiffness.

Lameness through a problem with the lower

legs or hooves can be seen when a horse is in its stable. The horse tries to keep its weight off one leg and makes very short steps on its bad leg preferring to put its weight on the opposite leg. This is best seen on firm ground.

Lameness that is caused by muscular problems is most often in the shoulder. The horse also makes short steps on one leg. This type of lameness is most readily seen on soft ground.

Leg and joint disorders

Leg and joint disorders have been divided into those inflammations that feel firm to the touch and can be clearly seen and the swellings caused by excess fluid in the joints which are not firm.

Firm swellings

CURB
Curb is a thickening on the back of the leg

Flexion test for splint

at the bottom of the hock of the ligament running from the hock to the cannon bone. At first the disorder is painful and causes lameness. Complete rest and cooling three times each day with water will cure the lameness but the thickening of the joint will remain.

RINGBONE AND SIDEBONE
Ringbone is an enlargement of the pastern at or just above the coronet, sidebone is a growth on the cartilage of the heel. Unless the growth of new bone sticks out above the coronet, this disorder is difficult to determine without X-rays. It is often caused by repeated concussion to the pastern during road work, although it can be genetically inherited. If the growth of new bone does not affect a joint, it may settle down after a period of rest.

SORE SHIN
Sore shins is a condition that affects young horses. It is an inflammation around one of both forecannons and its is caused by repeated pressure of work. It can also lead to inflammation of the tendon, causing lameness. The first essential treatment is rest.

SPLINT
A splint is the fusion of the slender splint bone to the cannon. It is more common in the forelegs, and is usually the result of concussion during work, or a blow. At first heat and pain are felt, and there is some lameness. Rest and cold-water therapy ease the discomfort until the fusion is complete. Soundness returns, although the bony enlargement will not disappear.

Soft swellings

WINDGALLS
Windgalls are soft swellings caused by a surplus of fluid on the joints. They occur mostly at the back of the leg, just above the fetlock. Windgalls in young horses are an indication of unsound legs, malformation of the bones, or problems caused by problem feet. No treatment is necessary but if the horse does become lame, consult a vet.

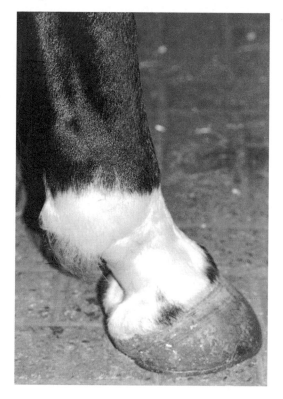
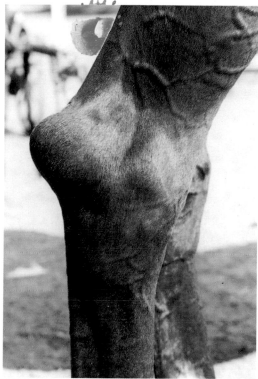

SPRAINED TENDONS

Sprained tendons are caused by hard galloping and jumping. The long flexor tendon at the back of the cannon bone is the most likely to be affected and the tendon becomes thickened with the tendon sheath puffy and feeling warm. Pressing the area will show that the horse is in pain. The horse will need at least three months complete rest.

CAPPED HOCK

There is a bursa, or fluid cavity, at the point of hock filled with excess joint fluid, causing a capped hock swelling. This is usually caused by bruising if there is insufficient bedding on the floor of the horse's box. Carriage horses can suffer from capped hock as a result of knocking their leg against the shafts. Generally no treatment is necessary but regular dousing with cold water may help in acute cases. There is usually a permanent marking of the hock afterwards.

THOROUGHPIN

Thoroughpin is a swelling of the hock. This is chronically infected causing an excess of fluid but also hard tissue to be formed. The swelling is usually not painful and the joint does not feel warm.

It is possible that the conformation of the horse was wanting. The condition is not susceptible to treatment, but does not cause lameness.

CAPPED ELBOW

A capped elbow like a capped hock is mainly caused by knocking or rubbing against the floor of a box or through the horse kicking itself when lying down. This does not cause lameness and the swelling is merely seen as a cosmetic fault.

Hoof disorders

There are a number of disorders that can affect the hooves of a horse, making the horse less or even unfit for work. Most hoof disorders can be prevented by regular visits from the farrier and daily cleaning of the hooves.

BRITTLE HOOF
The hoof wall can become hard and dry and consequently brittle. The cause is usually inadequate hoof-care. By ensuring the hooves are regularly oiled, the problem can be prevented. There are also many different preparations to encourage the growth of flexible new horn.

SOFT HORN
If the horn of a hoof is soft, it must be prevented from getting wet by treating it with hoof oil. A clean, dry box will also usually help improve matters.

HOOF-WALL CRACKS (SANDCRACKS AND GRASSCRACKS)
Grasscracks develop upwards from the lower, bearing surface of the hoof wall, and sandcracks extend downwards from the coronary band. Grasscracks usually cause little problem or distress but sandcracks can cause lameness. If a deep crack becomes infected, it needs to be trimmed back to new tissue. The crack may in severe cases need bonding with acrylic resin or holding together with a metal plate.

LAMINITIS
Laminitis is an infection of the sensitive laminae of the foot. It is most common in fore hooves. The causes can be: excessive use (such as a long ride on paved roads, or if a horse has put more weight on the leg because the opposite leg was lame), an allergic reaction, too much of a particular foodstuff (too much grass and too little exercise), and standing still too long in harness.
Laminitis can also be caused by other infections elsewhere in the body, such as an infection of the uterus or an afterbirth which has not been ejected. It is difficult to get a horse suffering from laminitis to move because of the pain. The horse arches its

Oiling the hoof

A clean stable is very important

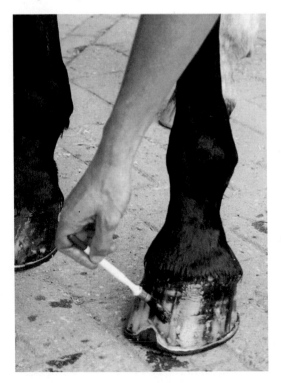

Special shoe for navicular disease

Special shoe for navicular disease

back, sticks its head well forward, and brings its rear legs under the body to relieve some of the weight on the forelegs. Call in the vet as soon as possible. If the problem does not heal quickly, it can become chronic so that the laminae separate from the hard tissue of the hoof and the pedal bone rotates. It can even lead to partial atrophy of the pedal bone. If this happens, the horse will only be able to be used for light work, with special shoes.

NAVICULAR DISEASE

Navicular disease is an infection of the navicular bone that is below the pastern and above the pedal bone, where it acts as a pivot. The infection causes a chronic, but intermittent lameness. The problem usually occurs with forelegs and is most prevalent in older horses that have worked hard for many years and over-stressed their forelegs. It cannot be cured but with horses that do not become totally lame, a specially adapted shoe can bring some relief and the horse remains able to work. The special shoe removes pressure on the diseased navicular bone.

NAIL PRICK

Nail prick is a wound in the sensitive tissues of the foot. The wound may be caused by a nail or some other sharp object. The injury mainly happens to hooves of the hindlegs because the forelegs disturb objects which then become lodged in the rear hooves. The lip of a loose shoe can also penetrate the foot. Wounds immediately be-

hind the point of frog are the most dangerous and can lead to incurable lameness.

Remove the object immediately but carefully to avoid it snapping off. If the wound bleeds, it is important to prevent any dirt getting in. The farrier can then trim the horn and flush the hole with iodine or some other strong antiseptic solution. If you keep the sharp object, the farrier will be able to see how deep the wound is. A tetanus injection is necessary.

THRUSH – INFECTION OF THE FROG

Thrush is an infection of the frog resulting in an accumulation of black, foul-smelling, moist matter. The hoof is actually rotting away. The affected horn is black and becomes so soft that it can easily be pricked.

The causes include: poor husbandry, dirty boxes, ill-fitting shoes, or bad trimming of the hoof. Hooves that have deep clefts in the frog are especially susceptible. To treat, the frog has to be thoroughly cleaned with all the affected matter cut away. This should be done by a vet or skilled farrier. The frog

Good hoof-care is essential

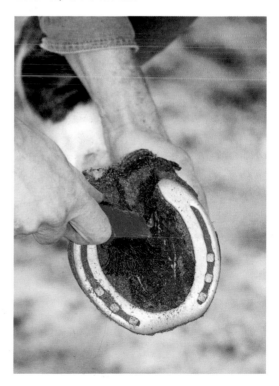

is then scrubbed with dilute iodine and then an antiseptic spray should be used. To prevent thrush, make sure the horse's box is dry and clean. If your horse is susceptible to infection then the hooves must be scraped out daily and the farrier needs to call more often to trim the excess hoof back to shape. Exercise is also important for your horse to ensure good circulation.

Stomach and intestinal disorders

DIARRHEA
Diarrhea is the excessive discharge of watery contents of the bowel. Diarrhea has a number of causes, including too much of one type of feed, a sudden change to a different diet, and anxiety (such as being transported in a horse box). Mild diarrhea normally clears itself up after a rest but if it persists, consult a vet.

COLIC
Colic is a general term for severe abdominal pain. Horses suffer more from this disorder than other animals. The three important types of colic are:
• Gaseous distension of the intestines (tympany), which is the most common form. The intestines become distended due to gas, causing pain.
• Impactive colic, caused by a hard mass of food material or digested food blocking the large colon at its narrow point. A special form is sand colic, resulting from a horse ingesting too much sand that builds up in the intestine. The most usual cause of impactive colic is too little exercise.
• A twisted gut (or intestinal catastrophy) in which the intestines have twisted themselves. Some cases can be cured by a timely operation but the general prognosis is poor.
Most cases of colic result from bad husbandry or the wrong diet. A horse that is suffering from colic makes this known by constantly looking at its belly. If the pain is bad, the horse will scrape its front hooves on the floor of the box and keep getting up and down in its box, and rolling. Warn the vet immediately colic is ascertained. Until the vet arrives, put the horse in a spacious stall with a soft floor or walk the horse gently. Before the vet arrives, the horse must not eat.

Sucking in air can cause gaseous colic

STOMACH AND INTESTINAL PARASITES
The most common stomach and intestinal parasites are worms. There are the large and small redworms, tapeworms, and pinworms. A horse that becomes slow and listless might be infested with worms. Horses ingest the larvae of worms from the droppings of infested horses when they graze. One way to reduce the worm problem is to collect the droppings from a pasture daily. Another important means is to give the horse a thorough worming treatment twice each year. If horses remain in the same pasture for some time, then worming is necessary every six weeks.

Horses can also be troubled by bot flies that lay their eggs on the horse's legs. When the larvae emerge, the horse ingests them by licking which carries them into the stomach where they attach themselves to the stomach wall. The horse suffers pain and is weakened. The larvae are fully grown by the spring and allow themselves to pass out with the droppings where they turn into flies. Within three weeks of their emerging, the process starts all over again.

Respiratory illnesses

Making a horse cough

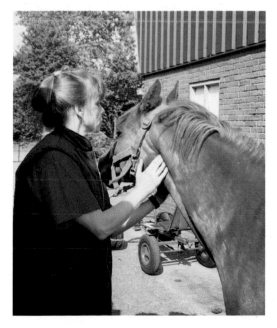

In order to check on the condition of the respiratory organs, it may be necessary to make the horse cough. This is done by pressing on the windpipe.

WHISTLING OR ROARING
The cause of whistling or roaring when a horse breathes is partial obstruction of the larynx due to paralysis of the vocal chord (usually the left side) with the result that opening and closing of the larynx is obstructed and breathing is made more difficult, resulting in a whistling sound. If the horse is intolerant of exercise, only an operation will make the horse fit to work.

HEAVES OR BROKEN WIND
Heaves or broken wind is a chronic lung illness in which connective tissue is formed in the lungs, making the horse short-winded. The first symptom of this problem is a deep, dull cough and another is double breathing.

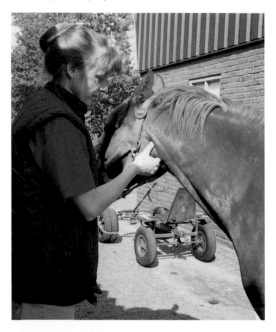

The horse breathes with difficulty, and often hastily, causing its flanks to heave. The horse gradually gets less good oxygen into its lungs because the elasticity of the lungs is impaired.

Heaves can result from an overlooked viral infection or through the horse continually ingesting dust. Specialist help is necessary to treat heaves. Good care with ample fresh air and a well-balanced diet usually are sufficient to enable most horses to be fit enough for light work.

STRANGLES

Strangles is a bacterial throat infection that is highly contagious, so a horse suffering from it must be separated from others. The horse will first seem off color and off its food, accompanied with a high temperature, abscesses in the mouth and discharge of pus from the nostrils. The lymph nodes in the head also become swollen – particularly those of the lower jaw. These must be coated with an ointment provided by the vet to make the abscesses burst. Once the abscesses have burst and their pus discharged, the horse finds considerable relief. Because of the pain caused by the swelling and the abscesses, the horse finds it difficult to move its head so it is helpful to provide its food and water at a height it can easily reach. The trough and water container can,

for example, be placed on a bale of straw. Infection of the lymph nodes elsewhere in the body of the horse is far more serious and can lead to death.

EQUINE INFLUENZA – FLU

Influenza is a viral infection of the upper respiratory system (nose, throat, and windpipe). The first symptoms of flu are a coarse, dry cough, and runny eyes and nose. The temperature can rise to 41°C (105.8°F) and the horse becomes sluggish. If the condition worsens, infected mucus is discharged and the muscles in the lower jaw become swollen.

The vet will usually give injections of antibiotics to prevent pneumonia. The horse needs to be kept away from other horses to prevent the flu from spreading. The horse will need several weeks rest and should not resume work until the cough has gone. Vets generally recommend vaccinating horses twice each year against influenza. Because of the infectious nature of the illness, many competitions will only accept entries from inoculated horses.

Vaccinating against influenza

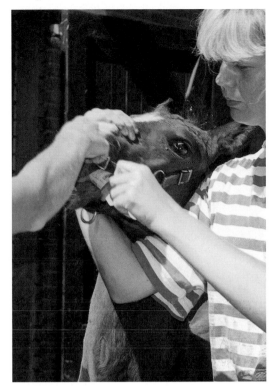

PNEUMONIA

Pneumonia can be caused by a bacterial or viral infection or foreign matter entering the lungs. Breathing with a horse with pneumonia is difficult, painful, more rapid, and shallow. If large parts of the lung are infected, the horse gets insufficient oxygen to keep the heart and other organs functioning and death will follow.

Call the vet immediately pneumonia is suspected. For bacterial pneumonia, a long course of antibiotics can cure the problem. A horse with pneumonia needs lots of fresh air.

CHOKE

Choke is a blockage of the esophagus or gullet somewhere between the throat and stomach. The cause might be a stuck apple but it is frequently due to dried bran or beet pulp. The horse becomes short of breath and coughs and food remnants come out of the nostrils and mouth. It is important that a vet frees the obstruction quickly. To prevent choke, it is best to moisten bran and beet pulp before feeding it to your horse.

ALLERGY TO HAY

An allergic reaction to hay is caused by sensitivity to fungal spores. There are various allergies found among horses, but an allergy to the fungal spores in hay is the most common.

The spores which cause the illness are not only found in hay but also in the air in the stable. A horse that is affected gets a stream of mucus and a racking, dry cough. If nothing is done, the cough can damage the tissues in the lungs. The horse has difficulty to take in sufficient oxygen. There are treatments that reduce the problem of mucus but it is far better to remove the cause of the allergy. Hay should be soaked first and wood shavings or peat dust are excellent substitutes for straw.

Good ventilation of the stable is essential, but a susceptible horse will probably be better staying out to pasture, night and day.

Illnesses diagnosed with a blood test

LYMPHANGITIS

Lymphangitis usually results from an infected wound or mud fever, and it most usually affects the hind legs. A swelling starts usually on the inside of the lower leg and spreads to the thigh. The horse becomes lame as a result, has a fever, and loses its appetite. Specialist treatment, including use of antibiotics, is the most successful solution.

MONDAY MORNING DISEASE – AZOTURIA

Monday morning disease gets its name because working horses go down with it following a day of rest on Sunday. It affects horses that are fed concentrates because they work hard. Through excess glycogen that is converted during work to lactic acid, a build up of lactic acid occurs that severely affects the muscles which are no longer able to function correctly.

The first symptom of Monday morning disease is sudden stiffness, followed by profuse sweating, and obvious signs of pain.

Taking a blood sample

If the horse urinates, the urine will be coffee colored. Through a metabolic accident, severe muscular cramps are caused that can seriously damage the muscles.

A horse discovered to have Monday morning disease must be rested at once. The horse may not even be capable of walking back to its stable. The vet should be called immediately. With good treatment and care, the horse can make a full recovery. The illness can be prevented by adjusting the feeding to the work the horse has to do.

Illnesses occurring with foals

There are various illnesses that can occur with foals.

PERSISTENT URACHUS

If urine drips from the navel, the umbilical cord has not properly withered. The leakage occurs from that part of the cord that had the function in the mother's body of removing the urine to the membrane in which the

A vet examines a foal

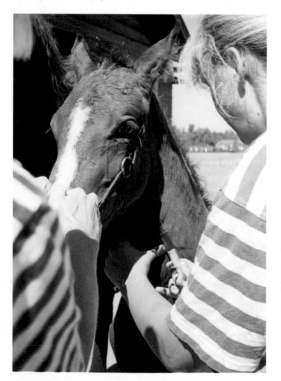

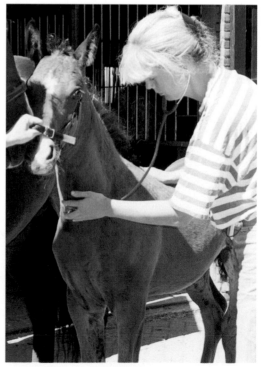

A vet inspects the mucous membranes

foal was enclosed. The vet can cure the problem surgically.

DIARRHEA
Some foals can suffer from diarrhea during the first forty-eight hours. This is caused by the change in their nutrition. The foal has to be removed from its mother, who should be milked.

During this time, the foal should only receive water.

Diarrhea can occur later in foals as well, suggesting an infection, but it can also be caused by the mare coming into season again, which can cause her milk to have a laxative effect.

JOINT ILL
Foals are prone to infection via a wound or the navel, which can enter the body via the bloodstream to cause inflammation of the joints. If this is not caught quickly, the foal may die.

The first symptom is lameness and the foal stops drinking, finds it difficult to lie down and get up, and has a temperature of around 40°C (104°F). The cause of this illness lies in inadequate hygiene during and after the birth.

DEVELOPMENT ORTHOPEDIC DISEASE
Abnormalities in the development of the bones in young animals can be caused by an imbalance of nutrients with the amount of energy used by the growing animal. Because of the complex range of causes, with some nutrients and minerals being in deficiency, yet others being in excess, specialist help is essential to uncover which dietary changes are necessary.

Poor conformation of the legs

The legs are extremely important to the agility and general flexibility of a horse and the way in which it moves. Good leg conformation makes it possible for a horse to work hard and makes a horse fast. Although the character of a horse can partially compensate for poor conformation of the legs, the same character would achieve so much more with better legs. The extent of the conformational defects determines how useful a horse will be.

In order to assess the conformation of a horse, it must first stand squarely on all four legs.

Conformational defects of the forelegs

NARROW IN FRONT
When a horse is *narrow in front,* the distance between the hooves is less then the width of the hoof and the feet may point very slightly inwards.

This causes the outside of the hooves to carry more load than the inside with a consequent greater risk of both joint and hoof problems. The horse's action is rickety, with a greater danger of hoof strike.

WIDE IN FRONT
With this stance, the space between the front hooves is too wide. This puts extra strain on the inside of the hooves and the same goes for the joints, leading to uneven pressure and wear. Horses that are wide in front have an awkward gait.

This is most prevalent in horses with small breasts.

PIGEON-TOED
The feet point inwards so that the outside of the hoof carries more load than the inside and is at a steeper angle. Sometimes just one

Conformational defects of the forelegs:
Normal, narrow in front, wide in front, pigeon-toed, and splay-footed

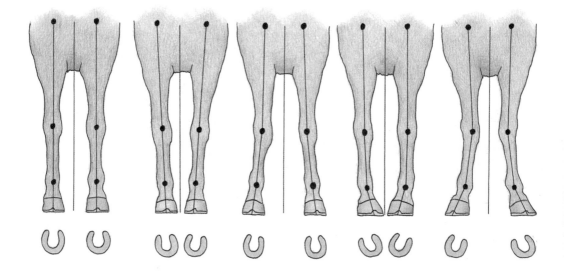

leg exhibits this deformity. Horses with this deformity have a "daisy-cutting" action. This is often coupled with oxbow legs.

SPLAY-FOOTED

With this stance, the feet point outwards with the result that the inner half of the hoof bears most of the weight. The horse has a powerful gait. Once the leg is lifted, it makes an inward arc before touching the ground. The chance of hoof strike is very great. This stance is usually coupled with legs that form an X-shape.

Conformational defects of the hindlegs

NARROW BEHIND

Viewed from behind, the horse has a narrow stance with hooves close together, meaning the chance of hoof strike is great.

WIDE BEHIND

The feet are far apart but the hocks are not drawn in as with cow hocks. Because the width between the hooves is too great, the hocks and cannon bones are unevenly laden, increasing the risk of a fracture. This conformational defect indicates unsound hindquarters.

SICKLE HOCKS

Splay-footed

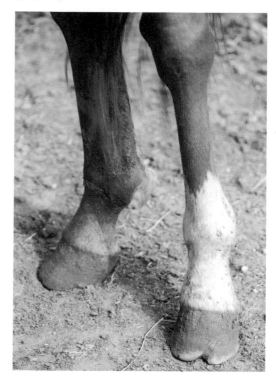

The conformational defect with the hooves turned in is less common on hindlegs. The same problems exist with sickle hocks as with pigeon-toed forelegs but the hocks are additionally at risk of injury.

Conformational defects of the hindlegs:
Normal, narrow behind, wide behind, sickle hocks, cow hocks

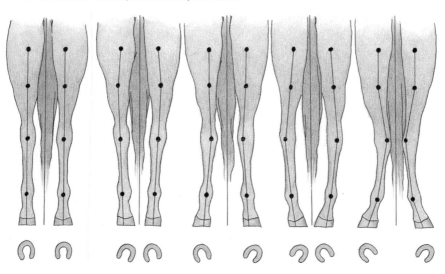

COW HOCKS

With cow hocks, the hocks are too close together, and the hooves are splayed. The hocks and cannon bones are unevenly laden increasing the chance of injury.

Gait abnormalities

There are a number of gait abnormalities which can be found in some horses. Most of these are caused by conformational defects with the legs.

TURNED IN AT THE HOCKS

A turned-in at the hocks action usually occurs with horses that are wide in front. Immediately the hoof touches the ground, it is turned outwards. The cause of the abnormal action is the wrong conformation of the hocks.

RUNNING

If a horse takes small trotting paces when it

It is important for a horse to have a consistent action

is asked to walk, it is running. This abnormality springs from incorrect training.

STRINGHALT

With this action, the horse brings its hindleg upwards from the knee with a backward movement. This sometimes cause the hoof to strike the belly. Painful tendons can be the cause of the *stringhalt*.

The gallop is the fastest of all the gaits of a horse

FORGING

Forging occurs when before the front hoof is being lifted, or at the moment it is being picked up, the rear hoof strikes against it. This can cause an injury to the frog and if the problem persists, the farrier can fit special shoes with double lips on either side instead of the normal central lip so that there is a reduced risk of metal striking the front hoof.

BRUSHING

Horses that suffer from *brushing* tend to bring their legs inwards in their gait with the result that the hoof brushes against the adjacent leg. Horses that have a *brushing* gait need to wear brushing boots to protect their legs.

PLAITING

A horse that *plaits* its legs tends to cross them over each other, which increases the chance of the horse tripping itself.

DAISY CUTTING

Horses that are pigeon toed tend to lift their legs outwards, making an outward curve which can injure their legs. The gait is sometimes known as daisy cutting because it looks like the horse is mowing the grass. Special shoes can help to reduce the problem.

TOE DRAGGING

With *toe dragging*, the front of the hoof tends to be slid along the ground. This problem mainly occurs with older horses.

Aftercare for a sick horse

The aftercare for a horse that has been ill is every bit as important as the initial treatment. The best period for a convalescent horse is the spring and summer when it can be put out to pasture. Of course the pasture has to be in good condition and have the required facilities. When pasture is not available and a horse has to be brought back to fitness in a stable, it is important to pay special attention to exercise and diet. While ill or lame, the horse will have had little if any concentrates. During the first weeks after initial recovery this should only be increased very slightly.

Exercise should ideally at first be done on the lunge rein. It is easy to observe the horse on the lunge and of course it easier for the horse without a weight to carry. After this, the horse can be taken for rides at a gentle pace. Regular work at a steady tempo, that is gradually increased in duration, is best for the horse.

First aid kit and medicines

When putting together a first aid kit and medicine cabinet for the stable, it is a good

The best place to convalesce is in pasture

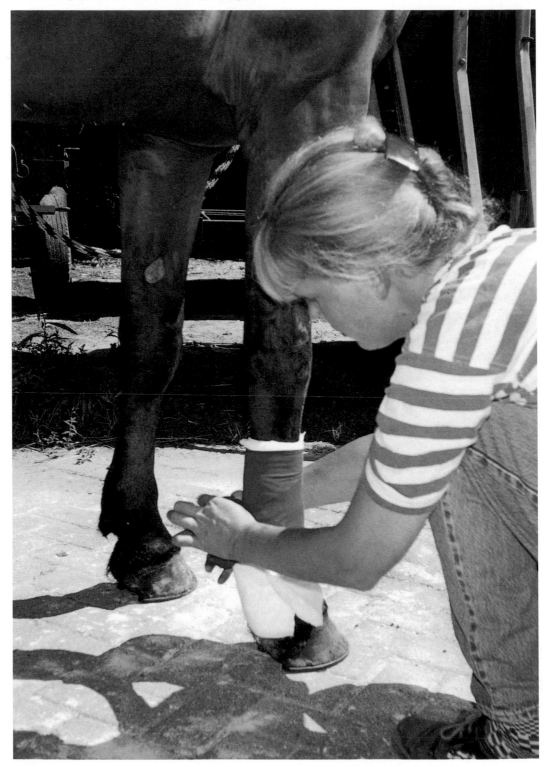

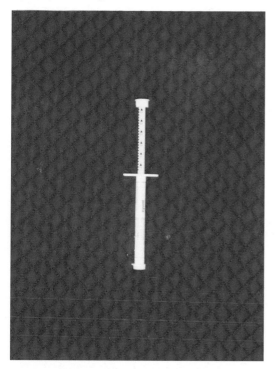

Injector for worming treatment

regularly over the horse when grooming it. Watch out for any abnormal behavior, swellings, places that clearly hurt the horse, or feel warm to the touch. For when you are not sure, a *thermometer* is a useful piece of equipment. Wounds of every variety are the most common occurrences: bruising, superficial wounds, and deep cuts which may also damage the tendons and bones. Bruises caused by knocks, falling, or being kicked by other animals can be helped by putting a pill under the horse's tongue which your vet can advise you about. Once superficial wounds have been cleaned with water, use an *antiseptic spray* that also protects the skin (blue spray). The first aid kit should include a number of rolls of *self-adhesive flexible bandages*, some *compression bandages*, cotton wool *gamgee* with gauze on both sides, *clean bandages*, and hydrophilic polyurethane dressings.

It is sensible to worm a horse regularly. If it is always in the same field then this needs to be done every six weeks. A *worming injector* in the stable medicine cabinet may help to remind you to do this chore. Make sure also that the *vet's telephone number* is kept in the same place so it can be found in an emergency.

There is little point in assembling a collection of pills and potions since the chances are they will be out of date when you actually need them.

idea to think of all the things that can happen and what you can sensibly do about it. The most important tools are your hands and eyes. Look carefully and run your hands

10 A horse of your own

The previous chapters are filled with information that is useful for those who own a horse, or those who are considering getting a horse of their own. Experience shows that there is far more to keeping a horse than just loving it. Even when you have ridden for many years through stables, you will be constantly confronted with new and unexpected situations. A horse is an individual with its own character and temperament. What is more, the horse's physical build plays an important part in the extent to which the horse enjoys its work. There is no overriding list of the characteristics which make for an ideal horse. No horse is perfect but then nor are their owners. The important point is to find a good combination between horse and rider, whereby there is mutual respect. Naturally, the rider must ensure that the horse is under their control. The other side to this is that a horse that trusts its rider will be far more prepared to put the effort in for that person.

Once you have a horse of your own, there is the opportunity to develop a bond with your horse. This can also happen with a horse that you look after for someone else, although in this case you will have the owner's wishes to comply with. The aim of this chapter is to deal in a logical sequence with all the likely matters that arise when buying a horse, the daily contact with the horse, and all manner of other practical points.

These are of interest to horse lovers even if you do not have your own horse. Finally, the chapter deals with various jobs that there are which work with horses.

RIDING SCHOOL

Even when you have your own horse or pony, it is still sensible to sign up for lessons with a riding school. The most experienced of riders can still benefit from good instruction. It is also useful to be able to ride different horses; horses that you do not intimately know and which cannot guess in advance what you are going to demand of them.

Bear the following points in mind when choosing a riding school.
• Are the boxes clean and well looked after?
• Are the staff friendly and helpful?

Left: a horse of your own

Riding school horse

• Do the horses and ponies all look fit, healthy, and content?
• Does the tack room look well organized and clean?
• Will they let you take a number of free lessons to find out if you are happy with everything?
• What is the accommodation like? Is it also possible to ride independently as well as take lessons?

LOOKING AFTER A HORSE OR PONY

It may seem the perfect arrangement: you take care of it and groom it, and in return you may ride it without having to worry about the cost of the stabling, feed, vet, or farrier. In reality you need to be very careful. Horse owners who like to groom their horse and enjoy being busy with it are most unlikely to offer it to someone else to look after. Don't give in to the urge to accept the first horse or pony you are offered to look after. Find out what is expected of you, how much time it will cost, and what sort of

horse or pony is in question. The insurance needs to be properly arranged. It may be best to enter into an agreement or form of contract between you. This will probably mean that you will pay a share of the costs but then your duties and rights will be set out in black and white.

BEFORE YOU BUY

If, in spite of your experience of caring for someone else's pony or grooming the horse you ride at the stables, you are still certain that your greatest wish is to have your own horse, then it may be time to buy a horse. There are a number of things you have to be aware of before doing so. These guidance notes are intended for amateurs. Professional riders have access to far more knowledge, support, and facilities than the recreational rider.

In the first place, the horse must be right for you. It must neither be too big nor too small for its rider but its build and weight are part of the consideration. If you are not very strong, then a powerful horse will quickly become your master. The character of the horse is also important. A quiet horse will be content with a fanatical rider that rides well. A spirited horse on the other hand will

have to be reminded constantly to calm down by an easy-going rider. The character

Professional once over

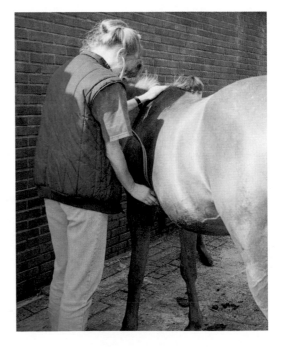

of a horse is very difficult to determine when you buy it. It may take up to six months before you really get to know your horse. There are certain things to bear in mind though.

• Try to see the horse in its box. Stable vices can often be seen straight away.

• If possible test ride the horse so that you can see how the horse reacts to the aids. Observe how it holds its head, ears, and tail, and watch if the horse moves forwards correctly. It is often a bad sign if the horse swishes its tail and pins its ears back.

• Get another rider to ride the horse as well. This gives you the chance to observe its action. A short session on the lunge rein is often very revealing. Beware, a slanted tail can indicate an unsound back.

• See how the horse reacts when you remove it from its box or well-known surroundings. Is it bold enough to work for you?

If you are still convinced the horse is right for you after this series of checks arrange to have it checked by a vet before the final sale is agreed. Visible faults can easily be ascertained but hidden problems will only come to light with a thorough professional inspection.

BUYING AND SELLING A HORSE

A horse is sold the moment that the buyer and seller have agreed which horse and what price it will be sold for. However, it is often the case the parties have a number of conditions attached to the agreement to buy and sell.

• The purchase is agreed subject to satisfactory report that the horse is free of visible or hidden fault from the vet.

• The horse is bought "on approval." If the purchaser finds the horse not suitable during an agreed period, the seller will take the horse back.

• The horse is bought on condition that it will be accepted for insurance.

HORSE SALES

In Europe horses are sometimes traded at a traditional horse market. In North America horses are more often purchased privately, through an agent, or at auction. Be aware that some sellers know many tricks to make a horse look acceptable for the day.

EXPENSE

Owning a horse is an expensive business. The biggest expenditure is for the horse

Horse market

itself and for its stabling. The amount you will have to part with depends on the type of horse, its age, and the extent to which it is already trained. A novice horse will be cheaper than a horse that has been schooled in the finer points of dressage. A horse that already has some experience is less likely to become frightened than a young, untrained horse. The combination of a novice horse and an inexperienced rider will often lead to an accident.

Stabling your horse also costs money. If you have your own stable or intend to have one built, follow the guidelines in Chapter 3. It is also possible to put your horse in livery. This costs a set amount of money each year, depending on the time you will be able to spare to care for and feed your horse. On the other side of the equation, the cost of lessons is likely to be much lower if you ride your own horse. Pasture for a horse needs lots of management and a good fence. If you want to use an electric fence, there are low voltage systems that work off the electric wiring but also battery systems.

You are not finished with the purchase of the horse and building of a stable. You will also need a good quality saddle and other tack, plus grooming equipment, blankets and rugs, a halter and leading rope, and food for your horse. Your horse will have to be wormed at least twice each year and also vaccinated against flu twice each year. The farrier will have to visit at least every eight weeks to keep the hooves in good order and fit new shoes. If your horse becomes ill, although most vets do their work as a calling, they will still present you with a bill.

On top of this, you need the right riding

Keeping a horse is an expensive business

Grooming helps you get acquainted

clothes, boots, and riding hat. The better you can ride, the more likely you are to want to compete. This will require special clothes, not to mention the entry money. If you want to take your horse to major competitions, then you will have to transport it there so you will need a trailer. In short a horse will cost a great deal of money before you even start to consider shampoos, boots to protect the horse's legs, a martingale etc.

GETTING TO KNOW EACH OTHER

The first few days will be very tense for both the brand new owner and their horse, which has been removed from surroundings it knows, possibly also away from other horses, to a totally new environment. It would not be sensible to put the horse out to pasture if you have a field. In its excited state, the horse could easily injure itself. It is better to keep it in the stable for a few days to give it a chance to get used to all the new smells, things, and people around it. If you believe it is calm enough to be taken out, first lead it quietly on the halter to inspect together its new play area.

Grooming is the best way to build a trusting relationship with a horse. Most horses enjoy being massaged and will quickly decide that there are advantages to their new owner. This way, you also get fully acquainted with the body of your horse. Do not get upset if at first the horse takes no notice of you or seems angry. You can come a long way in a week with patience and devotion.

The excitement and tension can make the droppings rather runny but this usually clears up quickly but it is wise to check the droppings. Try to match the same feeding that the horse previously had.

Behavior

A horse is a herd animal that once lived in the wild in large groups with a hierarchical order. If a new horse is put out to pasture with others, the horses will not necessarily immediately accept the newcomer. First they have to establish their position in the herd. Do not be surprised if there is some trampling and kicking between them, this is the quickest way horses know to establish appropriate status. Calm will usually be restored quickly.

COMPANIONSHIP

Because horses are naturally gregarious animals they do not like being stuck in a stable or placed in a field alone. Of course you can pay the horse as much attention as possible but you cannot be with it for twenty-four hours in every day. It is therefore a good idea to find some company for the horse. Not everyone can afford to keep more than one horse or pony but a pair of sheep or goats makes excellent companions. What's more, all sorts of parasites that can be harm-

Devoted company

ful for horses are killed off in the stomach of a sheep. Before you can place sheep in a field though the fence has to be fully secure. Make sure they cannot get under an electric fence.

Do not forget that sheep too need looking after. Once a year, the sheep have to be shorn and their hooves have to be taken care of. They too, like your horse, must be wormed. Otherwise, they are easy animals which can live outside all winter provided you supplement their grazing with additional fodder.

Donkeys are less suitable companions to share a field with horses. They are carriers of a parasite that their bodies can easily withstand but that makes horses extremely ill.

CATCHING

It can sometimes be very difficult to catch a horse or pony to take it out of the field. Immediately you appear carrying a halter, the horse disappears to the farthest corner of the field. If you do not possess one of those wonderful horses that trots up meekly

to you for its head collar, there are some things you can do to improve matters.

• Visit the field more often, not just when you want to ride your horse or the vet is visiting. It is nice for both of you if you give your horse a cuddle from time to time. Reward it occasionally with something nice to eat but do not make a habit of it because some horses become nippy as a result.

• If you do want to ride, do not walk straight up to your horse but make out that you have something else to do in the field. Most horses are so curious that they will come over to see what you are doing.

• Always remain calm, even when your horse will not let itself be caught immediately. Walk slowly after it. It will eventually have had enough of evading you.

• Difficult horses are best put out to pasture with a head collar on. This makes them easier to catch. Make sure the halter fits properly.

Foals are often more difficult to catch than adult horses. It can help to stoop down so that you are smaller and less threatening to the young animal.

Spirited stallion

work by really enjoying a roll on the ground as you put it out to pasture. The result may well be that the horse is dirtier than before you groomed it.

Yet horses have a perfectly good reason for rolling on the ground. In the first place, wild horses do it to strengthen the bonds within the herd. Horses from the same family always roll in the same spot where they transfer the scent of the other horses to themselves. Your horse is likely to have a set place in which it rolls. Secondly, strange as it may seem, the dust it picks up is intended to keep the coat clean. Dry dust absorbs grease and it also deters insects. In winter, mud forms an additional layer on the skin, which keeps the horse warm.

Finally, horses roll because they enjoy it. They can also scratch places that they cannot normally get to, which is why you should give stabled horses the chance from time to time to have a roll in a field. The danger for a horse if it rolls in its box, is that it might become stuck.

A horse should never be permitted to roll while it is working.

LIFTING A HOOF

Most horses have learned from a young age to lift a hoof so it can be scraped out but there are horses with which this can pose a problem. This requires a great deal of patience as the owner or person who looks after a horse. It helps if you check the feet frequently without actually doing anything to them so that the horse gets used to it without something unpleasant being associated. It is quite possible to put a horse off balance with your own weight when it is standing on three feet. Pulling very gently on the fetlock is an additional incentive.

Stand next to the horse or pony with your back to its head and let your hand slide down the leg as you talk to the horse. Take the horse by the fetlock and say "hoof" and then pull the leg upwards. If you have cleaned the hoof out, carefully lower the leg to the ground and reward the horse.

If you have a horse that is difficult about having its foot lifted, you must let the farrier know. If this is really bad, it may be necessary to give the horse a sedative in advance of the farrier's visit.

ROLLING

It can be extremely frustrating when you have just groomed your horse after a ride if the horse immediately undoes all your good

TEMPERAMENT

No two horses are the same. One may be rather lazy, the other timid or nervous, while a third might be high spirited. Horses

Docile horse

with a substantial proportion of full or hot blood will generally be more high spirited than, for instance, a Fjord Pony or Haflinger.

HOTTED UP
Quite apart from the extent of hotblood in its breeding, there are other reasons that are not inbred for a horse being "hotted up." A horse that is difficult to keep on the bit may be getting an inappropriate diet. Concentrates with a high proportion of oats can get a horse over-excited or it may simply be that the horse has been stabled too long. Some horses just get excited when they are in new surroundings for a competition. The excitement of the journey together with the atmosphere at the show or trials makes them go "out of their skin." The weather too plays a major role and the majority of horses get high spirited when the weather is fresh.

LETHARGIC HORSE
Just as with humans, lethargy may have its causes in a physical disorder. It could be that the horse has a viral infection or is infested with worms. If one or more hooves hurt that would make a horse less than enthusiastic to move. Beside physical causes, loneliness can cause a horse to lose its zest for life. Maybe it just finds its work too

repetitive and perhaps a little jumping practice might brighten the horse up. Remember though that a horse which has worked hard needs its rest and a lazy day out to grass can do wonders.

FRIGHTENED HORSE
A nervous horse is frightened. Perhaps it has had a bad experience in the past. If so, it is extremely important to win the horse's trust. The rider should always exude an air of calm and authority. If you are anxious, the horse will become anxious. The reason for this can be found by looking back at when horses lived in the wild. As potential prey, they had to be ready to flee from animals such as the puma at a moment's notice. A puma pumps its body full of adrenaline in readiness for the hunt. Once a horse smells adrenaline its immediate reaction is to take flight. If you are anxious, you will have adrenaline in your blood, with all the consequences that holds for the horse's behavior.

FEEDING
The amount of food that your horse needs is dependant on the work that it does. Generally it is possible to tell by looking at a horse if it is getting the right amount of feed. With horses but especially ponies that get a thick

A belly from eating grass

A field full of weeds

294

winter coat, it is necessary to feel with your hand whether the horse is getting enough to eat. Press your fingers against the flesh. You should not be able to feel the ribs.

Horses that are underfed have shoulders and ribcages that stick out. Horses and ponies that spend the entire day grazing in pasture often get a bigger belly than similar horses which are stabled. You must make sure a horse does not get overweight because it will then find it more difficult to work and the excess weight can also lead to breathing difficulties. Avoid giving too many apples, carrots, and bread to your horse.

If a horse has ample pasture, it has no need of additional feed and provided it has a salt and mineral lick, it will not require any other supplements either. If a change to your horse's feed becomes essential, you should make sure that it does not happen abruptly. The feeding regime should be adapted gradually.

DROPPINGS

Horses generally leave their droppings in one set place in a field and then do not graze in the vicinity of the droppings so that the pile gradually increases. The droppings are a breeding ground for all manner of parasites and they encourage the growth of weeds. It is sensible to remove the droppings from the field regularly and to mow the taller weeds, or you will be left with no grazing. But beware! There are horses with a mischievous bent. If you take your eye off the wheelbarrow full of horse manure for a moment, such horses find it great fun to tip the barrow over.

In really large areas of pasture, the droppings can be spread out with a harrow. Organic manure is less easily absorbed by the roots of the grass than fertilizer, resulting in tougher grass.

Apart from the manure in the field, you will also accumulate a great heap of dung from the stable. Horse manure is excellent for use in flower gardens once it is well rotted but not everyone, of course, has a large garden. You will probably have to give the manure away to keen gardeners or even have it taken away by a specialist company.

Some countries have regulations about the amount of manure that may be produced on sites of restricted dimensions.

EXERCISE

Exercise is essential for the physical well-being of your horse. It is not too great a problem to ride your horse every day during the summer, because even if you are working during the day, there is enough daylight in the evening to ride when you get home. Many horses can also be put out to pasture in the summer where they will get more exercise than when shut in a stable.

When the days become shorter and the temperature lower the problem of exercise becomes more acute. If the ground is frozen and slippery with snow or ice it may even be impossible to ride. It can then be useful to spread a circle of fresh dung on the ground so that you can exercise your horse on a lunge rein. You can also take your horse for a walk on the leading rein.

Transporting your horse

MEANS OF TRANSPORT

The most customary means of transporting horses and ponies is a horse trailer. There is a choice of single horse, one-and-a-half, and two-horse trailers. Even if you only have one horse, a two-horse trailer is the best solution because they have a more stable ride. Make sure that the horse and trailer are not too much weight for your car to pull. A compromise is to go for a one-and-a-half horse trailer.

There are also small horseboxes and truck-sized horseboxes, with and without sleeping accommodation. The average weights for different types of ponies and horse give a guide for considering trailers or horseboxes.
- Riding/carriage horse   550–650kg
  16–16.3hh (1.62–1.65m)   1,102–1,433lb
- Light warmblood   450–550kg
  15.8hh (1.60m)   992–1,102lb
- Fjord Pony   400–450kg
                                 881–992lb
- Riding pony   300–400kg
  (Welsh, New Forest etc.)   661–881lb
- Shetland Pony   200–225kg
                                 441–496lb

PREPARING A HORSE TO BE TRANSPORTED

A horse that is going to be transported must have a well-fitting head collar that should incorporate a quick release catch by which the horse can be simply released in an emergency. The legs need to be protected by bandages or travelling boots. The hooves and particularly the coronary band should be protected with over-reach boots. Protect

Two-horse trailer

Travelling boots

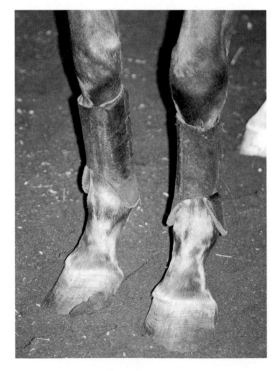

the tail by bandaging it. If the horse is likely to get cold, or will need a blanket when it has sweated a great deal, do not forget to take at least one that is right for its purpose. After hard work, a horse must be rubbed down before it is put back in the trailer. Prevent the horse soaking the blanket in the trailer through sweating.

LOADING UP
Provided the horse is willing to be loaded, the person leading the horse should walk beside the horse. This person leads the horse straight up the ramp and into the trailer with determination. While a helper fixes the crossbar, the person who led the horse in fastens the lead rope. Problem horses should be handled with patience and tact.

Tugging on the lead rope does not achieve anything because a horse will win any trial of strength with you. A lunge behind the hind-quarters often helps but if not there are various methods that have success such as backing the horse in, or putting a blindfold on, but these are methods that can only be tried with experienced people. Whatever you do, you must prevent the horse from becoming frightened.

Loading up

UNLOADING
The unloading must be done with some thought. When a horse has to back out of the trailer you must make sure that it is kept straight so that it does not stumble off the loading ramp. This means that the horse must be guided back. The first time it is done, it is best to have helpers on each side to prevent the horse stepping off the ramp. When unloading backwards, you must also prevent the horse from banging its head against the roof of the trailer or horsebox. With large horseboxes, in which horses travel sideways, there is no need to have to walk a horse out backwards.

ON THE ROAD
A trailer or horsebox must be well ventilated and sturdy. For longer journeys, the floor should be covered with straw to soak up the urine. To overcome boredom, hang up a hay net at breast height so that the horse has something to occupy it. However well you prepare for the journey, it will be stressful for the horse, regardless of how easily it seems to take everything. It is advisable on longer journeys to take a break every few hours. This benefits both the horse and the driver.

Valuable horses can be insured against theft, accidents, and illness

If you have to make a really long journey, arrange somewhere to stay to break the journey where there is stabling. Arrange everything in advance so that you are not confronted with unexpected problems.

INSURANCE
It is not necessary to insure most recreational horses and ponies but the rider should have third party liability insurance. The legal position regarding accidents that occur at a riding school varies from one country to another but in many instances, the riding school will be responsible for any accidents. Many associations and schools have collective insurance to cover their members, the cost of which is included in the subscription or charges for the lessons. It is sensible to check what the case is with the school or association you are considering. If you are taking care of someone else's horse for them, it is essential that there is proper insurance.

Valuable horses can be insured against theft, the costs arising from accidents, and illness. Most insurers are also prepared to offer life insurance policies on the horse.

The premium is dependant on the value of the horse, the type of cover, and its age. There are often minimum and maximum ages for cover. Up to a certain value, the horse has to be checked by an inspector from the insurance company. With more valuable horses, a full medical examination is often required, including X-rays.

FALLS
Riders who have never fallen off a horse are as difficult to find as the proverbial needle in a haystack. You are more likely to fall in the early days of riding because you will not yet have fully developed your sense of balance. The longer you ride, the greater your instinctive balance will be and the less will be your chances of falling off. You will also learn to sense the horse and almost read its thoughts. If you sense that a horse is going to buck or rear, you can urge it strongly forward and make it work hard. The horse will be so busy concentrating that it will forget all about trying to throw its rider.

Despite everything, your horse can take fright and rear up so much that you cannot

It is best to go for rides with other people

help but be thrown. The chances of the horse being surprised by something unexpected are far greater during rides away from the stables or school ring. Naturally you keep your eyes open for such possible problems but if you do get thrown try to remember:

• Try to fall as relaxed as possible
• The chances of serious injury are reduced if you remember to roll. Bend your head into your chest, fold your arms over your head, and pull your knees up. Try to avoid putting out a hand to break your fall because this will almost certainly mean that you break an arm.
• Remain calm. If you lie still on the ground, the horse is unlikely to trample on you.
• Only hold on to the reins if you're certain you will land on your feet.

There are also a number of things you can do to reduce the chance of an accident. Check the saddle and bridle to ensure that none of the straps is likely to break and that all buckles are properly fastened. A worn girth strap can be really dangerous. Make sure that you are properly protected. A hard hat is really essential for rides out on the road or cross country. Riding boots or shoes must have a definite heel to them to prevent your feet from sliding through the stirrup irons and they must not have any loose buckles or laces which could trap your foot in the stirrup. If you must ride alone, tell someone roughly where you are going and how long you expect to be away.

THE END OF A HORSE'S LIFE
This somewhat sombre subject does not get dealt with in most books about horses. You must accept though, if you buy a horse, that the day will come when you have to say farewell to it. With children's ponies, this usually occurs when the children have outgrown it and the pony will probably be sold on.
It could be that your horse will spend its last years with you and eventually you will notice that various signs of old age keep occurring. If the horse begins to really suffer, you will have to discuss with the vet what is best for the horse. In reality, few horses die a natural death. Should your horse die, or have to be destroyed by the vet, you will probably need to arrange with the knackers to remove it.

Fortunately there is always new life!

Working with horses

Many riders – especially the younger ones – dream of working with horses. Unfortunately, not everyone can realize this dream. There are a number of jobs which bring you into contact with horses.

VETERINARY SURGEON
To become a vet, you will have to study hard for many years at university. Although many people choose this profession because of their love of horses, the reality of working with horses is not very high.

Most vets deal with pets because of the reduction in the numbers of livestock in agriculture so that there are fewer large animals. If a vet does get to work with horses, he or she will be mainly confronted with lameness and respiratory illnesses.

EQUINE DENTIST
Most horses have their teeth dealt with by a vet but dental problems are a very small part of a vet's training and most vets' experience is restricted to rasping sharp edges off teeth. The profession of equine dentist is still little known. Most people who carry on this profession have spent part of the practical work experience while at university with a

specialist in this field. The work is not heavy but often has to be carried out in awkward positions.

To work in a Shetland Pony's mouth, an equine dentist must kneel down but a large draft horse can present different problems if it lifts its head up. This specialist deals with the sharp edges of teeth that result from grinding fodder between the upper and lower jaws. Some horses experience problems with the changing of teeth. Milk teeth usually sit like a lid on top of the permanent teeth but occasionally the milk teeth will not fall out. Other matters that are dealt with include misplaced teeth.

FARRIER

Special training is needed to become a farrier. It is heavy work, constantly dealing with new and different horses, some of which want to resist. For this reason there are strict entrance standards to assess if someone is suitable.

During a farrier's training, they learn anatomy of the horse but also metalwork and the use of all kinds of specialist tools on a living

Groom

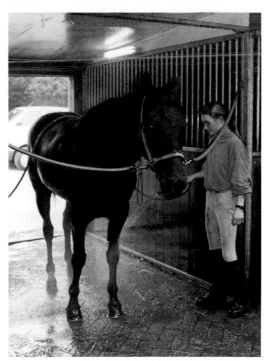

animal. Someone who cannot cope with a trimming knife and hoof pincers will not make a good farrier. The training includes a period working with a qualified farrier. The trade can only be truly learned through practical experience.

GROOM

Many horse publications are full of advertisements seeking grooms. Grooms are people who look after horses. It is hard work, which is not always properly valued. Grooms have to get up early and they usually work six days every week. The work varies from mucking out stables, feeding horses, and grooming them to helping out at competitions. All this effort might be rewarded by letting you ride from time to time. There is not really a training to become a groom but a course in stable and horse management will certainly help.

WORKING WITH HORSES IN
THE FORESTRY

Horses used to be the main means of pulling anything before tractors. Horses were still a common sight on farms for a while after World War II. Every farmer had at least one

horse to work his land. Today, horses are still used in some countries in Europe to haul timber in places where tractors cannot go.

MOUNTED POLICE

Many a young horse-mad child dreams of becoming a mounted police officer. Every police force has a selection procedure for its mounted police that is just as tough as the way they choose their horses. Not every trainee police officer who completes their basic training will be considered for the mounted section but if you do get chosen, you will get to know some quite exceptional horses. One of the main roles of a police horse is crowd control – holding back large numbers of people. The training for a police horse is extremely thorough and usually starts when a horse is four years old.

The horse has to be trained in a kind of dressage to a very high standard and also to learn to cope with all manner of obstacles. The horses are also taken out onto the streets, at first usually in a column of horses, then in pairs, and finally on their own. After the initial training, the horses

usually have a period of rest. The training is continued with the horses getting used to smoke, fire, and other frightening occurrences that they could encounter in their work. The horses must remain calm and trust their rider under all circumstances.

HORSES IN TOWN TRAFFIC

Horses that have to work alongside traffic in towns must be fully at ease with the buses and cars that race past them. They are treated as slow moving vehicles and must obey the rules of the road.

Horses in town traffic

Appendix

Foundation sires

One of the three foundation sires of the Thoroughbred, the *Darley Arabian* was foaled in Syria, about 1700. Thomas Darley acquired the yearling in exchange for a gun. Imported to England, the stallion was never raced. His entire career was as a stud; whether he covered ordinary or finer-bred mares, he consistently sired swift racers.

The *Byerly Turk*, foaled about 1679, was a war horse imported from Turkey by a Captain Byerly. The Byerly Turk is the second of the Thoroughbred foundation sires.

The third foundation sire, the *Godolphin Barb*, was one of a group of Barbs sent by the Bey of Tunis to the King of France, who preferred heavy war horses. The unpopular Barb was eventually hitched to a Parisian watercart. Brought to England and sold to Lord Godolphin, the Barb was to sire even more outstanding race horses than the Darley Arabian.

Messenger is considered the founding sire of North America's trotting, pacing and saddle horses. His sire was Mambrino, a descendant of the Darley Arabian and himself a foundation sire – of the English coach horse.

Messenger's son, Messenger's Mambrino, was the grandsire of *Rysdyk's Hambletonian*, an outstanding sire of Standardbred trotting horses. Hambletonian's sire, Abdallah, was ugly and bad-tempered but passed on the marvellous messenger bloodlines.

Denmark, American saddlebred sire, was foaled in Kentucky, about 1850. His exact parentage is not established, but is thought to have been mainly Thoroughbred. Denmark is the foundation sire of the five-taited American Saddlebred.

Allen F-1, Thoroughbred foaled in 1886 in Lexington, Kentucky, is considered the founding sire of the Tennessee Walking Horse.

Janus, an English Thoroughbred imported to Virginia, stood at stud between 1756 and 1780. He was stocky and well muscled, a rather untypical Thoroughbred, and is considered the foundation sire of the American Quarter Horse.

Justin Morgan is the only foundation sire whose progeny immortalize his name. Foaled in Vermont about 1793, reputedly sired by Beautiful Bay, a Thoroughbred import, on a mare of the Wild-airstrain, he combined Thoroughbred and Arab characteristics. Three of his sons – Bulrush, Sherman and Woodbury – established three prepotent "families" of Morgans.

Well-known sires

Arkelshof's Sunlight, Welsh Pony
Color: chestnut
Sire: Solway Master Bronze
Dam: Derwen Chestnut lady
Arkelshof's Sunlight is one of the most influential stallions for Class B Welsh Ponies. He has produced ten approved stud stallions.

Bar Flit, Quarter horse
Color: buckskin
Sire: Fritz Command
Dam: Saucy Bar Flit
Bar Flit was world champion western riding horse three times. One of his best known progeny is Commander Flit Fritz.

Brown's Liberty Light, Hackney
Color: dark brown
Sire: Amarilla The Sorcerer
Dam: Brown's Tip Top
Brown's Liberty Light is one of the most important stallions in the Hackney Stud Book. A number of his male progeny became approved studs.

Cambridge Cole, Hackney
Color: brown
Sire: Walton Searchlight
Dam: Cambridge Madge
Cambridge Cole is the third stallion that was at stud after 1960 for a specialist carriage horse stud. Cambridge Cole's progeny includes many champions. A number of his sons became approved Hackney studs.

Christiaan, Fjord Pony
Color: Cream
Sire: St. Restrup Falk
Dam: Annette
Christiaan has produced many successful stallions and mares. Three of his approved stud stallions are Harald, Lars, and Kurt.

Colonel, Gelderland
Color: chestnut
Sire: Mentor
Dam: mare of Tourbillon
Colonel lived to an old age. His grandfather Tourbillon was an Anglo-Norman.
The presence of Colonel is highly regarded for the breeding of both riding and carriage horses.

Conquistador, Welsh Pony
Color: chestnut
Sire: Hamad Ox (fullblood Arab)
Dam: Sheila
This stallion with Arab blood sired four successful stud stallions.

Doc Bar, Quarter horse
Color: sorrel
Born from a daughter of Music Mount
Doc Bar won many western riding trophies, particularly for cutting competitions. One of his best known progeny is Doc's Cinch Bet.

Hendrik, Groningen
Color: black-brown
Sire: Gambo
Dam: Nezelly
Hendrik sired 17 approved stallions of which the most important are Dijkgraaf and Harro.

Joost, Holstein
Color: brown
Sire: Consul
Dam: Ulana
Joost was an outsanding jumper leading to great interest in his progeny. Joost sired a number of approved stud stallions.

Laski Fra Haeli, Icelandic
Color: chestnut
Sire: Hafeti Fra Brautarholt
Dam: Fluga Fra Haeli
Laski Fra Haeli was overall champion in 1970. He became an approved stud in 1982 for three years and sired three approved studs.

Lucky Boy, Thoroughbred
Color: dark brown
Sire: Compromise
Dam: Séjanne
Lucky Boy has sired numerous successful Thoroughbreds and horses that have done well in various areas of equestrian sport.

Maestoso Morana, Lipizzaner
Color: grey
Sire: Maestoso Allegra x
Dam: 19 Morana
Deze stallion that was born in 1955 was approved by the then stallions approval committee for three years.

Noran Ox, Arab
Color: chestnut
Sire: Oran Ox
Dam: Nerina Ox
The Arab stallion Noran, originating in England, has been very influential in the breeding of riding horses and ponies. He also produced sons that were outstanding showjumpers.

Ooigaard Damgaard, Fjord Pony
Color: cream
Sire: Oygard
Dam: Lady Damgaard
This stallion has 585 sons and daughters registered. His progeny included the stallions Oostman and Gustaaf grandsons Pastor and Tjostar.

Oregon, Gelderland
Color: brown
Sire: Kurassier
Dam: Derka
Oregon is the foundation stallion for carriage horse breeding in the Netherlands. Oregon's progeny include 13 approved stallions of which the most important are: Tamboer, Gloriant, Hoogheid, Indiaan and Jonkheer.

Revel Tobias, Welsh Pony
Color: brown
Sire: Revel Crusader
Dam: Brierwood
Revel Tobias's progeny were immensely successful and included nine approved studs.

Rigoletto, Dutch Warmblood
Color: grey
Sire: Ramzes
Dam: Idee
Rigoletto produced a number of successful showjumping horses.
His male progeny included nine approved studs of which the most important are Turijn and Romein.

Snowboy, Appaloosa
Color: leopard
Sire: Zane Grey
Dam: Busking
Snowboy won a number of championships. He produced two stud stallions.

Spotlight of Marswood, Shetland Pony
Color: black
Sire: Rustic Sprite of Standen
Dam: Rose Blossom of Marifield
Spotlight of Marswood produced 59 approved studs and 67 approved grandsons. His best known sons are Waldheer, Timmy, Randolf, and Orson.

Twyford Thunder, Welsh Pony
Color: cream
Sire: Twyford Grenadier
Dam: Mountain Torrent
This stallion was several times approved for three years. He has produced five approved stallions.

Westman, Fjord Pony
Color: cream
Sire: Hans
Dam: Gerda
Westman has produced 423 sons and daughters that have been registered. His approved sons are Einar, Hans, and Ivar.

Zane Grey, Appaloosa
Color: leopard
Sire: Flesh Light
Dam: Brown Spot
The Appaloosa stallion Zane Grey is one of the most influential stallions in the Appaloosa studbook. He produced five approved sons.

Acknowledgements

The author's thanks are due to the following companies, organizations, and persons for the information and advice they gave and for making it possible to take photographs:

Burgmeyer Quarterhorses, Vorstenbosch NL
Arthur's Western Store, Vorstenbosch
Duindigt Racecourse NL
Riding Federation Centre, Ermelo NL
de Galgenbergh Riding Stables, Garderen NL
Mister Ed. western riding stables de Galgenbergh, Garderen
Riding Association De Garder Riders and De Garderreenties Ponyclub
Dutch Endurance Club
Haras Le Pin Stud, Cluny (F)
Heja, riding equipment and horse trailers, Garderen
Gebroeders van der Wiel N.V., saddlers
Appaloosa stud de Woldhoeve, Peize NL
Mini-Appaloosa stud De Brummerhoeve, 's-Hertogenbosch NL
Holland T.T.S. BV
Rieky Burgmeijer
Ceesje van Nunen
Henk van Nunen
Yvonne Schutte, riding instructor, Garderen
Femke Dijkstra, de Nieuwe Heuvel Riding Stables, Lunteren NL
Jan de Zwaan, farrier, Hierden NL
John Pijnappel, vet, Nijmegen
Ellen Kral, vet, de Veluwe Horse Clinic, Vierhouten NL
Martine Carriere, vet, Ermelo NL
Restaurant Poppe, Apeldoorn
Bert Wiekema,
Jan and Ankie van den Brink
Bert van Veen, Henk Heetebrij, Reint Knoppert, Dirk de Ruiter, Elspeet NL
Ria Lubbers
Ginny Rozema
Nelleke Dijkhuizen
Claudia Boon
Christel Jongboer
Anouschka van Hierden
Leen en Mies Kouwenhoven, Pijnacker NL
Tobias Wegener
Harry Kock, Peter Kruyssen, Henk Hermsen, Fred Schutte
Zuzanne Miezgiel
Henk Vink, Barneveld NL
and many others.

In the preparation of the English edition, the help of the British Horse Society, the veterinary surgeon Paul Cooper, MRCVS, and Pru Ormandy of the Plumtree Riding Centre was invaluable.

Index

Abcesses	276
Achal-Teké	14
Achenbach grip	203
Aids	124, 217, 289
Aids to move forwards	173
Albino	65
Allergies	272
American Saddlebred	15
American Standardbred	16
American Welsh Pony	57
Andalusian	16,23
Antibiotics	276-278
Anus	81
Appearance	13
Apple in throat	277
Approaching a fence	171
Appuyer	156
AQHA course	235
Arab	9–10
Arab pure bred	20
Ardennais	22
Automatic balancing rein	139
Automatic drinking bowl	95
Azoturia	278
Back cinch	224
Back jockey	225
Back jockey and skirt	225
Balancing rein	139
Bandages	140, 141, 283, 296
Barrel race	236
Bars of the feet	111
Base coat	263
Base-coat hairs	63, 263
Bay	64
Bedding material	97
Beet pulp	277
Before buying	288
Behavior	291
Bell signals	180
Belly protector	141
Birth	84,85
Bit	137, 220
Biting	88
Blacking the hooves	239
Blanket	19
Blaze	67–68
Blinkers	195
Blood tests	278
Blue spray	269
Body	61
Body roller	121
Bone tissue	270
Boot pullers	143
Boot wedge	143
Boots	140, 143, 296
Boots, horse	283
Boredom	87
Bosal	220–221, 229
Bowing	204
Bowline	221
Brabant draft horse	22
Bran	102, 277
Branding	72
Breast harness	191
Breathing	263-265, 275, 277
Breeds	9
Bridle	12
Bridle paths	255
Broken wind	275
Browband	219–220
Brushing	283
Bucking	89
Buckskin	50
Buxton bar	197
Buying and selling a horse	289
Camargue horse	24
Can't see back	225
Cannon bone	266, 270. 271
Canter, changing the	235
Cantering in circles	216
Cantle	134
Cap	165
Capped elbow	271
Capped hock	271
Capriole	167
Carrots	102–103
Carthusian Andalusian	17
Catching	292
Cavalletti exercises	173–174
Cavalletti schooling	174–175
Cavesson	122
Changement	158, 223
Changing hand	130
Chaps	228
Character	288
Check up	288
Cheek-piece	131
Chestnuts	268
Chin strap	131
Choke	277
Cinch	216
Classes in competition	230
Classic showjumping competitions	186
Cleveland Bay	24
Clipping	115
Clothing	227, 236
Clover-leaf	210
Clydesdale	56
Coat	293
Coldblood	10
Colic	263, 274
Collected	148
Collected canter	150
Colored	271
Combination fence	176
Combined nose-band	132
Companionship	291
Competitions	229–230, 235, 238, 290, 294
Conformation	231
Connemara Pony	25
Convalescence	283
Coronary band	69, 111, 272
Costs	289
Cough	263, 275–277
Courbette	165
Course	233, 235
Course builder	183
Course builder's assistants	184

Cow hocks	281	Figures	154
Cow sense	237	Finger loop	194
Cowboy	215, 237	First aid and medicines	283
Cream	64-65	Fjord Pony	28, 117, 268
Crest of mane	62, 266	Flags	181
Cross-country obstacles	248	Flat bottom stirrup	226-227
Crush box for veterinary inspection	82	Flehmen	75, 78
Curb	270	Flexion test	270
Curry comb	108	Flying change	158, 233
Cutting	228, 237–239	Foals	12, 71, 85, 87, 97, 119, 278
Cutting saddle	225–226	Fodder	263, 274, 279, 290
		Forehand	61
Daisy cutting	283	Forelegs, poor conformation	279
Damp	266, 271–272	Forelock	62
Dandy brush	109	Foreplay	82
Dapple grey	66	Forging	283
Dartmoor Pony	26	Forging – shoe to prevent injury	283
Dentist, equine	300	Fork	222
Descending a slope	257	Formation dressage	167
Development	59	Forward seat	235
Development orthopedic disease	279	Four-in-hand reins	194
Diarrhea	274, 279	Freestyle reining	235–236
Discharge	276	Freeze branding	72
Dismounting	125	French Trotter	18
Double-pointed show	230	Friesian	31
Draft horses	10, 302	Frightened horse	294
Dressage	226, 232–233, 235	Frock coat	142
Dressage arena	159	Frog	111, 273
Dressage clothing	161	Frog, infection of	273
Dressage test	205	Front strap	131
Driving	191	Full collar harness	193, 197
Droppings	274	Full mouthed	70
Dry legs	62	Fungal infection	267
Dry work	238		
Dummy cow	239	Gait abnormalities	282
Dun	64	Galloping	254
Dung heap	79	Gelderland mare	38
Dust	276	Gelding	70
Dust, allergy to	279	General Studbook	27
Dutch Draft Horse	42	General-purpose saddle	134
Dutch Draft Horse (Belgian type)	22	Getting acquainted	290
Dutch Warmblood	38	Getting into the driving seat	200
		Girth	135, 136
Eel stripe	67	Gloves	144
Endurance	248	Glycogen	278
Ennobling	10	Grass	272
Eventing	246–248	Grass belly	294
Excitement	274	Graze	268
Exercise	272, 295	Grey	64–65
Exercise wheel	98	Groningen stallion	38
Exmoor Pony	28	Groom	205, 301–302
		Grooming	108–109, 290
Falls	299	Grooming corner	98
False martingale	197	Grooming equipment	290
Farrier	112, 270, 273, 283, 290, 293, 301	Ground line of fence	178
Fast trotting	241	Guardians	24
Fault in jumping	184	Gullet	98, 124
Fear	274	Gymnastic exercises	127
Feather	72		
Feeding	274, 294	Hackamore	133
Feeding trough	93	Hackney	31
Feeds	279	Haflinger	32
Fence	100	Hair loss	266
Fence work	238	Half circle	130
Fences and obstacles	182, 233	Halt	216, 233
Fencing	100, 290, 292	Halter	136, 230, 290, 296
Fender	222–223	Halter show	230–231
Fever	278	Halting	201
Few Spot	19	Handler	13

Hard horn	272
Hard swellings of the legs	270
Harness rack	198
Hat	142
Hay	102, 104
Hay allergy	277
Hay net	297
Hay storage	95
Head collar	136, 230, 290, 296
Headpiece	131, 137, 195, 220, 290
Headstall	219–220
Healthy horse	263
Heartbeat	264–265
Heaves	275
Height	14
Herbivores	77
Herd	78, 293
Herd animals	89
Herdholders	239
High jump	176
High nose-band	132
Highly sensitive	266
Hindlegs, poor conformation	281
Hindquarters	61
Hitching knot	92–93
Hocks	270–271, 282
Holstein	33
Hoof	68, 111–113, 272, 282–283
Hoof disorders	272
Hoof nails	113
Hoof pick	111
Hoof wall	111, 272
Hooves	283, 294
Horn	273
Horse and pony nuts	102–103
Horse ball	87
Horse blankets	93
Horse length	244
Horse sales	9, 289
Horse trials	246–248
Horses in traffic	303
Hosing down	110
Hotted up	294
Hunger	264
Hunter	34, 36, 47
Hunter classes	236
Hunter half-bred	25
Hunter under saddle	236
Hunting	236, 249
Hunting stock	145
Huntsman	250
Icelandic Pony	35, 268
Imaginary vertical	236
Impactive colic	274
Impulsion	147
In season	81, 83, 279
Infection	266, 270, 272–273, 276–277
Influenza	276
In-hand classes	221, 230
Inoculations	269, 290
Insects	293
Insurance	287, 299
Intestines	274
Irish Draft Horse	36
Jobs with horses	300
Jockey	245
Jodhpurs	142

Jog	215, 233
Joint ill	279
Judges and jury	161, 230–231, 233
Jump off	182
Jumping the water jump	178
Junior western horse	214, 229
Kentucky Saddler	15
Kladruber	36–37
Knee roll	134
Koniks	37
Kür to music	162
Lactic acid	278
Lady's saddle	135
Lameness	269–273, 278
Laminitis	272
Landing (in showjumping)	172–173
Large circle	130
Large figure eight	130
Leading rope	220–221
Left-hand, riding to the	128
Leg disorders	270
Legs	271
Legs, poor conformation	279
Legs, position of	271, 279, 280, 282
Leopard	19
Lethargic horse	294
Levade	165
Lever bit	133
Lice	266
Line-up	230, 232
Lipizzaner	39
Liver chestnut	66
Liverpoool bit	196
Loading and unloading horsebox	297
Loire	47
Loneliness	294
Looking after a horse or pony	272, 274, 287, 288
Lope	215–216, 232–233
Low nose-strap	131–132
Lower leg	267
Lunge	120–121
Lunge rein	289
Lungeing whip	121
Lungeing with an assistant	120
Lungs	277
Lymph glands	276
Lymph node infection	278
Mail coach	204
Maine	47
Malopolski	17
Mane	115–117
Mange	265
Manger bars to prevent spillage	91
Manure	263, 290, 295
Manure heap	79
Marathon (driving trials)	205
Mare	70, 81–82
Martingale	138
Mating	82
Mealy muzzle	28, 67
Medium trot	149
Merlins	57
Midges	268
Mineral lick	93
Miniature Horses	41
Miniature Shetland Pony	52

Mites	266	Preparing to show western horses	239
Moment of suspension	172	Pressure marks	266
Monday Morning Disease	278	Private driving competitions	208
Monté racing	19	Przewalski's Horse	49
Morgan	51	Puissance	186
Morocco	48	Pulling comb	114
Mounted police	302	Purchasing a horse	289
Mucking out	96	Pus	276
Mucus membranes	263	Putting out to pasture	100
Mud fever	266, 278		
Mud fever ointment	267	Quarter horse	50–51
		Quick release catch	91, 194, 296
Nail prick	273		
Narrow behind	281	Race	244
Narrow in front	279	Racing saddle	245
Nasal discharge	276	Raising a foot	293
Native breed	9	Ram's head	73
Navicular bone	273	Ram's nose	13
Navicular disease	273	Ranchwork chaps	228–229
Neck reining	216–217	Rearing	125
New Forest Pony	43	Recreational carriages	210
Nits	266	Recreational driving	208
Noriker	44	Red roan	64–65
Nose strap	220	Reflective clothing	259
Nose-band	131	Refusal	185
Novice horse	119, 290	Reining	235–237
Numnah	135	Reining back	150, 153, 235
Nutritional disorders	279	Reining saddle	225–226
		Reins	131, 136, 200, 216, 220, 229
Oats	294	Reins, dressage and jumping	134
Oiling the hoof	272	Resistance	220
One-ear headstall	219	Respiratory disorders	275
Open plain animals	77	Resting	259
Orlow trotter	45	Reverse (in western riding)	232-233
Over-reaching	231	Reverse turn on the hindquarters	154
Overo	46	Riding breeches	142
Overtaxing	270, 272	Riding clothes	290
Oxbow	227	Riding equipment	220
		Riding etiquette in school ring	130
Pack Horse	260	Riding horse	11, 114, 260
Paint	46–47	Riding permits	255
Palomino	66	Riding school	290
Parasites	292	Riding school horse	287
Parasites, stomach and intestines	274	Riding stallion	70
Part-coloured	64	Riding straight ahead	152
Partitioning pasture	101	Rigging dee	224
Pas de deux	163	Right-hand, riding to	128
Passage	158	Ring steward	230
Pasture	99, 290	Ringworm	267
Paying respect (to officials)	161, 230	Roan	19
Pedal bone	273	Roaring	275
Pelham bit	133	Rollback	216–217, 235
Penalty seconds	237	Rolling	292–293
Penning	237	Root of tail	266
Percheron	47	Roping saddle	225–226
Persistent urachus	278	Rosettes	145, 196
Piaffe	159	Running	282
Piebald	48, 64		
Pigeon toed	281–283	Saddle	226, 266, 290
Pinto	47	Saddle blanket	226
Pirouette	157	Saddle cushions	134, 226
Pit pony	53	Saddle flaps	134
Pivot moment, showjumping	170	Saddle strings	225
Plaiting	283	Saddlehorn	220
Plumb line	236	Saddling up	122
Pneumonia	276–277	Salt lick	93
Poisionous	78, 101	Sand colic	274
Pole bending	237	Scabs	267
Polo pony	250, 251	School figures	130

Schooling ring	129
Scissors	114
Scissors bit	220, 229
Scraping the foreleg	88
Seat	123, 213, 224–225
Selle Français	18
Senior horse (western riding)	214, 229
Serpentine	130
Set distance trotting race	242
Sexual urge	82
Shafts	134
Shagya Arab	51
Shedding hair	110
Sheep	291
Shetland Pony	9, 52–53, 268
Shire Horse	53–54
Shoeing nails	113
Shoes	111–113, 272–273, 283
Shoulder in	155
Show ring chaps	228–229
Showing for breed registration	13
Showing halter	221, 231
Showjumping arena	180
Showjumping course	179
Showjumping horse	170
Showjumping shoes	140, 296
Showjumping whip	169
Showmanship	231
Side saddle	135
Signalling	74
Single fence	175
Skewbald	48, 64
Skin ailments	265
Skin care	106
Skirt	225
Sliding shoe	227
Sliding stop	216–217, 227, 235
Small circle	130
Smearing petroleum jelly on hooves	272
Snaffle	131, 133, 220, 229
Snip	67, 74
Snowflake	19
Sock	69, 72
Soft brush	109
Soft leg swellings	270
Sole	111–112
Solid coloured	64
Sore shin	270
Sorraia pony	17
Special shoes for splint	270
Speed games	226, 236, 237
Spin	217–218, 235
Spin, learning to	218
Splay-footed	280
Splint	270
Split ear headstall	220
Sponge	110
Spotted	64
Sprained tendon	271
Spread fence	176
Spring clip	91
Spurs	141, 227
Square	63, 279
Stable	94, 272, 293
Stable cat	76
Stable tools	98
Stable vices	288
Stabling	289
Stall	96
Stallion	81–82, 293
Stallion plait	239
Standard grip for driving	199
Standing square	14, 62
Standing still	129, 153, 213
Star markings	67, 74
Steeplechase	246
Step	254
Stiffness	278
Stirrup	222–223
Stirrup iron	134, 226–227, 236
Stockings	69
Stomach and intestinal disorders	274
Stopping on the bit	150
Straight profile	13
Strangles	276
Straw	97
Stringhalt	282
Sucking in air	87
Sun blisters	266
Sunburn	266
Supplementing feed	102
Surroundings	290, 294
Sweat scraper	134
Sweating	278
Sweet itch	267–268
Sweets	105
Swellings	270–271
Swishing the tail	79
Tack	131, 139, 236
Take off (in showjumping)	172
Team dressage	166
Team penning	237
Temperament	293
Temperature	263–264, 276
Tennessee Walking Horse	55
Test	232–233, 235, 239
Test of ability	207
Test ride	289
Testing the mare	83
Tetanus injection	269, 273
Thermometer	264
Thoroughbred	9, 27
Thoroughpin	271
Three-day event	246–248
Throat latch	131, 137
Thrush	273
Tie strap	222–223
Tobiano	46
Toe dragging	283
Too heavily built	62
Toxin	269
Track	129, 233
Trail	233–234, 236
Trail riding	218–219
Trailer	296
Training	119, 246
Training rig	243
Transport	296
Travers	156
Trekking	261
Trimming the hoof	112
Triple bar	177
Trot	215
Trotting horses, training	242
Turnback men	239
Turned in hocks	282
Tush	71

311

Twins	86
Twisted gut	274
Two-handed driving grip	199
Two-wheeled gigs and traps	209
Umbilical cord	278
Unhitching	198
Unloading	297
Upright hairs	66
Urine	278
Veterinary checks	206
Veterinary surgeon	266–271, 273–274, 276–279, 290, 300–301
Viral infection	276
Vocal chords	275
Vulva	81
Walk	215, 232–233
Walking the course	182
Wall (showjumping)	186
Warble Fly	268
Warmblood	11
Warming-up for competition	160, 180
Warts	268
Water jump	177
Waxing up	84
Weaving rack	88
Weighing in	245
Weights	296
Welsh Cob	57

Welsh Mountain Pony	57
Welsh Pony	57
Western horsemanship	232–233, 236
Western pleasure riding	232, 236
Western rider	213
Western riding competitions clothing	228
Western saddle	221, 226
Western seat	213
Whip	121, 124
Whippers-in	250
Whiskers	73, 114
Whistling	275
Whitener	239
Wide behind	281
Wide in front	279
Wind	274
Windgall	270, 271
Windpipe	276
Winner	241
Wood shavings	97
Working	237–238
Working classes	237
Working through	148
Working with horses in forestry	302
Worming	292
Worms	274, 294
Wound	266, 268, 269, 273, 277–278, 283
Yearling	86
Young horse	270